American Actors, 1861-1910:

An Annotated Bibliography

American Actors, 1861-1910:

An Annotated Bibliography

of Books Published in the United States

in English from 1861 through 1976

by

Ronald L. Moyer

The Whitston Publishing Company
Troy, New York
1979

To LoAnn

PREFACE

In 1968, Dr. Alfred E. Rickert observed that the "number of works and reprints recently available is evidence of the increasing interest in the theatre of the nineteenth century."[1] This growing interest has more recently been demonstrated by the founding of *Nineteenth Century Theatre Research,*[2] a scholarly journal devoted exclusively to work in this era, by the publication of the "Nineteenth Century" issue of the *Educational Theatre Journal,*[3] and by the continuing publication of new and reprinted works concerned with nineteenth-century theatre. This growing attention paid to the field of nineteenth-century theatre has included an increased interest in the specific area of nineteenth-century American acting. During the ten years from 1963 through 1972, numerous new and reprinted books which contain substantial information on pre-World War I American actors were published, including Garff B. Wilson's *A History of American Acting,*[4] which emphasizes nineteenth-century actors.

Yet, despite the growth of interest in this field, there are currently no guides to the literature which deals with nineteenth-century American actors and which are annotated with specific reference to those actors. Wilson's useful history of American acting contains references in the "Notes" to the sources of the materials which he uses in that book. These citations are neither complete indications of the sources relevant to the study of the actors whom he discusses, nor are they descriptive of the general contents of the works he utilized. Similarly, Cole and Chinoy's *Actors on Acting*[5] and Richard Moody's *Dramas from the American Theatre: 1762-1909*[6] contain useful but incomplete and non-descriptive bibliographies on American actors.

Blanch M. Baker's *Theatre and Allied Arts*[7] is a fine annotated bibliography of books dealing with the theatre and theatre-related subjects. Yet this volume contains few entries for books published prior to 1885 and none for books published after

1950. Furthermore, the bibliography is selective and most of the annotations are brief. *Performing Arts Books in Print: An Annotated Bibliography,* edited by Ralph Newman Schoolcraft,[8] is a useful volume, but it contains references only to those books in print at the time of publication. A third annotated bibliography, the American Educational Theatre Association's *A Selected Bibliography and Critical Comment on the Art, Theory, and Technique of Acting,*[9] is less useful than either Baker's or Schoolcraft's works, even though it is specifically concerned with actors and acting. Not all of the entries in this bibliography are annotated, most of the annotations are too brief to be useful guides to the material contained in the works listed, and it is highly selective, with less than three hundred entries for all periods of Western acting.

In addition to the above-named works, most general histories of American theatre—for example, those written by Barnard Hewitt, Glenn Hughes, and Garff Wilson[10]—include bibliographies containing entries on American actors. These are selective, non-descriptive lists. Various serials, such as the *Tulane Drama Review* and the *Dramatic Index,* contain useful bibliographical information which is spread over years of publication or lost in lengthy, unannotated compilations.

It is desirable that complete, descriptive bibliographies of all types of materials dealing with American actors and acting from the beginnings to the present be compiled. Such reference works, properly indexed, would facilitate scholarship in the fields of American theatrical and cultural history. The performance of such a task as this would require many years and/or numerous researchers. It is the compiler's hope that this bibliography will be the beginning of such a project.

§

Definition of "American Actors, 1861-1910"

For the purposes of this study, the term "American Actors, 1861-1910," is defined as actors and actresses who resided in the United States and who performed on the English-language legitimate stage in America for at least part of their adult professional stage careers during the years 1861-1910. The actors' places-of-birth and legal nationality are not considered: for instance, such foreign-born players as Helena Modjeska, Charles Fechter, and George Arliss are included. The actors' most important period of activity need not have occurred between 1861 and 1910, as long as some portions of their adult stage careers do fall within this time-span; for example, James Murdoch and John Barrymore, whose major periods of theatrical activity were, respectively, before 1861 and after 1910, are included. Actors who did not reside in the United States are excluded from the study, even if they made extensive American tours: for example, such performers as Tommaso Salvini, Henry Irving, and Sarah Bernhardt are not included.

§

The Purpose of the Study

During the period 1861-1976 over three hundred and fifty books which contain substantial information concerning American Actors, 1861-1910, were published in the United States in the English language. The purpose of this study are: (1) to compile a complete listing of the titles of these books, with full bibliographical data for each entry, (2) to provide descriptive annotations of the contents of each work, with special reference to material pertinent to the study of American Actors, 1861-1910, (3) to provide an alphabetical index of actors of the period which refers the reader to books containing substantial information on those actors, (4) to provide an index to the short titles of the annotated works, (5) to provide an index to the authors, editors, writers of introductions, etc., for those books, and (6) to make this information available to scholars and students in a single reference work.

§

The Scope of the Study

The entries in this study are for books published in the

English language in the United States from 1861 through 1976 which contain substantial biographical, descriptive, critical, pictorial, and/or theoretical material by or about American Actors, 1861-1910. The works included in the bibliography of this study must meet all of the following criteria:

(1) Published books, printed as originals or as reprints in the United States of America;
(2) Books published from 1861 through 1976;
(3) Books printed in the English language;
(4) Books pertaining to American Actors, 1861-1910:
    (a) Containing substantial autobiographical, biographical, descriptive, pictorial, and/or critical references to one or more such actors, with specific references to the years 1861-1910, or
    (b) Containing substantial theoretical and/or practical statements concerning acting made by one or more such actors.

Materials which may meet the above criteria, but which are not included in the bibliography are:

(1) Biographical reference works pertaining to many professions (e.g., *Dictionary of National Biography, Dictionary of American Biography,* and "Who's Who" collections other than those specifically relating to theatre);
(2) General cultural histories;
(3) General histories of international theatre;
(4) General histories of American theatre;
(5) International histories of acting;
(6) Play scripts, play anthologies, and published promptbooks;
(7) Works concerned solely with the events surrounding the assassination of Abraham Lincoln.

§

Procedure

The initial step in the compilation of the bibliography was

the gathering of titles for a working bibliography. This list was collected through the examination of reference works, scholarly publications, and available unpublished dissertations. Full bibliographical data, including reprints, variant editions, etc., was obtained by checking each entry in the working bibliography through the Library of Congress and National Union catalogues.

The books listed in the basic bibliography were then located and obtained either in libraries which the compiler was able to visit personally or through the services of Interlibrary Loan. These works were examined and, if relevant to the study, annotated for inclusion in the final compilation. Bibliographies and other book references in each volume obtained were searched for additional entries to the working bibliography. When at variance with Library of Congress or National Union listings, bibliographical data noted from the original work is included in the final study. Bibliographical information omitted in the original work but discovered elsewhere is included in the entries and it is enclosed by square brackets.

Upon completion of the compilation of bibliographical data and the annotation of the works included, the entries were ordered alphabetically by author or editor; or, when no author or editor was indicated, by title. Each entry was then numbered. Indices of actors, titles, and authors were compiled; a brief summary of the work was composed; and, finally, a recommendation for further research was written. The actor index alphabetically lists individual American Actors, 1861-1910, and refers the reader to specific entries which contain substantial information on those actors. The title index is an alphabetical list of the short titles of the works annotated in the bibliography, with the number of the entry for each respective title. The author index is an alphabetical listing of authors, editors, pseudonyms, writers of prefaces and introductions, etc., with the entry number(s) for the work(s) to which each person contributed.

§

Organization

Each entry in the annotated bibliography is included in a

single alphabetical listing which is arranged by author or editor. If the author or editor used a pseudonym, his works are listed under his real name. If there is more than one author or editor for a single work, the entry is arranged according to the surname of the author or editor who is listed first in the original publication. If authorship is anonymous, the entry is placed alphabetically according to title. Numbering of the entries is continuous.

The *Index to Actors* lists American Actors, 1861-1910, who are given substantial coverage in one or more of the works annotated. Following each actor's name is a listing of entry numbers referring to the specific works containing substantial information on that actor. This index also includes references by entry numbers to works which provide general coverage on American Actors, 1861-1910. A book having general coverage is defined as one which contains substantial information on over fifty American Actors, 1861-1910, or one which contains only brief references to a number of American actors of that period. In order to obtain a more specific indication of the limitations of works providing general coverage, the reader may consult the annotations of those works.

The next aspect of the study is the *Index to Titles*. This index consists of an alphabetical listing of the short titles of the works annotated in the final compilation. Each title is followed by the entry number for that work.

The study is concluded by an *Index to Authors*. An alphabetical list of authors, editors, pseudonyms, writers of prefaces and introductions, etc., who contributed to the annotated books comprises this section. Following each "author's" name is a listing of entry numbers for specific works to which he contributed.

§

Entries

The entries in the annotated bibliography contain full bibliographical data for each of the works included and a descriptive annotation for each work. The following bibliographical information is included for each entry:

(1) The full names of the authors or editors for each work (if known), including pseudonyms;
(2) The full title of each work;
(3) The names of authors of prefaces and introductions, editors of the original composition, etc.;
(4) The number of volumes, if more than one, in each work;
(5) The place of publication;
(6) The name of the publisher;
(7) The year of publication or copyright; and
(8) The number of pages in the work.

This information is provided for the first publication of each work in the United States. Changes in the bibliographical information are noted for: (1) each subsequent publication of the work in the United States by a different publisher, (2) each publication of the work in the United States under a variant title, (3) each American publication of a revised edition of the work, and (4) each reprint of the work which has been published in the United States. The following sample indicates the correct reading of the bibliographical data for a standard entry:

Winter, William. *Life and Art of Edwin Booth.* New York: Macmillan, 1893; rpt. New York: Greenwood, 1968. xii, 308 pp.

Ibid. New ed., rev. New York: Macmillan, 1894; Boston: Joseph Knight, 1894. 437 pp.

This book by William Winter was first published in New York City by Macmillan and Company in 1893. It is paged to xii forward of the main body of the work, and thereafter to page 308. This first edition was reprinted by the Greenwood Press of New York City in 1968. In 1894, both Macmillan and Company and the Joseph Knight Company of Boston published a new, revised edition of Winter's original work. As of the end of 1976, the revised edition had not been reprinted.

The annotation following each entry includes four sections: descriptive comment, "Illustrations," "Features," and "Actors." The descriptive comment immediately follows the bibliographical data and is primarily descriptive of the general contents of the work being discussed. This comment is intended to define the general nature of the work, the approximate time period covered by the work, and the nature of the materials concerning American Actors, 1861-1910, which are contained in the work. Unless otherwise noted, all materials quoted in the annotations have been selected from the work being annotated. The compiler's brief evaluations of some of the works under consideration are included, but criticism is not a primary aim of the study.

Following the comment, each entry includes a section headed "Illustrations." In this section the number and types (e.g., photographs, engravings, etc.) of illustrations are noted, and an indication of the subjects of the illustrations is given.

The next section in each annotation is "Features." When they are contained in the work under consideration, the features are listed in the following order: preface, foreword, author's note, etc.; acknowledgements; introduction; table of contents; list of illustrations; documentation; bibliography; appendices, chronologies, special lists, etc.; and index. In some cases, brief descriptions of the features are included. Under "documentation," the note that "sources of quotations are identified by author and/or title and/or date" indicates that the documentation form utilized in the work is inconsistent: sometimes identifying sources by author, sometimes by author and title, or by title alone, or by author and date, etc.

Each annotation concludes with a section headed "Actors." This section comprises an alphabetical list of the American Actors, 1861-1910, about whom substantial information is included in the work being annotated. Individual actors are listed in this section only if substantial coverage is provided for less than fifty actors of the period. If more than fifty American Actors, 1861-1910, are given substantial coverage or if a number of such actors are given only brief mention, the book will be considered to be providing general coverage, and this will be indicated in the "Actors" section.

Abbreviations

The following abbreviations are used in this study. The authority for these abbreviations is *The MLA Style Sheet,* Second edition (New York: The Modern Language Association of America, 1970).

©	:	copyright
comp.	:	compiler, compiled by
ed., eds.	:	editor(s), edition(s), edited by
e.g.	:	for example
enl.	:	enlarged
etc.	:	and so forth
illus.	:	illustrated, illustrator, illustration(s)
introd.	:	introduction
N.B.	:	take notice
n.d.	:	no date (in a book's imprint)
n.n.	:	no name (of the publisher)
no. nos.	:	number(s)
n.p.	:	no place (of publication)
p., pp.	:	page(s)
pt., pts.	:	part(s)
pseud.	:	pseudonym
rev.	:	revised (by), revision, review, reviewed by
rpt.	:	reprint, reprinted
vol., vols.	:	volume(s)

NOTES

[1]Alfred E. Rickert, rev. of *English Melodrama*, by Michael R. Booth, *Educational Theatre Journal*, XX (March, 1968), p. 113.

[2]*Nineteenth Century Theatre Research*, I (Spring, 1973).

[3]*Educational Theatre Journal*, XXIV (October, 1972).

[4](Bloomington, Ind.: Indiana University Press, 1966).

[5]Toby Cole and Helen Krich Chinoy, eds., *Actors on Acting: The Theories, Techniques and Practices of the Great Actors of All Times Told in Their Own Words*, rev. and enl. ed. (New York: Crown, 1970).

[6](Boston: Houghton Mifflin, 1969).

[7]*Theatre and Allied Arts: A Guide to Books Dealing with the History, Criticism, and Technic of the Drama and Theatre and Related Arts and Crafts* (New York: H. W. Wilson, 1952).

[8](New York: Drama Books Specialists, 1973).

[9](Ann Arbor, Mich.: American Educational Theatre Association, 1948).

[10]Barnard Hewitt, *Theatre U.S.A., 1668 to 1957* (New York: McGraw-Hill, 1959); Glenn Hughes, *A History of the American Theatre 1700-1950* (New York: Samuel French, 1951); and Garff B. Wilson, *Three Hundred Years of American Drama and Theatre: From "Ye Bare and Ye Cubb" to "Hair"* (Englewood Cliffs, N.J.: Prentice-Hall, 1973).

TABLE OF CONTENTS

PREFACE..v
    Definition of "American Actors, 1861-1910"......... vi
    The Purpose of the Study vii
    The Scope of the Study..........................vii
    Procedure viii
    Organization ix
    Entries....................................x
    Abbreviations xiii

THE BIBLIOGRAPHY 1

CONCLUSION 247
    Summary...................................247
    Recommendations for Further Research............248

INDEX TO ACTORS 249

INDEX TO TITLES 255

INDEX TO AUTHORS............................263

THE BIBLIOGRAPHY

1.   Abbott, Lyman. *Silhouettes of My Contemporaries.* Garden City, New York: Doubleday, Page, 1922. x, 361 pp.

This book is composed of nineteen "portraits of men who I [Abbott] believe have contributed something toward the progress which is making out of this world a better world." Included is an essay on Edwin Booth which emphasizes the actor's spiritual faith and high ideals. This chapter contains brief quotations from some of Booth's letters.

Illustrations. One photograph of the author.

Features. Preface; table of contents.

Actors. Edwin Booth.

2.   Adams, W[illiam] Davenport (comp.). *A Dictionary of the Drama: A Guide to the Plays, Playwrights, Players, and Playhouses of the United Kingdom and America, from the Earliest Times to the Present.* Vol. I, A-G. Philadelphia: J. B. Lippincott, 1904; rpt. New York: Burt Franklin, 1964. viii, 627 pp.

In a single alphabetical listing, plus an "Addenda," this volume includes brief, factual comments on selected theatres (entered under city), playwrights, actors, vocalists, managers, scenic artists, composers, writers on theatre, plays, and characters in plays. All subjects had achieved prominence on the British or American stage, but they need not be native to those places. Concerning performers, the compiler writes: "Of the living, no biographical particulars are furnished, beyond an occasional record of the date or place of birth; otherwise the particulars relate solely to *rôles* (and especially 'original' *rôles*) . . . . Deceased players are treated, as a rule, more fully, selected criticisms being sometimes given, as well as references to biographical and critical authorities."

Illustrations. None.

Features. Preface; bibliography: occasional references in individual entries; "Addenda."

Actors. General.

3.   Aldrich, Mrs. Thomas Bailey [Lilian Woodman]. *Crowding Memories.* Boston and New York: Houghton Mifflin, © 1920. viii, 295 pp.

This volume of reminiscences concerns the period from the early 1860s to the death of Thomas Bailey Aldrich in 1907. Along with copious comments on her famous husband, the author provides anecdotes and descriptions of many of the leading literary figures of the late nineteenth century, among whom are Howells, Clemens, Longfellow, Wilde, and Dickens. Memories of Edwin Booth, dating from Civil War days and the last few years of Booth's life, are also included.

Illustrations. Twenty-one photographs of people, places, and correspondence associated with Thomas Bailey Aldrich.

Features. List of illustrations; index.

Actors. Edwin Booth.

4.   Alger, William Rounseville. *Life of Edwin Forrest, the American Tragedian.* 2 vols. Philadelphia: J. B. Lippincott, 1877; rpt. New York: Benjamin Blom, 1972. Vol. I: 431 pp.; Vol. II: 433-864 pp.

This massive biography was written with Forrest's permission and aid.   In preparing this work, the author utilized published and manuscript biographies and criticisms, letters and papers left at Forrest's death, correspondence and conversations with the actor's friends, and correspondence and conversations with Forrest (during the period 1868-72).   The first volume traces Forrest's life from his birth to the Astor Place Riot of 1848.   Letters, specific dates, and descriptions and criticisms of the actor are included, along with the author's disquisitions on various philosophical, artistic, and moral subjects.   The second volume departs from chronological narrative in order to examine various aspects of Forrest's personal and professional qualities, and includes more of the author's views.   Many reviews and appreciations, mostly uncredited, are included in this volume.   Evaluations and some description of the following of Forrest's characterizations are included: Volume One—Rolla, William Tell, Damon, Brutus (in Payne's *Brutus*), Virginius, Spartacus, and Metamora; Volume Two—Richelieu, Macbeth, Richard III, Hamlet, Coriolanus, Othello, and Lear.

Illustrations. Fourteen engravings, mostly of Forrest in various characterizations.

Features. Vol. I: Prefatory note; table of contents (for both volumes); list of illustrations (for both volumes); documentation: most letters are dated, few criticisms are adequately identified. *Vol. II:* Documentation: most letters are dated, few criticisms are adequately identified; Appendix I: "The Will of Edwin Forrest"; Appendix II: "The Forrest Medals and Tokens"; index (for both volumes).

Actors. Edwin Forrest.

5.   Alpert, Hollis. *The Barrymores.* New York: Dial, 1964. xviii, 397 pp.

This book is a generally chronological biography of

Lionel, Ethel, and John Barrymore. The anecdotal narrative emphasizes their careers in theatre, film, and radio, but it also contains much information on their offstage lives. Little critical comment and few specific dates are included. Slightly more than one-third of the book concerns the pre-1911 period.

Illustrations. Seventy-five photographs, mainly of Lionel, Ethel, and John Barrymore, including many of scenes from plays and films.

Features. Prologue; table of contents; partial bibliography in the "Prologue"; index.

Actors. Ethel Barrymore, Georgie Drew Barrymore, John Barrymore, Lionel Barrymore, Maurice Barrymore, John Drew II, Mrs. John Drew, Helena Modjeska.

6.   Altemus, Jameson Torr. *Helena Modjeska.* New York: J. S. Ogilvie, 1883; rpt. New York: Benjamin Blom, 1971. 217 pp.

This volume consists of two sections: the first is a biography of Helena Modjeska to the summer of 1883 and the second is a collection of essays pertaining to her acting. The biography, comprising over one-half of the text, is a narrative of the actress' youth, European career, and early English-language career. Anecdotes and excerpts from reviews, but few specific dates, are included in this portion. The essays include an 1882 article by Mme. Modjeska in which she makes general statements on the requisite attributes of an actor. Also contained in this section are lengthy reviews of Modjeska performances by various American and English critics, including Henry Labouchere, Clement Scott, William Winter, and John C. Freund, which embody evaluations and some descriptions of the dramas and her characterizations.

Illustrations. Two engravings of Helena Modjeska.

Features. Introduction; table of contents; documentation: sources of quotations are identified by author and/or name of periodical (no dates).

Actors. Helena Modjeska.

7. *The American Stage.* Chicago: H. Sellschopp, © 1894. Unnumbered.

This volume is composed of eighty full-page illustrations of theatre personnel who were prominent during the last quarter of the nineteenth century. American actors, some pictured in roles, predominate. There is no commentary included.

Illustrations. Eighty full-page photographs of prominent theatre personnel.

Features. None.

Actors. General.

8. *American Stage Celebrities.* Chicago: Hunt & Wall, © 1894. 144 pp.

Each of the sixty-six portrait photographs in this book is accompanied by a very brief biographical sketch of its subject. The subjects were all connected with the American stage in the 1890s and were primarily, although not exclusively, American-born performers. The biographies usually indicate the subjects' general lines of business, most popular roles, and major engagements. Specific dates are occasionally indicated.

Illustrations. Sixty-six photographs, mostly of American actors and singers.

Features. Introduction.

Actors. General.

9. *The American Stage. Schiller Theatre Souvenir.* Chicago: American Stage Publishing, [1895]. Unnumbered.

> This volume is composed of portraits of sixty-one people active in the American theatre, as native performers or as touring stars, at the time of publication. Each photograph is accompanied by a very brief biographical sketch.

> *Illustrations.* Sixty-one portrait photographs of men and women connected with the theatre.

> *Features.* None.

> *Actors.* General.

10. *The American Stage of Today: Biographies and Photographs of One Hundred Leading Actors and Actresses.* Introd. by William Winter. New York: P. F. Collier, 1910. [174 pp.]

> Entries for one hundred performers prominent on the American stage at the time of publication comprise this volume. Each entry contains a brief biographical sketch and several photographs (from two to fourteen, many in roles) of its subject. Such actors as Viola Allen, David Warfield, Nazimova, Louis James, and Arnold Daly are included. Winter's ten-page introduction surveys actors of the past and present.

> *Illustrations.* Hundreds of photographs of performers prominent on the American stage during the first decade of the twentieth century.

> *Features.* Introduction by William Winter; table of contents: alphabetical listing of the subjects.

> *Actors.* General.

11. *The American Theatre: A Sum of Its Parts. Collection of the Distinguished Addresses Prepared Expressly for the Symposium, "The American Theatre—A Cultural*

Process," at the First American College Theatre Festival, Washington, D.C., 1969. Preface by Henry B. Williams. New York and Hollywood: Samuel French, © 1971. x, 431 pp.

Each of the sixteen addresses included in this volume surveys a specific aspect of American theatre, for example, "European Influences on American Theatre: 1700-1969," "The Producer's Many Roles (The Producer: 1750-1969)," "Broadway Book Musicals: 1900-1969," "The University Theatre Begins to Come of Age: 1925-1969," and "Black Drama in the American Theatre: 1700-1970." Among the authors are Francis Hodge, Alan S. Downer, Lawrence Carra, Ned Bowman, Bernard Beckerman, and many other notable scholars and theatre professionals. Richard Moody's essay on "American Actors and Acting Before 1900" is an overview of prominent players, with brief comments on their dominant characteristics. Discussing over two score performers, Moody includes such figures as Forrest, Cushman, Edwin Booth, MacKaye, Rehan, Maude Adams, Mansfield, and Herne. Other phases of the careers of some major actors are touched upon in Barnard Hewitt's essay on producers and Helen Krich Chinoy's article on directors from 1860 to 1920. Summary and evaluation predominate in these addresses.

Illustrations. None.

Features. Preface by Henry B. Williams; table of contents; documentation: varies (many of the essays are thoroughly documented); bibliographies are provided for many of the essays.

Actors. General.

12. Archer, William. *The Theatrical 'World' for 1893.* London, 1894; rpt. New York: Benjamin Blom, 1969. xxxv, 307 pp.

Ibid. *The Theatrical 'World' of 1894.* Preface by George Bernard Shaw. "Synopsis of Playbills of the Year" by Henry George Hibbert. London, 1895; rpt.

New York: Benjamin Blom, 1971. xxxiii, 417 pp.

Ibid. *The Theatrical 'World' of 1895.* Prefatory letter by Arthur W. Pinero. "Synopsis of Playbills of the Year" by Henry George Hibbert. London, 1896; rpt. New York: Benjamin Blom, 1971. xxxix, 445 pp.

Ibid. *The Theatrical 'World' of 1896.* Introd., "On the Need for an Endowed Theatre," by William Archer. "Synopsis of Playbills of the Year" by Henry George Hibbert. London, 1897; rpt. New York: Benjamin Blom, 1971. lviii, 423 pp.

1893: This volume collects, from various periodicals, the author's reviews of dramatic performances at London's West End theatres during 1893. The reviews comprise, in varying mixtures, comments on the plays and on the specific productions. Included are criticisms of Augustin Daly's troupe.

1894: This volume contains the same sorts of materials as the 1893 volume, except for the 1894 year.

1895: This volume contains the same sorts of materials as the 1893 volume, except for the 1895 year.

1896: This volume contains the same sorts of materials as the 1893 volume, except for 1896.

Illustrations. None (each volume).

Features. *1893:* Author's note; "Epistle Dedicatory to Mr. Robert W. Lowe"; table of contents; separate indices for theatres, plays, authors, actors, actresses, and "Managers, Critics, &c."
1894: Preface by George Bernard Shaw; author's note; table of contents; epilogue; "Synopsis of Playbills, 1894" by Henry George Hibbert (chronological listing of productions, with title, author, theatre, cast, opening and closing dates); separate indices for theatres, plays, authors, actors, actresses, and "Managers, Critics, Composers, &c."

> *1895:* Prefatory letter by Arthur W. Pinero; author's note; table of contents; epilogue; "Synopsis of Playbills, 1895" by Henry George Hibbert; separate indices for theatres, plays, authors, actors, actresses, and "Managers, Critics, Composers, &c."
>
> *1896:* Introduction, "On the Need for an Endowed Theatre"; author's note; table of contents; "Synopsis of Playbills, 1896" by Henry George Hibbert; separate indices for theatres, plays, authors, actors, actresses, and "Managers, Critics, Composers, &c."

Actors. *1893:* Ada Rehan.
   1894: General.
   1895: General.
   1896: Ada Rehan.

13. Arliss, George. *My Ten Years in the Studios.* Boston: Little, Brown, 1940. xii, 349 pp.

This anecdotal narrative follows the author's life from the commencement of his film career in 1928 to 1938. Few specific dates are indicated, but cast lists of Arliss' 1928-37 films are included. Although the author focuses on his film career and personal life during these years, he does insert many scattered statements pertinent to his general attitudes toward theatre and his approach to acting.

Illustrations. Thirty-seven photographs, primarily of the author in scenes from several of his films.

Features. Preface; list of illustrations.

Actors. George Arliss.

14. —. *Up the Years from Bloomsbury: An Autobiography.* Boston: Little, Brown, 1927; New York: Blue Ribbon Books, 1927. 321 pp.

In this anecdotal narrative, the author recounts his life from childhood in the 1870s to the time of publication. Emphasizing his theatrical experiences, he devotes approximately two-thirds of the book to the period before 1911, mainly in England. Over one-third of the text relates to his American career. He comments briefly on the preparation for and the performance of various roles and recollects incidents concerning several of his co-workers, including Belasco, Mrs. Fiske, Blanche Bates, and John Mason.

Illustrations. Eighteen photographs, mostly of George Arliss.

Features. Table of contents; list of illustrations; index.

Actors. George Arliss.

15. Arthur, Sir George C. A. *From Phelps to Gielgud: Reminiscences of the Stage through Sixty-Five Years.* Introd. by John Gielgud. London, 1936; rpt. Freeport, New York: Books for Libraries, 1967; rpt. New York: Benjamin Blom, 1972. 256 pp.

This volume of reminiscences of the London stage concerns the years from the 1870s to the 1930s. The author comments on actors, such as the Bancrofts, Irving, Bernhardt, and Gielgud, and theatrical topics, such as "Burlesque and Musical Comedy," "Diction," and critics. Personal observations and hearsay are utilized in the anecdotes and reflections comprising the various chapters. Sections on Mme. Modjeska's and Mary Anderson's visits to England in the 1880's, including evaluations of their performances, are included.

Illustrations. Ten photographs of actors, mostly British.

Features. Author's note; introduction by John Gielgud; table of contents; list of illustrations; index.

Actors. Mary Anderson, Helena Modjeska.

16. Ball, Robert Hamilton. *The Amazing Career of Sir Giles Overreach: Being the Life and Adventures of a Nefarious Scoundrel Who for Three Centuries Pursued His Sinister Designs in Almost All the Theatres of the British Isles and America, the Whole Comprising a History of the Stage.* Princeton, New Jersey: Princeton University Press, 1939; rpt. New York: Octagon Books, 1968. xiii, 467 pp.

Writing on the English and American stage history of Philip Massinger's *A New Way to Pay Old Debts,* the author focuses primarily on those actors who have notably portrayed the play's main character—Sir Giles Overreach. The author treats the English and American stages separately and he has "grouped the presentations under the actors [who played Sir Giles] , and treated these groups chronologically according to the actor's *first* performance of the part."   Specific dates of productions, cast lists, and copious quotations from contemporary criticisms, containing evaluations and descriptions of performances, are included.   Over one-sixth of the text concerns American productions of the period 1861-1910.   In addition to the more substantial material on Booth and Davenport, the author comments briefly on many other American players.

Illustrations. Fourteen photographs, paintings, and engravings, mostly of actors as Sir Giles Overreach.

Features. Preface; table of contents; list of illustrations; thorough documentation; bibliography; Appendix A: "The Stage Versions of *A New Way to Pay Old Debts*"; Appendix B: "Addenda [to the known presentations of *A New Way to Pay Old Debts*] "; index.

Actors. Edwin Booth, E. L. Davenport.

17. [Ball, William Thomas Winsborough] . *Life and Memoires of William Warren, Boston's Favorite Commedian. With a Full Account of His Golden Jubilee. Fifty*

Years of an Actor's Life. Boston: James Daly, [1888?]. 70 pp.

This brief volume is an admiring tribute to William Warren, Jr. Among the materials included are a sketchy outline of the actor's life, year-by-year lists of his new roles during his thirty-six seasons in Boston, a description of the celebration of his golden anniversary on the stage, and several appreciations of him which were written after his death. Unfortunately, sources of quoted materials are not indicated. Although some considerations of Warren's acting are included, this is primarily a tribute to Warren, the man.

Illustrations. Seven, mostly photographs of William Warren, Jr.

Features. Lists of roles which Warren first played in Boston.

Actors. William Warren, Jr.

18.   Bancroft, [Lady] Marie, and [Sir] Squire Bancroft. *The Bancrofts: Recollections of Sixty Years.* New York: E. P. Dutton, 1909; rpt. New York: Benjamin Blom, 1969. xii, 462 pp.

This volume of reminiscences is drawn from the Bancrofts' experiences, primarily in London, during the last half of the nineteenth century and the beginning of the twentieth. The authors recollect theatre conditions, productions, and scores of friends and associates—in and out of the theatre. Anecdotes, many letters to the Bancrofts, and brief descriptions and appreciations, but few dates, are included. In addition to those listed below, the authors comment briefly on a few American actors, for example, Joseph Jefferson III, Edwin Booth, and John Sleeper Clarke.

Illustrations. Thirty-seven photographs and drawings of the Bancrofts and some of their friends.

Features. Preface; table of contents; list of illustrations; index.

Actors. Dion Boucicault, Charles Coghlan, E. A. Sothern.

19.   Bandmann, Daniel E. *An Actor's Tour: Seventy Thousand Miles with Shakespeare.* Ed. by Barnard Gisby. Boston: Cupples, Upham, 1885. x, 303 pp.

This book is the German-born actor-author's chronicle of his extensive tour through the South Pacific and the Orient during the early 1880s. Although replete with anecdotes and the author's opinions of his encounters, it contains little infomation relative to theatre.

Illustrations. One painting of the author as Hamlet.

Features. Preface by Barnard Gisby; table of contents.

Actors. Daniel E. Bandmann.

20.   Barclay, G[eorge] Lippard (ed.). *The Life and Remarkable Career of Adah Isaacs Menken, the Celebrated Actress. An Account of Her Career as a Danseuse, an Actress, an Authoress, a Poetess, a Sculptor, an Editress, as Captain of the "Dayton Light Guard," as the Wife of the Pugilist John C. Heenan, and of "Orpheus Kerr."* Philadelphia: Barclay, 1868. 63 pp.

This book contains a biographical sketch of Adah Isaacs Menken and a miscellany of writings by, to, and about her, including some of her poetry. Both factual and anecdotal materials concerning this "virtuous" actress are included. Miss Menken's lengthy—and probably spurious—account of her capture by Indians in Texas is inserted.

Illustrations. Three drawings, one portrait and two fanciful scenes from Adah Isaacs Menken's life.

Features. Brief biographical sketches of seven actors and

actresses.

Actors. Adah Isaacs Menken.

21.   Barnabee, Henry Clay. *Reminiscences of Henry Clay
        Barnabee: Being an Attempt to Account for His Life,
        with Some Excuses for His Professional Career.* Ed. by
        George Leon Varney. Boston: Chapple Publishing,
        1913; rpt. Freeport, New York: Books for Libraries,
        1971. 461 pp.

> This volume of miscellaneous reminiscences proceeds,
> with many tangents, from the author's youth (he was
> born in 1833) to 1906. The many anecdotes primarily
> concern the author's career in musical theatre, especially
> his connection with the Boston Ideal Opera Company
> (later, The Bostonians). Brief comments on several actors
> and singers, for example Richard Mansfield, Charlotte
> Cushman, and William Warren, Jr., numerous excerpts
> from periodical reviews, and a few dates are included.
> The volume concludes with selections from appreciative
> letters written by many of the author's friends and co-
> workers.

> *Illustrations.* One hundred and fifty-four photographs of
> the author, other performers, and places.

> *Features.* Introduction by George Leon Varney; table of
> contents; documentation: sources of quota-
> tions are usually indicated by title and/or date;
> lists of the author's roles with the Boston Ideal
> Opera Company and The Bostonians, pp. 339-
> 40 and p. 426.

> *Actors.* Henry Clay Barnabee, William Warren, Jr.

22.   Barnes, J[ohn] H. *Forty Years on the Stage: Others (Prin-
        cipally) and Myself.* New York: E. P. Dutton, 1915.
        vi, 320 pp.

> Dealing primarily with his acting career during the period

1871-1914, the author writes with the intention of using his career as "a peg on which to hang impressions and anecdotes of men and women and places and circumstances which can hardly fail to prove entertaining reading for many, both inside and outside my own calling." The author's recollections mainly concern the English stage, but, having performed with many American actors in both England and America, he includes brief comments on many American actors, such as John McCullough, Mary Anderson, and Joseph Jefferson III. Few specific dates are included.

Illustrations. Thirty-three photographs of the author, other actors, and other acquaintances of the author.

Features. List of illustrations; index.

Actors. General.

23. Barrett, Lawrence. *Edwin Forrest.* Boston: James R. Osgood, 1881; Boston: Houghton Mifflin, 1893; rpt. St. Clair Shores, Michigan: Scholarly Press, 1969; rpt. New York: Benjamin Blom, 1969. 171 pp.

This life of Edwin Forest is based mainly on earlier biographies. Primarily narrative, with some specific dates, anecdotes, and criticisms, approximately one-fourth of the book concerns the post-1860 period. The author provides some anecdotes and evaluations from his personal experiences with Forrest and reflects on many incidents in Forrest's life. Little specific description of Forrest's acting is included.

Illustrations. Seven, including one photograph and six engravings and facsimiles, of Edwin Forrest, Mrs. Forrest, and materials related to the actor's life.

Features. Table of contents; list of illustrations; documentation: sources of quotations are indicated by author and/or title and/or date; index.

Actors. Edwin Forrest.

24.   Barron, Elwyn A[lfred]. *Lawrence Barrett: A Profession-al Sketch.* Chicago: Knight & Leonard, 1889. 98 pp.

> This chronological narrative of Lawrence Barrett's career, emphasizing the period 1856-1889, is, in the author's words, "necessarily cursory, brief glimpses of a career that is rich in exceptional interest." The work is a usable summary of Barrett's career to 1889, but it provides few specific dates or anecdotes and it is almost entirely admiring of the actor. The book contains numerous excerpts from newspaper reviews which evaluate and/or describe briefly Barrett's performances in many of his most notable roles, but does not document the sources of the quotations.

Illustrations. Five photographs of Lawrence Barrett.

Features. Introduction.

Actors. Lawrence Barrett.

25.   Barry, John D[aniel]. *Julia Marlowe.* Boston: Richard G. Badger, ©1899. 87 pp.

Ibid. Boston: E. H. Bacon, 1907. 117 pp. Illus.

> *1899 ed.:* In this chronological narrative, emphasizing the period 1887-99, the author traces Julia Marlowe's acting career to the time of publication. Along with lengthy quotations from critiques published in various periodicals, the author includes his own brief evaluations of the actress' major characterizations. Comments on Robert Taber—Miss Marlowe's co-star and husband—and brief comparisons of Miss Marlowe's portrayal with those of other actresses, for example Mary Anderson, Ada Rehan, and Helena Modjeska, are included. Few specific dates are provided.

> *1907 ed.:* This edition reprints the full text of the 1899

edition and extends the narrative of Miss Marlowe's career through the summer of 1907. The actress' professional relationship with E. H. Sothern, especially their London season of 1907, is emphasized. Several excerpts from British criticisms are included.

Illustrations. 1899 ed.: Seventeen photographs of Julia Marlowe.
1907 ed.: Thirty-eight photographs of Julia Marlowe.

Features. None.

Actors. 1899 ed.: Julia Marlowe, Robert Taber.
1907 ed.: Julia Marlowe, E. H. Sothern, Robert Taber.

26. Barrymore, Ethel. *Memories: An Autobiography.* New York: Harper & Brothers, © 1955; rpt. New York: Kraus Reprint, 1968. x, 310 pp.

Covering the years from the 1880s to the 1950s, the author reminisces about her theatrical, social, and personal life. She comments on many productions and scores of friends—both in and out of the theatre world. She includes anecdotes relating to most members of the Drew-Barrymore family. Over one-half of the book concerns the pre-1911 period.

Illustrations. Seventy-three, mostly photographs of the author and other members of the Drew and Barrymore families.

Features. Table of contents, list of illustrations; documentation: most sources of quotations are indicated by author and/or title and/or date; index.

Actors. Ethel Barrymore, John Drew II, Mrs. John Drew.

27. Barrymore, John. *Confessions of an Actor.* Indianapolis,

Inc.: Bobbs-Merrill, © 1926. Unnumbered.

This book of loosely strung and mostly humorous anecdotes and recollections concerns the author's life from the
1890s to the mid-1920s. Occasional brief descriptions of
stage business and a lengthy letter from Bernard Shaw
concerning Barrymore's London *Hamlet* of 1925 are included. The author inserts passing comments on other
members of the Drew-Barrymore family. Approximately
one-half of the text relates to the pre-1911 period.

Illustrations. Thirty-four, mostly photographs of John
Barrymore.

Features. None.

Actors. John Barrymore.

28.   —. *We Three: Ethel—Lionel—John.* Akron, Ohio, and
New York: Saalfield Publishing, © 1935. Unnumbered.

This friendly reminiscence of Ethel, Lionel, and John
Barrymore, with brief glimpses of other members of the
Drew-Barrymore family, emphasizes the post-1910 period,
but provides some information on earlier years. Anecdotes and material concerning family relationships, individual personalities, and the author's approach to acting
are included.

Illustrations. Forty-nine photographs of Drews, Barrymores, and related materials.

Features. None.

Actors. Ethel Barrymore, John Barrymore, Lionel Barrymore.

29.   Barrymore, Lionel, as told to Cameron Shipp. *We Barrymores.* New York: Appleton-Century-Crofts, © 1951;
New York: Grosset & Dunlap, © 1951. viii, 311 pp.

This volume of reminiscences and reflections proceeds chronologically from the author's youth in the 1880s to the time of publication. Nearly one-half of the text deals with the pre-1911 period. Anecdotes and opinions concerning the author's stage and film career predominate, but information on his offstage life and memories of numerous actors, authors, directors, and managers are included. The comments on other actors pertain mostly to members of the Drew-Barrymore family. The author's remarks on his attitude toward and approach to acting are scattered throughout the book.

Illustrations. Nineteen photographs of the author and members of his family.

Features. Table of contents; list of illustrations; documentation: rare partial indications of the sources of quotations; appended list of Lionel Barrymore' stage appearances (includes theatres, dates of opening, and cast lists); Lane-Drew-Barrymore family tree (inside front cover); index.

Actors. Ethel Barrymore, John Barrymore, Lionel Barrymore, Maurice Barrymore.

30. Bates, Finis L[angdon]. *The Escape and Suicide of John Wilkes Booth, or the First True Account of Lincoln's Assassination, Containing a Complete Confession by Booth Many Years after the Crime, Giving in Full Detail the Plans, Plot and Intrigue of the Conspirators, and the Treachery of Andrew Johnson, then Vice-President of the United States, Written for the Correction of History.* Boston: G. M. Smith, © 1907; Memphis, Tennessee: Historical Publishing, © 1907; Memphis, Tennessee: Pilcher Printing, 1907; Naperville, Illinois, Atlanta, and Memphis, Tennessee: J. L. Nichols, [1907]; Parkersburg, West Virginia: White, 1908. 309 pp.

The author attempts to prove that John Wilkes Booth did not die in 1865, that Wilkes Booth later lived as John

St. Helen, and that he committed suicide in 1903 while using the name David E. George. The author was St. Helen's attorney in the early 1870s and was St. Helen's audience for a lengthy confession concerning the Lincoln conspiracy, assassination, and escape. The author reproduces this long-remembered confession in the form of a direct quotation. The author's later investigations of the "John Wilkes Booth" identity are detailed, along with sketchy accounts of "Booth's" later activities. The author's conclusions are highly dubious and many of his "facts" are in error.

Illustrations. Thirty-one photographs, tintypes, and drawings of John Wilkes Booth, people associated with the Lincoln assassination or with Booth, and fanciful scenes; some of the tintypes and photographs are apparently retouched.

Features. Preface; table of contents; list of illustrations.

Actors. John Wilkes Booth.

31.   Bates, Helen Marie [Leslie]. *Lotta's Last Season.* Brattleboro, Vermont: Printed by E. L. Hildreth for the author, 1940. 306 pp.

This book is divided into two sections: a narrative of "Lotta's Last Season" and the author's autobiography. Having been the leading lady in Lotta Crabtree's company during the star's last season of performing, the author affords an unusually intimate backstage view of the "inimitable" Lotta and her redoubtable mother. Both sections contain anecdotes concerning other members of the Crabtree troupe and other actors with whom the author was acquainted, such as Edwin Booth.

Illustrations. Four photographs of Lotta Crabtree.

Features. Foreword; table of contents.

Actors. Lotta Crabtree, Helen Leslie [Bates].

32.   Belasco, David. *The Theatre Through Its Stage Door.* Ed.
by Louis V. DeFoe. New York: Harper & Brothers,
1919; rpt. New York: Benjamin Blom, 1969. 246 pp.

> In the several essays comprising this volume the author
> advances his ideas on a number of theatrical topics, in-
> cluding actor-training, the acting profession, play produc-
> tion, and cinema. Although most of his discussion deals
> in generalities, he includes some anecdotes from his act-
> ing, directing, and producing experience. He comments
> briefly on such actors as David Warfield, Nance O'Neill,
> John McCullough, and Robert Taber.
>
> *Illustrations.* Thirty-one photographs of the author,
>   actors, scenes from Belasco productions,
>   and areas in the Belasco Theatre.
>
> *Features.* Foreword; table of contents; list of illustra-
>   tions.
>
> *Actors.* David Belasco, Mrs. Leslie Carter, Frances Starr.

33.   Bennett, Joan, and Lois Kibbee. *The Bennett Playbills.*
New York, Chicago, and San Francisco: Holt, Rinehart, and Winston, © 1970. xi, 332 pp.

> This book is an anecdotal biography of the Wood-Morri-
> son-Bennett theatrical family from the end of the eigh-
> teenth century to 1967. Among those members of the
> family who are included are William F. Wood, Rose Wood,
> Lewis Morrison, Richard Bennett (the author's father),
> Mabel Adrienne Morrison (her mother), Constance Bennet
> (her sister), and the author. The careers of the author, her
> father, and her grandfather (Lewis Morrison) are empha-
> sized. Approximately one-fourth of the book relates to
> the 1861-1910 period.
>
> *Illustrations.* Thirty-eight, mostly photographs of the
>   Wood-Morrison-Bennett family.
>
> *Features.* Preface; acknowledgements; documentation:
>   some sources of quotations are partially identi-

fied.

Actors. Richard Bennett, Lewis Morrison, Mabel Adrie-
enne Morrison [Bennett] , Rose Wood.

34.   Binns, Archie, in collaboration with Olive Kooken. *Mrs.
Fiske and the American Theatre.* Foreword by George
Freedley. New York: Crown, © 1955. x, 436 pp.

This admiring narrative of Minnie Maddern Fiske's life is,
according to George Freedley, writing in the foreward,
"the definitive Fiske biography." The book contains
anecdotes, specific dates, and much quoted material.
The quotations are drawn from reviews, appreciations,
and letters, and they include many autobiographical
statements by Mrs. Fiske.   Well over one-half of the
volume concerns the pre-1911 period, emphasizing the
years following her marriage to Harrison Grey Fiske in
1890.   Comments on many of Mrs. Fiske's fellow-actors,
for example John Mason, Maurice Barrymore, Tyrone
Power, and Lotta Crabtree, are included.

Illustrations. Sixty-two, mostly photographs of Minnie
Maddern Fiske.

Features. Foreword by George Freedley; preface; list of
illustrations; documentation: most sources of
quotations are indicated by author, occasionally by title, and rarely by date; appended lists
of "Produced Plays written by Minnie Maddern
Fiske," "Plays written by Minnie Maddern
Fiske but not produced," "Some parts played
by Minnie Maddern as a child," "Other plays in
which Minnie Maddern appeared as a star,"
"Theatre Programs" (1871-1931; includes most
of Mrs. Fiske's productions and a few of Miss
Maddern's; includes dates, theatres, and cast
lists); index.

Actors. George Arliss, Minnie Maddern Fiske, Emily
Stevens.

35.   Blum, Daniel. *Great Stars of the American Stage: A Pictorial Record.* New York: Greenberg, © 1952. Unnumbered.

This volume consists of entries for one hundred and fifty "stars" whose main periods of popularity range from the late nineteenth century to the middle of the twentieth century. Each entry contains a brief biographical sketch and several photographs (up to twenty; most in roles). The author's arbitrary choices range through such figures as Lillian Russell, John Drew II, the Barrymores, the Lunts, Walter Huston, Eva Le Gallienne, Uta Hagen, Brando, and Maureen Stapleton. Not all of the subjects are American, nor are they all primarily dramatic actors: such performers as Olivier, Gielgud, W. C. Fields, and Eddie Cantor are included. Approximately one-half of the profiles concern performers who made their adult, American debuts prior to 1911.

Illustrations. Hundreds of photographs of performers notable on the American stage.

Features. Foreword; index.

Actors. General.

36.   —. *A Pictorial History of the American Theatre, 1900-1950.* Foreword by Helen Hayes. New York: Greenberg, © 1950. 276 pp.

Ibid. *A Pictorial History of the American Theatre, 1900-1951.* New York: Greenberg, © 1951. 304 pp.

Ibid. *A Pictorial History of the American Theatre.* [rev., 3rd ed.] New York: Grosset & Dunlap, 1953. 304 pp.

Ibid. *A Pictorial History of the American Theatre, 1900-1956.* New York: Greenberg, 1956. 319 pp.

Ibid. *A Pictorial History of the American Theatre, 100 Years, 1860-1960.* Philadelphia: Chilton, © 1960;

New York: Bonanza, © 1960. 384 pp.

Ibid. *A Pictorial History of the American Theatre, 1860-1970.* New 3rd ed., enl. and rev. by John Willis. New York: Crown, © 1969. 416 pp.

1950 ed.: This volume contains, in a season-by-season arrangement, thousands of portrait, character, and production photographs of actors and productions on the American stage during the period 1900-50. Although many of the illustrations are of poor quality or are rather small, this is an invaluable record of the American theatre.

1951 ed.: This edition is the same as the 1950 edition through the 1948 season. There are some additions to and deletions from the illustrations for 1949 and 1950. Coverage is extended through the 1951 season.

1953 ed.: This edition is the same as the 1951 edition through the 1948 season. There are some additions to and deletions from the illustrations for 1949-51. Coverage is extended through the 1952 season.

1956 ed.: This edition is the same as the 1953 edition through the 1952 season. Coverage is extended through the first half of the 1956 season.

1960 ed.: Photographs and engravings covering the period 1860-99 are added. There are some deletions of photographs for the period 1900-49, but the 1950-55 illustrations are the same as in the 1956 edition. Coverage is extended through the first half of the 1960 season.

1969 ed.: This edition is the same as the 1960 edition except two full-page portraits are omitted and coverage is extended through the first half of the 1969 season.

Illustrations: Thousands of portrait, character, and production illustrations, almost totally photographs (each edition).

Features. Foreword by Helen Hayes (each edition); index (each edition).

Actors. General.

37. Bodeen, DeWitt. *Ladies of the Footlights.* Pasadena, California: Login Printing and Binding, © 1937. 133 pp.

> This book is composed of twenty brief biographical articles on prominent actresses who had appeared on the West Coast. These sketchy biographies include some anecdotal material and tend to be romantic or sensationalistic. In addition to the actresses noted below, there are articles on Lola Montez, Lillie Langtry, Bernhardt, Duse, Adelaide Neilson, and Ellen Terry.

> *Illustrations.* Eight pen-and-ink drawings of actresses.

> *Features.* Table of contents.

> *Actors.* Mary Anderson, Lotta Crabtree, Pauline Cushman, Fanny Davenport, Julia Dean Hayne, Matilda Heron, Laura Keene, Julia Marlowe, Adah Isaacs Menken, Helena Modjeska, Clara Morris, Ada Rehan, Lillian Russell, Catherine Sinclair.

38. Booth, Edwin, and William Winter. *Between Actor and Critic: Selected Letters of Edwin Booth and William Winter.* Ed., with an introd. and commentary, by Daniel J[ude] Watermeier. Princeton, New Jersey: Princeton University Press, 1971. ix, 329 pp.

> This volume contains one hundred and eighteen letters from Booth to Winter, with excerpts from twenty additional letters, the six known extant letters from Winter to Booth, and one letter from Edwina Booth Grossman to Winter. "The letters are arranged chronologically and divided into ten chapters corresponding to periods of Booth's professional activity. . . Through a series of headnotes [the editor has] tried to orient the reader towards the content of each letter, put it in context and provide a narrative continuity from one letter to the next." The letters, which emphasize the period 1869-90,

provide rare insight into Booth's personality, as well as containing information on his career. Brief comments on other actors of the period are included. Watermeier's commentary and biographical introduction are clear, informative, and well-documented.

Illustrations. Nineteen engravings and photographs of Booth, Winter, letters, and places.

Features. Preface; introduction (contains brief biographies of Booth and Winter); table of contents; list of illustrations; thorough documentation; selected bibliography; "Biographical Note" (indicates years of birth and death for persons mentioned in the text); index.

Actors. Lawrence Barrett, Edwin Booth, Joseph Jefferson III.

39.　　—. *Edwin Booth: Recollections by His Daughter, Edwina Booth Grossman, and Letters to Her and to His Friends.* New York: Century, 1894; rpt. New York: Benjamin Blom, 1969; rpt. Freeport, New York: Books for Libraries, 1970. vi, 292 pp.

Letters written by Edwin Booth to his daughter and to many of his friends during the period from 1860 to 1893 comprise ninety per cent of this book. The remainder is Mrs. Grossman's memoir of her father. The memoir contains miscellaneous anecdotes and appraisals of Booth's domestic and professional character, based on Mrs. Grossman's observations and on incidents which were told to her. The letters include anecdotes, comments, and reflections on a wide variety of matters concerning Booth's personal and public activities.

Illustrations. Fourteen photographs, drawings, and paintings, mostly of Edwin Booth.

Features. List of illustrations; index.

Actors. Lawrence Barrett, Edwin Booth.

40. Boucicault, Dion. *The Art of Acting.* Introd. by Otis Skinner. Notes by [James] Brander Matthews. New York: Published for the Dramatic Museum of Columbia University by the Columbia University Press, 1925. 66 pp.

> In the introduction, Skinner presents a general consideration of acting. He includes his own ideas and anecdotes and those relating to other players, including Joseph Jefferson III. The Boucicault essay, originally delivered as an address in 1882, deals with the teachable aspects of acting, focusing on speaking, walking, gesture, and approaches to characterization. The author presents some general "rules," specific examples, and a few anecdotes elucidating desirable and objectionable stage techniques. Matthews' notes include a brief biographical sketch of Boucicault and short quotations on acting and the teaching of acting by Coquelin, Bronson Howard, and William Charles Macready.

> *Illustrations.* None.

> *Features.* Introduction by Otis Skinner; table of contents; notes by [James] Brander Matthews.

> *Actors.* Dion Boucicault, Otis Skinner.

40a. Bowen, Croswell, with the assistance of Shane O'Neill. *The Curse of the Misbegotten: A Tale of the House of O'Neill.* New York: McGraw-Hill, © 1959. xviii, 384 pp.

> This romantic and highly anecdotal biography of Eugene O'Neill is based on the author's interviews with scores of friends and family of his subject, as well as on letters and published materials. Commentary on the plays is brief and simplistic, with the emphasis being placed on the "cursed" personal lives of O'Neill and his family. The work contains descriptions of James O'Neill's life and his relationship with Eugene.

> *Illustrations.* None.

Features. Preface; acknowledgments; table of contents; documentation: sources of quotations are identified by author and/or title and/or date; list of "Premiers of Eugene O'Neill's Plays in America;" index.

Actors. James O'Neill.

41.   Bradford, Gamaliel. *American Portraits, 1875-1900.* Boston and New York: Houghton Mifflin, 1922. xiii, 249 pp.

An essay on Joseph Jefferson III is one of eight biographical articles in this book. The Jefferson portrait emphasizes the actor's personal qualities in relation to both his stage career and his personal life. Anecdotes, quotations by and about Jefferson, and a little biographical data are included.

Illustrations. Eight photographs, paintings, and drawings of the subjects of the essays; one photograph is of Joseph Jefferson III.

Features. Preface; table of contents; list of illustrations; extensive documentation; index.

Actors. Joseph Jefferson III.

42.   —. *As God Made Them: Portraits of Some Nineteenth-Century Americans.* Boston and New York: Houghton Mifflin, 1929. 295 pp.

Among the seven biographical essays comprising this volume is one on Edwin Booth. Anecdotes, quotes from Booth's letters, comments by the actor's acquaintances, the author's interpretation of Booth's character, and some biographical data are included in this essay. The emphasis is on Booth's personal qualities, rather than on his artistic endeavors: Bradford writes, ". . .my interest in the artist is only as he explains and illustrates the man."

Illustrations. Eight photographs, paintings, and crayons, mostly of the subjects of the essays; one photograph of Edwin Booth is included.

Features. Preface; table of contents; list of illustrations; extensive documentation; index.

Actors. Edwin Booth.

42a. Bradley, Edward Sculley. *George Henry Baker: Poet and Patriot.* Philadelphia: University of Pennsylvania Press, 1927; rpt. New York: Benjamin Blom, 1972. xi, 372 pp.

This fine, respectful biography of the American man of letters and diplomat traces Baker's life (1824-90) and provides extensive descriptions and commentaries on his major literary works—especially his dramas.   Drawing upon his subject's correspondence and manuscripts, as well as published materials, the author supplements his strongly factual account with intelligent conjecture concerning Baker's activities.   Of special interest are comments on the E. L. Davenport (1855), Lawrence Barrett (1882), and Otis Skinner (1901) productions of *Francesca da Rimini,* including comments on script alteration, approaches to the play, and critical reception.

Illustrations. Thirteen photographs, prints, and paintings of Baker, productions of his plays, and miscellaneous subjects.

Features. Prefaces; table of contents; list of illustrations; documentation: sources of quotations are identified by author and/or title and/or date; bibliography; "A Chronological List of the Writings of George Henry Baker;" index.

Actors. Lawrence Barrett, Otis Skinner.

43. Brady, James Jay. *Life of Denman Thompson (Joshua Whitcomb).* New York: E. A. McFarland & Alex.

Comstock, © 1888. 83 pp.

This book is a souvenir of the 1888 production of Denman Thompson's *The Old Homestead* at the Academy,
New York City. Primarily concerned with the characters
and the dramatic milieu of this play and its predecessor—
Joshua Whitcomb—the volume also contains a biographical sketch of Thompson, notes on the stage history and
development of *Joshua Whitcomb/The Old Homestead*,
and some tributes to the play.

Illustrations. One photograph of Denman Thompson;
thirty-seven drawings of Thompson, his
parents and homes, scenes from *The Old
Homestead,* and fanciful scenes; three playbills from Thompson's career.

Features. Introduction; table of contents; documentation: sources of quotations are identified by
author and/or title.

Actors. Denman Thompson.

44.   Brady, William A. *The Fighting Man.* Indianapolis, Indiana: Bobbs-Merrill, © 1916. 227 pp.

This volume consists of the author's reminiscences of the
last third of the nineteenth century and the early years
of the twentieth. Over one-half of the book relates to his
activities as a prize-fight promoter, but some information
on his own acting and early theatrical production experiences is included.

Illustrations. Twenty-one, mostly photographs of author's
acquaintances.

Features. None.

Actors. William A. Brady.

45.   —. *Showman.* New York: E. P. Dutton, 1937. 277 pp.

The author reminisces informally about his life from the 1870s to the 1930s, emphasizing the years prior to 1904. He recollects events from his own brief acting career in the 1880s, but he deals primarily with his rather checkered career as a theatrical producer and sports promoter. He includes brief comments on some actors, for example Wilton Lackaye and David Warfield.

Illustrations. Nineteen photographs of the author and various associates, including several actors.

Features. List of illustrations.

Actors. William A. Brady.

46.　Brazier, Marion Howard. *Stage and Screen.* Boston: M. H. Brazier, © 1920. 130 pp.

The author, writing "of some of the players known to me personally or professionally, from the standpoint of the theatre goer since the middle sixties," devotes approximately two-thirds of this book to the stage and the remainder to the silent screen. She briefly records her personal reactions to dozens of actors and actresses who performed during the period from the 1860s through the 1910s. She frequently refers to individual roles, but rarely provides specific descriptions.

Illustrations. Eighty-four photographs of actors and actresses.

Features. Table of contents; list of illustrations.

Actors. Charlotte Cushman, William Seymour.

47.　Brereton, Austin. *The Life of Henry Irving.* 2 vols. New York: Longman, Green, 1908; rpt. 2 vols. in 1. New York: Benjamin Blom, 1969. Vol. I: xx, 381 pp.; Vol. II: x, 364 pp.

The author of this biography of Henry Irving was a friend

of his subject for a quarter of a century. Utilizing statements by the author, Irving, and various critics, the work
concentrates on Irving's life and especially on his career,
but it also contains comments on many of the actor's
associates and friends. A section on Edwin Booth's London engagement of 1880-81 is included.

> *Illustrations. Vol. I:* twenty-three photographs, drawings,
> paintings, etc., mainly of Henry Irving.
> *Vol. II:* twenty-two photographs, drawings,
> paintings, etc., mainly of Henry Irving.

> *Features.* Preface (Vol. I); table of contents (each vol.
> for that vol.); lists of illustrations (each vol. for
> that vol.); documentation: sources of quota-
> tions are identified by author and/or title and/
> or date; bibliography (each vol.: Vol. I—to the
> end of 1883; Vol. II—1884-1908); "Parts
> Played by Henry Irving" (1857-1903; Vol. II);
> index (Vol. II for both vols.).

> *Actors.* Edwin Booth.

48.   Briscoe, Johnson. *The Actors' Birthday Book: An Author-
itative Insight Into the Lives of the Men and Women of
the Stage Born Between January 1 and December 31.*
3 series. New York: Moffat, Yard, 1907-09. First
Ser.: 285 pp.; Second Ser.: 288 pp.; Third Ser.: 296
pp.

> *First Ser.:* This volume, "meant as an artistic souvenir,
> more than as a reference work," consists of a chronologi-
> cal listing of the days of the year, with each date accom-
> panied by a brief biographical sketch of a living theatre
> worker (mostly, but not exclusively, American actors)
> who was born on that day. Some dates are omitted due
> to "the thoughtlessness of actors in not having been born
> on these particular dates." Factual accuracy is attempted
> in the brief surveys of the actors' careers. This miscel-
> laneous collection of biographies includes information
> on many little-remembered performers. There are three
> hundred and forty-five biographies.

Second Ser.: Observing the same general aim as the First Series, this volume reproduces a few biographical sketches from the earlier book and includes biographies of a small number of deceased performers. Three hundred and sixty-three biographical sketches are included. *Third Ser.:* This volume deviates from the aim of the previous books of this series in the following manner: ". . . the compiler has endeavored in this third, and last, book to include as many of our leading players as possible. In order to do this, of course, the most important biographies of the other books are reproduced in this one, with the addition of over eighty new names. . . ." Containing over four hundred biographical sketches, this volume contains more than one entry for some dates.

Illustrations. First Ser.: eighty-four photographs of some of the subjects of the sketches.
Second Ser.: ninety-eight photographs of some of the subjects of the sketches.
Third Ser.: ninety-two photographs of some of the subjects of the sketches.

Features. Introduction (each vol. for that vol.); table of contents (an alphabetical listing of the subjects of the biographical sketches; each vol. for that vol.); list of names of subjects treated in the First Series (Second Series).

Actors. General (each vol.).

49. Brougham, John. *Life, Stories, and Poems of John Brougham.* Ed. by William Winter. Boston: James R. Osgood, 1881. xi, 461 pp.

This memorial volume is composed of four main sections: autobiographical materials by Brougham, a supplementary memoir by Winter, a reminiscence of the actor's association with the Lotos Club of New York by Noah Brooks, and a selection of thirteen short stories and twenty-three poems written by Brougham. The autobiographical writings include fragmentary pieces concerning Brougham's youth and early career, a synopsis of his

career, an interview with him which was originally published in the *New York Herald* (no date given), extracts
from Brougham's diaries of 1853-54 and 1878-80, and his
will. Winter's memoir contains reprints of two of his own
obituaries of Brougham, two poetic tributes to the actor,
and miscellaneous reminiscences and information concerning the actor. Factual, anecdotal, and eulogizing materials
predominate in this book; criticism and description of
Brougham's acting are omitted.

Illustrations. Eight photographs and drawings of Brougham and scenes from his stories, and one
facsimile manuscript page.

Features. Preface by William Winter; table of contents;
list of illustrations; documentation: sources
of some quotations are partially indicated.

Actors. John Brougham.

50.   Brown, T[homas] Allston. *History of the American Stage,
Containing Biographical Sketches of Nearly Every
Member of the Profession That Has Appeared on the
American Stage, from 1733 to 1870.* New York: Dick
and Fitzgerald, 1870; rpt. New York: Benjamin Blom,
1969; rpt. New York: Burt Franklin, 1969. 421 pp.

In this pioneering collection of information, the hundreds
of biographical sketches are concerned chiefly with performers who resided in or visited the United States, but
some non-performers (e.g., managers) are included. The
entries are arranged alphabetically according to the last
names of the subjects; husband and wife are usually given
a single entry under the husband's name. An alphabetically-arranged appendix contains additional entries and
addenda to entries in the main body of the work. Most of
the entries are brief, but this book is useful in suggesting
major functions, some times and places of activities, etc.,
for the persons included. The work is especially useful
for comments, however brief, on minor figures about
whom information is difficult to find. The entries vary
widely in quality and length and are sometimes marred

by factual errors.

Illustrations. Eighty portrait engravings of actors.

Features. Preface; appendix containing additional entries and addenda to entries in the main body of the work.

Actors. General.

51. —. *A History of the New York Stage, from the First Performance in 1732 to 1901.* 3 vols. New York: Dodd, Mead, 1903; rpt. New York: Benjamin Blom, 1964. Vol. I: xii, 523 pp.; Vol. II: x, 652 pp.; Vol. III: ix, 671 pp.

This history is arranged by separate entries for over four hundred New York theatres. The entries are ordered according to the dates of the openings of the theatres. Each entry contains a chronological record of the entertainments held in the subject-theatre. Specific dates, titles of productions, cast lists or the names of the stars, and miscellaneous comments are included. The author inserts short biographical sketches of many prominent actors and provides descriptive or evaluative comments on several, many of whom he had personally observed.

Illustrations. None.

Features. Preface (Vol. I); tables of contents (each vol. for that vol.); indices (Vol. III): "Index" (theatres and play titles), "Brief Index of Actors," "Brief List of Theatre Riots," "Brief List of Benefits," "List of Theatres Destroyed by Fire," "Brief List of Male Characters Impersonated by Women," "Notable Events Connected with the Stage in America."

Actors. General.

52. Browne, Walter, and F. A. Austin (eds.). *Who's Who on*

the Stage: The Dramatic Reference Book and Bio-graphical Dictionary of the Theatre.   Containing Re-cords of the Careers of Actors, Actresses, Managers, and Playwrights of the American Stage. New York: Walter Browne & F. A. Austin, ©1906. 232 pp.

Browne, Walter, and E. DeRoy Koch (eds.). *Who's Who on the Stage, 1908:   The Dramatic Reference Book and Biographical Dictionary. Containing Careers of Actors, Actresses, Managers, and Playwrights of the American Stage.* New York: B. W. Dodge, 1908. 467 pp. Illus.

1906 ed.: This volume contains "biographies, not only of hundreds of actors and actresses, including all the stars and many lesser lights, but also of managers, playwrights, musical composers, opera singers, and the most prominent of vaudeville artists." Most of the subjects were American and were living at the time of publication. The brief sketches present factual data concerning the subjects' careers and, occasionally, private lives. Many specific dates and, for actors, major roles are indicated. Although alphabetical order is not scrupulously observed, "All named with the same initial. . .will be found together."

1908 ed.: This edition updates biographical sketches which originally appeared in the 1906 edition and adds entries for many persons who were not included in the earlier work. The arrangement is alphabetical.

Illustrations. 1906 ed.: Seventy-six portrait photographs of many of the subjects of the biographical sketches.
1908 ed.: Fifty-one portrait photographs of many of the subjects of the biographical sketches.

Features. 1906 ed.: Preface.
1908 ed.: None.

Actors. General (both editions).

53. [Buck, Lillie West Brown] , Amy Leslie [pseud.] . *Some Players: Personal Sketches.* Chicago and New York: Hubert S. Stone, © 1899. 624 pp.

Ibid. New York: Duffield, 1906. 436 pp. Illus.

1899 ed.: This volume contains complimentary (sometimes adulatory) sketches of prominent performers of the end of the nineteenth century. Bits of biography, anecdotes, personal appreciations, criticisms, and descriptions of the subjects on and off the stage are included, much derived from the author's personal acquaintance with her subjects. In addition to the actors noted below, the author comments briefly on other American actors, such as David Warfield, Robert Taber, and Henry Miller, as well as foreign actors, opera and comic opera celebrities, and variety performers.

1906 ed.: This edition is composed of sketches from the 1899 edition. These biographies concern American, English, and European actors of the legitimate state only.

Illustrations. 1899 ed.: Thirty-five photographs of some of the subjects of the sketches.

> *1906 ed.:* Twenty-four photographs of some of the subjects of the sketches.

Features. Table of contents; list of illustrations (both editions).

Actors. 1899 ed.: Viola Allen, Julia Arthur, Maurice Barrymore, Edwin Booth, William H. Crane, Fanny Davenport, Minnie Maddern Fiske, William Gillette, Nat C. Goodwin, James H. Herne, May Irwin, Joseph Jefferson III, Thomas Keene, Richard Mansfield, Julia Marlowe, Helena Modjeska, Clara Morris, Cora Urquhart Potter, Ada Rehan, Stuart Robson, Annie Russell, Lillian Russell, Otis Skinner, E. H. Sothern, James H. Stoddart, Fay Templeton.

> *1906 ed.:* Same as the 1899 edition except this edition omits Viola Allen, May Irwin, Lillian Russell, and Fay Templeton.

54.   Bulliet, C[larence] J[oseph]. *Robert Mantell's Romance.*
       Boston: John W. Luce, © 1918. vii, 256 pp.

> This popularly-written biography of Robert B. Mantell,
> covering the period from the 1860s through 1917, was
> written by a long-time friend and sometime business asso-
> ciate of the actor. The author had access to Mantell's
> personal papers and conversations. Although primarily
> writing a chronological narrative, the author digresses
> "Any time [he feels] like interrupting the narrative to
> insert something out of its order or even something
> wholly irrelevant. . . ." The author emphasizes Mantell's
> career after the latter's American debut in 1878, although
> he also includes information concerning Mantell's youth
> and early career in Ireland and England. Anecdotes,
> appreciations of the actor's work, and biographical data,
> including many specific dates, are contained in this book.

> *Illustrations.* Twenty-seven,   mostly   photographs   of
>   Robert B. Mantell.

> *Features.* Prologue; table of contents; list of illustrations.

> *Actors.* Robert B. Mantell.

55.   Burke, Billie, with Cameron Shipp. *With a Feather on My
       Nose.* New York: Appleton-Century-Crofts, © 1949.
       ix, 272 pp.

> This volume comprises the author's reminiscences about
> her life and career from the last decade of the nineteenth
> century into the 1940s. Primarily anecdotes, with some
> description and reflection, over one-third of the book
> concerns the pre-1911 period (she debuted in America in
> 1907). Major portions of the book concern the author's
> marriage to Florenz Ziegfeld, Jr., and her work under the
> management of Charles Frohman. Briefer passages relate
> to actors and playwrights of the author's acquaintance,
> such as John Drew II, Maxine Elliott, and Booth Tarking-
> ton.

> *Illustrations.* Seventeen, primarily photographs of Billie

Burke and her friends.

Features. Table of contents; list of illustrations; appended lists of productions in which Billie Burke appeared in London, 1903-07, and New York, 1907-44 (includes date of opening, theatre, and cast).

Actors. Billie Burke.

56. Burroughs, Marie. *The Marie Burroughs Art Portfolio of Stage Celebrities: A Collection of Photographs of the Leaders of Dramatic and Lyric Art.* 14 parts. Chicago: A. N. Marquis, ©1894. Unnumbered.

Two hundred and eight-two photographs of "the most noted dramatic, operatic, and musical artists of the world who have, within recent years, found favor with the American public" comprise this work. Miss Burroughs is pictured nine times; one portrait of each of the other artists is included. Each photograph is accompanied by a biographical note which provides a very brief identification of the subject. Most of the subjects were living American performers; a few had died within the decade prior to publication or were English or European artists who toured in the United States.

Illustrations. Two hundred and eighty-two photographs of dramatic and musical performers (twenty-one in Parts 1 and 2; twenty in each of the other parts).

Features. Introduction (pt. 2); publisher's note (back cover of each part); note: "The Great Singers" (inside front cover of Pts. 12, 13, and 14); lists of contents for the entire work (inside back cover of Pts. 12, 13, and 14).

Actors. General.

56a. Cahn, William. *The Laugh Makers: A Pictorial History of*

American Comedians. Introd. Harold Lloyd. New York: Putnam, © 1957. 192 pp.

Ibid. *A Pictorial History of the Great Comedians.* New York: Grosset and Dunlap, © 1970. 224 pp.

1970 ed.: This popularly-written work contains brief discussion of major American comedians, comics and clowns from the 1790s to the 1960s. Anecdotes, comments by the performers, excerpts from routines, undocumented historical notes, and critical quotations are used to sketch the major features of variety, film, and legitimate stage performers. Among those mentioned are Joseph Jefferson III, Harrigan and Hart, May Irwin, Weber and Fields, and George M. Cohan.

Illustrations. Hundreds of drawings, prints, and photographs, mainly of American comedy performers.

Features. Acknowledgments; introduction (by Harold Lloyd in 1957 edition only); table of contents; no documentation; index.

Actors. General.

57. Carlisle, Carol Jones. *Shakespeare from the Greenroom: Actors' Criticism of Four Major Tragedies.* Chapel Hill, North Carolina: University of North Carolina Press, © 1969. xiv, 492 pp.

The author's aim is "to present a coherent and useful account of the best Shakespearean criticisms by English and American actors, past and present: concerning *Hamlet, Othello, King Lear, and Macbeth.*" The chapter devoted to each play is divided into three sections: "The Play" ("structure, language, 'meaning,' theatrical effectiveness," etc.), "The Characters" (the "heroes" and some other major roles), and "From Criticism to Theatre" (attempting "to illuminate the process by which an actor translates his critical ideas about Shakespeare into terms that can be realized on the stage"). Hundreds of, usually, brief quotations by scores of actors from the Restoration to the middle of the twentieth century are incorporated into the author's commentary. Included are comments by such American players of the 1861-1911 period as Edwin Booth, Charlotte Cushman, Edwin Forrest, and Frederick Warde.

Illustrations. None.

Features. Preface; table of contents; thorough documentation; appendix: "Biographical Sketches of the Actor-Critics"; index.

Actors. Edwin Booth, James H. Hackett.

57a. Carpenter, Frederic I. *Eugene O'Neill.* New York: © 1964. 191 pp.

The first third of this volume comprises a biography of O'Neill, relating his life to this plays. The balance of the work consists of descriptions and criticisms of O'Neill's "best" dramas. This useful introduction to the playwright's life and work contains commentary on O'Neill's relationship with his father and a comparison of the elder O'Neill with the James Tyrone of *Long Day's Journey Into Night.*

Illustrations. None.

Features. Preface; acknowledgments; table of contents; thorough documentation; selected bibliography; brief chronology of Eugene O'Neill's life; index.

Actors. James O'Neill.

58. Carroll, David. *The Matinee Idols.* New York: Arbor House, © 1972. 160 pp.

By means of brief comments and photographs of actors, the author presents a popularly-written account of American "matinee idols" in the theatre and film. Defining a "matinee idol" as "a male entertainer whose appeal is primarily to the female sex," the author discusses actors from Edmund Kean to John Barrymore. The sketches contain bits of biographical information and brief descriptions of the actors' personalities and performance styles. Approximately one-third of the book concerns "American actors, 1861-1910," including such players as Wilkes Booth, Fechter, Frank Mayo, Maurice Barrymore, Robert B. Mantell, and Henry Miller.

Illustrations. One hundred and eighty-seven, mostly photographs of actors.

Features. Introduction; table of contents; documentation: sources of quotations are rarely and, then, only partially identified; index.

Actors. General.

59. Carson, William G[lasgow] B[ruce]. *Dear Josephine: The Theatrical Career of Josephine Hull.* Norman, Oklahoma: University of Oklahoma Press, © 1963. xii, 313 pp.

Slightly over one-third of this narrative of Josephine Sherwood Hull's life concerns the pre-1911 period, including information on her youth, college days (Radcliffe), and early stage career (as Josephine Sherwood). This section contains brief comments on such actors as Robert Taber, Julia Marlowe, and Wilton Lackaye. Married to Shelley Hull in 1910, she retired until 1920, a year after her husband's death. Her post-1920 career included work in radio, film, television, and the theatre. She was in the original productions of *You Can't Take It With You, Arsenic and Old Lace, Harvey,* and *The Solid Gold Cadillac.* The book contains quotations from the actress' diaries (1897-1953) and letters, various reviews, and other appreciations of her and her work. Many specific dates are indicated.

Illustrations. Twelve photographs of Josephine Sherwood

Hull and other people.

Features. Preface; table of contents; list of illustrations; documentation: sources of some quotations are indicated by author, title, and/or date; bibliography; index.

Actors. Shelley Hull, Josephine Sherwood (known as Josephine Hull following her marriage in 1910).

60.   —. *Letters of Mr. and Mrs. Charles Kean Relating to Their American Tours.* St. Louis: Washington University Press, 1945. ix, 181 pp.

Eighty-five letters written by Charles Kean and Ellen Tree Kean concerning their American tours comprise this volume. Written during the period from 1830 to 1866, approximately one-half of the letters were written after 1860. Primarily concerned with the Keans' personal and professional activities, the letters contain brief comments on some American actors, notable Ben DeBar in his managerial role.

Illustrations. Seven photographs, engravings, and facsimiles of the Kean's and manuscript letters.

Features. Preface; introduction; documentation: thorough; index.

Actors. General.

61.   Chapman, John, and Garrison P. Sherwood (eds.). *The Best Plays of 1894-1899.* New York: Dodd, Mead, 1955. vii, 279 pp.

This volume contains brief surveys of the theatrical seasons from 1894/95 through 1898/99, short digests (including some dialogue) for a "representative" play for each season, and a listing of plays produced in New York City from June 15, 1894 through June 15, 1899. Synopses are given for Henry Arthur Jones' *The Case of Rebel-*

lious Susan, David Belasco's *The Heart of Maryland,* William Gillette's *Secret Service,* James M. Barrie's *The Little Minister,* and Sir Arthur Wing Pinero's *Trelawny of the Wells.* Sherwood's compilation of the plays produced in New York is arranged chronologically by the date of the New York opening and it includes the following information: number of performances, genre (e.g., "Musical comedy," "Play," etc.), author/composer/lyricist, theatre, and date. Cast lists for New York premieres and performances by notable companies are included, usually without indication of specific roles performed by individual actors. Some miscellaneous notes concerning performers or productions are inserted. The lack of an index to actors and the usual omission of role designations hinders this work's usefulness in tracing actors' activities.

Illustrations. None.

Features. Introduction by Garrison P. Sherwood; table of contents; two indices: one for authors, composers, and lyricists, and one for plays.

Actors. General.

62.   Charters, Ann. *Nobody: The Story of Bert Williams.* New York: Macmillan, © 1970. 157 pp.

This work chronicles Bert Williams' life and career, emphasizing the period from the beginning of his partnership with George Walker in 1893 to his death in 1922. Anecdotes, some factual data, descriptions, and criticism are included, along with music and lyrics for ten of Williams' songs. Apparently well-researched, including many quotations from Williams' and his contemporaries, the book is poorly documented.

Illustrations. Twenty-four photographs, engravings, and drawings of Bert Williams, George Walker, and other performers, production scenes, sheet music covers, programs, and playbills.

Features. Table of contents; documentation: sources of

quotations are usually indicated by author and/ or title; list of cylinder recordings by Bert Williams; Williams discography; music and lyrics of ten songs associated with Williams; index.

Actors. George Walker, Bert Williams.

63. Clapp, Henry Austin. *Reminiscences of a Dramatic Critic, with an Essay on the Art of Henry Irving.* Boston & New York: Houghton Mifflin, 1902. ix, 241 pp.

> After many years as the distinguished drama critic of the Boston *Advertiser,* the author published this volume of "recollections which. . .have remained most vivid in his memory." Chapters on various theatrical subjects of the last half of the nineteenth century, including several essays on individual actors, are contained in the book. Clapp evaluates and describes the art of the American players noted below, as well as J. L. Toole, Charles Matthews, Salvini, Adelaide Neilson, and Henry Irving. He includes briefer comments on other actors, for example Joseph Jefferson III, Maude Adams, and Richard Mansfield.

> *Illustrations.* Six photographs of actors who are discussed by the author.

> *Features.* Prefatory note; table of contents; list of illustrations; index.

> *Actors.* Edwin Booth, Charlotte Cushman, Charles Fechter, E. A. Sothern, William Warren, Jr.

64. Clapp, John Bouve, and Edwin Francis Edgett. *Players of the Present.* Introd. by Evert Jansen Wendell. 3 parts. New York: Dunlap Society, 1899-1901; rpt. 3 parts in 1 vol. New York: Benjamin Blom, 1969; rpt. 3 parts in 1 vol. New York: Burt Franklin, 1970. vi, 423 pp. (Part I: A-H, vi, 160 pp.; Part II: I-Q, 161-294 pp.; Part III: R-Z, 285-423 pp.).

This work is composed of over one hundred and fifty biographical sketches of actors who were alive, although not
necessarily active on the stage, at the time of original publication.   The entries are arranged alphabetically.   Although Wendell notes that the compilation is not exhaustive and that many actors are omitted because the authors
were "unable to secure information sufficiently definitive
to prepare satisfactory articles," this is a highly useful
work.   A typical sketch provides information concerning
its subject's birth, education, theatrical debut, major roles,
and associations with specific theatres and other actors.
Usually, just the year or approximate period of an event is
mentioned, but specific dates are occasionally indicated.
Some anecdotes and quotations from the subjects are included; criticism is avoided.   In some instances, notes concerning an actress are included in her husband's sketch
(e.g., Maud Durbin Skinner and Katherine Corcoran
Herne).

Illustrations. Twenty-eight photographs and engravings,
mostly of actors.

Features. Introduction by Evert Jansen Wendell; documentation: sources of quotations are indicated
by author and/or title; index.

Actors. General.

65.   —. *Plays of the Present.* Preface by Douglas Taylor. New
York: Dunlap Society, 1902; rpt. New York: Benjamin Blom, 1969. ix, 331 pp.

A selective, alphabetical listing of plays popular in America during the last half of the nineteenth century, emphasizing the two decades prior to publication, comprises this
volume.   Each entry includes a comment which contains
varying amounts and types of information.   Among the
types of material included in the comments are dates and
cast lists of original and/or major revivals of the drama,
brief statements concerning plot or character, and occasional critical evaluations.

Illustrations. Thirty-four photographs of actors in roles.

Features. Preface by Douglas Taylor; index.

Actors. General.

66.   Clark, Susie C[hampney]. *John McCullough as Man, Actor and Spirit.* Boston: Murray and Emery, 1905. 359 pp. Illus.

  Ibid. New York: Broadway, 1914. 368 pp.

  Over two-thirds of this adulatory volume consists of biographical data, anecdotes, and appreciations of John McCullough's personal qualities and professional abilities. The appreciations include reminiscences by McCullough's friends, obituaries, memorial orations, and newspaper reviews. The reviews evaluate and, occasionally, describe his major characterizations. Several of the actor's speeches are quoted and many specific dates are indicated. The remainder of the book contains accounts of several "contacts" with the deceased actor through psychic mediums.

  Illustrations. Five photographs, mostly of John McCullough in various roles.

  Features. Introduction; table of contents; list of illustrations; documentation: sources of quotations are identified by author and/or title and/or date; index.

  Actors. John McCullough.

67.   Clarke, Asia Booth. *The Elder and the Younger Booth.* Boston: James R. Osgood, 1882. 194 pp.

  Approximately one-third of the text in this book is devoted to a life of Edwin Booth by his sister. The remainder is a life of their father—Junius Brutus Booth. The biography of Edwin emphasizes his professional activities. Over one-half of this section pertains to the 1861-81 period. The narrative of Edwin's life includes many specific dates and anecdotes, but little evaluation or description of his personality or performances.

Illustrations. Seven, including an engraving and a painting
of Edwin Booth.

Features. Table of contents; lists of illustrations; documentation: sources of quotations are identified
by author and/or title; index.

Actors. Edwin Booth.

68.   —. *The Unlocked Book: A Memoir of John Wilkes Booth
by His Sister.* Foreword by Eleanor Farjeon. New
York: G. P. Putnam's Sons, 1938; rpt. New York:
Benjamin Blom, 1971. 205 pp.

The heart of this volume is Mrs. Clarke's memoir of John
Wilkes Booth. The last page of the manuscript of this
personal, chronologically-arranged reminiscence is dated
1874. The life of Wilkes Booth is mainly anecdotal, but
it includes the author's opinions of her brother's character and personality. Also included are an excerpt from
Mrs. Clarke's *Life of the Elder Booth* describing the
Booth's Maryland homestead, a poem about Wilkes Booth
by a General Tyrrel, six unidentified periodical clippings
saved by Mrs. Clarke which pertain to Wilkes Booth, and
nine letters relating to various members of the Booth
family. Brief comments on Edwin Booth, John Sleeper
Clarke, and Junius Brutus Booth, Jr., are included. Little
of the material concerns theatrical activities.

Illustrations. Sixteen, mostly photographs and engravings
of various members of the Booth family.

Features. Foreword by Eleanor Farjeon; table of contents; six periodical clippings relating to John
Wilkes Booth; nine letters by, to, or concerning
various members of the Booth family.

Actors. John Wilkes Booth.

69.   Clarke, Joseph I[gnatius] C[onstantine]. *My Life and Memories.* Introd. by Rupert Hughes. New York: Dodd, Mead, 1925. xv, 404 pp.

>   The author recounts incidents from his life, emphasizing the last half of the nineteenth century. Memories of his childhood in Ireland, youth in London, and maturity in America, and of his activities as an Irish nationalist, journalist, and playwright are coupled with anecdotal reminiscences of many of his acquaintances. Personal recollections of Sarah Bernhardt, Sir Henry Irving, and the American actors noted below are included along with chapters on such figures as Roscoe Conkling, Edison, Parnell, and John D. Rockefeller.

>   *Illustrations.* Eight photographs, mostly of the author and his friends.

>   *Features.* Introduction by Rupert Hughes; table of contents; list of illustrations.

>   *Actors.* Margaret Anglin, Grace George, John McCullough, Richard Mansfield, Julia Marlowe.

70.   Cochran, Charles B[lake]. *The Secrets of a Showman.* Foreword by James Agate. New York: Henry Holt, 1926. xx, 436 pp.

>   The author recollects incidents in his life from childhood in the 1870s through 1923. He is mainly concerned with his experiences in the theatre and prize-fight worlds, primarily in London. In America during the 1890s, the author was associated with Richard Mansfield as an actor, private secretary, and friend, and he includes substantial comment on Mansfield's offstage life.

>   *Illustrations.* Thirty-five photographs, paintings, and drawings of the author and several associates.

>   *Features.* Foreword by James Agate; table of contents; list of illustrations; documentation: sources of

quotations are identified by author; index.

Actors.   Richard Mansfield.

71.   Cohan, George M[ichael]. *Twenty years on Broadway and the Years It Took to Get There: The True Story of a Trouper's Life from the Cradle to the "Closed Shop."* New York: Harper & Brothers, © 1925; rpt. Westport, Connecticut: Greenwood, 1971. 264 pp.

Using a brisk, informal style, the author sketches his theatrical career from the 1880s into the 1920s. He presents anecdotes, narration, and opinions, mostly related to his struggles for recognition in variety and drama. He includes information on his performing, writing, and producing activities, but provides little specific description. Over eighty per cent of the book pertains to the pre-1911 period.

Illustrations. Fifteen, mostly photographs of members of the Cohan family.

Features. Table of contents; list of illustrations.

Actors. George M. Cohan, Jerry J. Cohan, Josephine Cohan.

72.   [Cohan, Alfred J.], Alan Dale [pseud.]. *Familiar Chats with Queens of the Stage.* New York: G. W. Dillingham, 1890. viii, 399 pp.

This book is composed of twenty-nine "gossipy sketches, or interviews, or notes" concerning popular, late nineteenth-century actresses, mainly Americans. The sketches contain bits of biography, descriptions of the subjects, occasional brief evaluations, and frequent, often lengthy, quotations from those subjects who were interviewed. Along with considerations of the actress' offstage personalities, some indications of their working methods and attitudes toward the theatre are included.

Illustrations. Twenty-eight photographs of the actress-subjects (excepting only Clara Morris).

Features. Introduction; table of contents; list of illustrations.

Actors. Mary Anderson, Georgie Drew Barrymore, Louise Beaudet, Agnes Booth, Mrs. D. P. Bowers, Georgia Cayvan, Rose Coghlan, Lotta Crabtree, Fanny Davenport, Effie Ellsler, Pauline Hall, Marie Jansen, Nellie McHenry, Marion Manola, Sadie Martinot, Helena Modjeska, Clara Morris, Minnie Palmer, Lillie Post, Cora Urquhart Potter, Ada Rehan, Lillian Russell, Isabella Urquhart, Rosina Vokes, Marie Wainwright.

73. Cole, Toby, and Helen Krich Chinoy (eds.). *Actors on Acting: The Theories, Techniques and Practices of the Great Actors of All Times as Told in Their Own Words.* New York: Crown, © 1949. xiv, 596 pp.

Ibid. New revised edition. New York: Crown, © 1970. xvii, 715 pp.

This immensely valuable work collects over one hundred selections dealing with the art and craft of the Western actor from the fourth century, B.C., to the middle of the twentieth century. Most of the contributors are actors. Each section of the text is preceded by an historical note and each contributor receives a biographical sketch. Theories, anecdotes, and descriptions are included. Less than one-tenth of the volume concerns "American actors, 1861-1910," but it includes comments by or about such figures as Edwin Booth, Boucicault, Mansfield, Gillette, and Mrs. Fiske.

1970 ed.: Historical and biographical notes are updated from the 1949 edition. Thirty selections, mostly concerning the twentieth century, are added to those contained in the first and sixteen are deleted. The same selections concerning "American actors, 1861-1910" are retained from the first edition.

Illustrations. None.

Features. *1949 ed.:* Introduction; table of contents; documentation: the source of each selection is fully indicated; extensive bibliography; indices: "Art of Acting Index: Major References by Actors to Fifty Fundamentals of Acting," "General Index."
1970 ed.: Introduction (revised); table of contents, documentation: the source of each selection is fully indicated; extensive, revised, bibliography; "General Index."

Actors. General.

74.   Coleman, John. *Players and Playwrights I Have Known: A Review of the English Stage from 1840 to 1880.* 2 vols. Philadelphia: Gebbie, 1890. Vol. I: 329 pp.; Vol. II: 399 pp.

This work of reminiscence is mainly organized by chapters devoted to several of the author's professional acquaintances, such as Macready, Mme. Vestris, Tom Robertson, and Charles Fechter. These chapters contain anecdotes and evaluations of the subjects based on the author's experiences with them and some hearsay. The chapter on Fechter concerns that actor's sojourn in England during the 1860s. The section on F. B. Chatterton includes a lengthy account of Chatterton's business dealings with Dion Boucicault.

Illustrations. Fifty engravings and photographs, mainly of English actors of the mid-1880s.

Features. Tables of contents (each vol. for that vol.); lists of illustrations (each vol. for that vol.).

Actors. Dion Boucicault, Charles Fechter.

75.   Coleman, Marion Moore. *Fair Rosalind: The American Career of Helena Modjeska.* Cheshire, Connecticut:

Cherry Hill Books, 1969. iv, 1019 pp.

This thorough and scholarly volume traces Helena Modjeska's life and career in the United States from 1876 to 1909, with a brief glimpse at her life prior to her arrival in America. Narration, anecdotes, and criticism/description of her acting are included. The author employs extensive quotations from Mme. Modjeska's own writings, including pesonal letters, and from contemporary sources. Specific dates are consistently indicated. Among the many actors mentioned briefly are John McCullough, Fanny Janauschek, Clara Morris, and Robert Taber.

Illustrations. Twenty-four, mostly photographs and drawings of Helena Modjeska and her friends and relations.

Features. Introduction; acknowledgments; extensive documentation; "Chronological List of Plays Presented by Modjeska" (includes title and the city and date of her debut in each play; 1877-1900); "Alphabetic List of Plays Presented by Modjeska"; "Modjeska on the American Stage: Known Professional Appearances" (extensive list, 1877-1907; includes specific date, play, theatre, and city); index.

Actors. Lawrence Barrett, Maurice Barrymore, Edwin Booth, Helena Modjeska, Otis Skinner.

76. Cook, Doris E[stelle]. *Sherlock Holmes and Much More, or Some of the Facts About William Gillette.* Hartford, Connecticut: The Connecticut Historical Society, 1970. vii, 112 pp.

This book is a well-documented, though brief, biography of William Gillette from the 1860s until his death in 1937. Factual and anecdotal material concerning his personal and professional lives, numerous quotations from his letters, and many evaluations of him are included.

Illustrations. Twenty-one photographs, mostly of William

Gillette, scenes from his plays, and his houses.

Features. Foreword, table of contents, list of illustrations, thorough documentation.

Actors. William Gillette.

77.   Copeland, Charles Townsend. *Edwin Booth.* Boston: Small, Maynard, 1901. xvii, 159 pp.

With the aid of previous biographical works, the author traces Edwin Booth's life and career. The narrative is frequently interrupted by discussions of various subjects concerning Booth, and it becomes very sketchy after the actor's German triumph in 1883. The author, who had seen Booth act numerous characters between 1878 and 1891, describes and evaluates portions of portrayals, occasionally noting changes in Booth's execution of his characterizations. Some excerpts from Booth's letters are included.

Illustrations. One portrait photograph of Edwin Booth.

Features. Preface; brief bibliography; chronology of major events in Edwin Booth's life; "Sargent's Portrait of Edwin Booth at 'The Prayers,' " poem by Thomas Bailey Aldrich.

Actors. Edwin Booth.

78.   Coquelin, Constant, Henry Irving, and Dion Boucicault. *The Act of Acting: A Discussion.* Explanatory note by [James] Brander Matthews. New York: Published for the Dramatic Museum of Columbia University by the Columbia University Press, 1926. 93 pp.

This volume is composed of the following five articles, all originally published in 1887: "Actors and Acting" by Constant Coquelin, "M. Coquelin on Actors and Acting" by Henry Irving, "Coquelin—Irving" by Dion Boucicault, "A Reply to Mr. Henry Irving" by Coquelin, and "A Reply to Mr. Dion Boucicault" by Coquelin. All of the essays center on the debate concerning the relative merits of physical technique and inspiration in the acting of tragedy and comedy. All of the authors cite examples, primarily continental, to illustrate their ideas. Boucicault writes more from the vantage point of a dramatic author than from that of an actor.

Illustrations. None.

Features. Table of contents; explanatory note on the original publications of the articles by Brander Matthews.

Actors. Dion Boucicault.

79. Cosgrave, Luke. *Theater Tonight.* Hollywood: House-Warven, © 1952. 245 pp.

In this anecdotal narrative, the author traces his life from his youth in the 1860s to 1949, with nearly three-fourths of the book concerning the pre-1911 period. The author emphasizes his career as a barnstorming actor in the mid- and far west from the 1880s to the 1920s, presenting an interesting picture of the life of an itinerate trouper. During the 1920s and '30s, he was a film actor. Many dates are indicated.

Illustrations. Twenty-one photographs, mostly of Luke Cosgrave.

Features. Documentation: sources of quotations are indicated by author and/or title and/or date.

Actors. Luke Cosgrave, James Cruze, F. W. George, Grace George (Rena Marcells), John Shanks Lindsay, Charles H. Murray.

80. Courtney, Marguerite [Taylor]. *Laurette.* Introd. by Samuel Hopkins Adams. New York: Rinehart, © 1955. xiii, 433 pp.

Ibid. Introd. by Brooks Atkinson. New York: Atheneum, 1968. xiii, 445 pp.

This biography of Laurette Taylor was written by the actress' daughter. The reminiscences of Miss Taylor's friends, the author's memories, and materials written by and about the actress are utilized in this anecdotal narrative. Also included are excerpts from reviews, eulogies, and letters. Nearly one-fourth of the volume concerns the pre-1911 period, with information on Miss Taylor's early career in melodrama and comedy.

1968 ed.: This edition contains the same text as the earlier edition. An introduction by Brooks Atkinson replaces that by Samuel Hopkins Adams and an index is added.

Illustrations. Thirteen photographs of Laurette Taylor and her family.

Features. 1955 ed.: Introduction by Samuel Hopkins Adams; acknowledgements; table of contents; documentation: sources of many quotations are identified.
1968 ed.: Introduction by Brooks Atkinson; acknowledgements; table of contents; documentation: sources of many quotations are identified; index.

Actors. Laurette Taylor.

81.   Crane, William H. *Footprints and Echoes.*   Introd. by Melville E. Stone. New York: E. P. Dutton, © 1927. ix, 232 pp. Illus.

The author reminisces about his life, emphasizing his theatrical career from the mid-1860s through the 1910s. Writing with great warmth, he offers scores of anecdotes, opinions on theatrical matters, personal memories of old friends, and some short descriptions of productions. Among the many actors mentioned briefly are John Wilkes Booth, John McCullough, Lawrence Barrett, and Frank Mayo.

Illustrations. Forty-one, mostly photographs of the author.

Features. Introduction by Melville E. Stone; list of illustrations; documentation: most sources of quotations are identified by author and/or title; index.

Actors. William H. Crane, Joseph Jefferson III, Stuart Robson.

82.　Creahan, John. *The Life of Laura Keene. Actress, Artist, Manager and Scholar. Together with Some Interesting Reminiscences of Her Daughters.* Philadelphia: Rodgers Publishing, 1897. 254 pp.

The author, an old friend of Laura Keene and of her daughters, devotes approximately two-thirds of this volume to various aspects of Miss Keene's career and personality during the third quarter of the nineteenth century. The remainder of the book consists of reminiscences concerning and letters from the actress-manager's daughters—Clara Stella Taylor and Emma Taylor Rawson. The materials pertaining to Miss Keene include many periodical reviews and appreciations, lengthy quotations from books by Joseph Jefferson III and Kate Reignolds-Winslow, selections from interviews with and letters from Miss Keene's professional associates, and biographical data, including many specific dates. An article by Miss Keene on the art of Edwin Booth is included. Largely biased in favor of his subject, the author attempts to vindicate her from the derogatory comments and factual errors of earlier writers, especially William Winter.

Illustrations. Fourteen photographs, engravings, and crayon pictures of Laura Keene and members of her family.

Features. Preface; table of contents; list of illustrations; documentation: many sources of quotations are identified by author and/or title and/or date; partial listing of Laura Keene's roles (pp.

124-27); index.

Actors. Edwin Booth, Joseph Jefferson III, Laura Keene, Kate Reignolds, Emma Taylor.

83.   Daly, Joseph Francis. *The Life of Augustin Daly.* New York: Macmillan, 1917. xi, 672 pp.

This biography, written by the subject's younger brother, is concerned mainly with Augustin Daly's theatrical career after the Civil War. The chronological narrative contains passing references to most members of Daly's stock companies and to many other prominent actors of the day, such as Lester Wallack, Lawrence Barrett, Joseph Jefferson III, etc. The dates of numerous production premiers and many cast lists are indicated. Of special note are copious quotations from letters by, to, and concerning the subject of this volume. Much of the correspondence relates to actors employed by Daly.

Illustrations. Sixteen, mostly photographs of Augustin Daly and actors.

Features. Preface; publisher's foreword; no table of contents, but a listing of contents heads each chapter; list of illustrations; index.

Actors. Edwin Booth, John Drew II, Mrs. G. H. Gilbert, James Lewis, Richard Mansfield, Ada Rehan.

84.   Davidge, William [Plater]. *Footlight Flashes.* New York: American News, 1866. xii, 274 pp.

Noting that "Opinions of the merits of my contemporaries I have most carefully avoided. . .," the author sets down vagrant memories culled from his nearly forty years on the stage. Anecdotes experienced by or told to the author and generalized descriptions and opinions concerning theatrical procedures and personnel predominate. Autobiographical information extends only into the mid-1850s.

Illustrations. Fifteen line-drawings, mostly of theatrical equipment.

Features. Table of contents; list of illustrations.

Actors. William P. Davidge.

85. Davies, Acton. *Maude Adams.* New York: Frederick A. Stokes, © 1901. 110 pp.

> The author traces Maude Adams' career through her performance in Rostand's *L'Aiglon,* emphasizing the period following 1889. For information concerning her early life, he relies on reminiscences by Annie Adams (Maude's mother) and David Belasco. The author's own observations and opinions dominate the account of the actress' New York career in the 1890s. Lengthy selections from an interview with Miss Adams (c. 1892-93), some evaluations and descriptions of her acting, criticisms of plays in which she appeared, and brief comments on her personal character, but few specific dates, are included.

> *Illustrations.* Twenty-one photographs of Maude Adams, mostly in various roles.

> *Features.* List of illustrations.

> *Actors.* Maude Adams.

86. DeAngelis, Jefferson, and Alvin F. Harlow. *A Vagabond Trouper.* New York: Harcourt, Brace, © 1931. 325 pp.

> This book is an anecdotal chronicle of Jefferson DeAngelis' life from his birth in 1859 to the time of publication. Being true to the title, approximately eighty per cent of the book deals with the period prior to 1887, the year in which the author feels he ended his vagabondage. Although information concerning the author's career in variety, comic opera, and legitimate theatre is included, the book emphasizes his offstage experiences. Few

specific dates are indicated.

Illustrations. Twenty-seven photographs and drawings, mostly of Jefferson DeAngelis.

Features. List of illustrations.

Actors. Jefferson DeAngelis.

87.   DeFontaine, F[elix] G[regory] (ed.). *Birds of a Feather Flock Together, or Talks with Sothern.* New York: G. W. Carlton, 1878. xiii, 250 pp.

Anecdotes and reminiscences concerning E. A. Sothern comprise this volume. The editor has collected remembered conversations, published articles and letters, and unpublished letters, including copious quotations from Sothern, John T. Raymond, Stephen Fiske, and Mrs. J. R. Vincent. Among the matters considered are Sothern's personal characteristics, development of roles, attitudes toward playwriting, and famous practical joking. Specific historical references—dates, places, etc.—are not included.

Illustrations. Nine engravings, mostly of E. A. Sothern in roles.

Features. Introduction; table of contents, list of illustrations.

Actors. E. A. Sothern.

88.   DeMille, Cecil B[lount]. *The Autobiography of Cecil B. DeMille.* Ed. by Donald Hayne. Englewood Cliffs, New Jersey: Prentice-Hall, 1959. viii, 463 pp.

This book primarily concerns the author's association with the motion picture industry from 1913 until his death in 1959. The early portion of the book, however, deals with his youth and with his early career as a stage actor, including material on his father—the playwright

Henry C. DeMille—and David Belasco. Anecdotes and opinions abound; some dates are indicated.

Illustrations. Ninety-three photographs and drawings of Cecil B. DeMille, his associates, family, and films.

Features. Editor's preface by Donald Hayne; table of contents; epilogue by Donald Hayne; appended chronological list of motion pictures directed by Cecil B. DeMille (partial cast lists are included); index.

Actors. Cecil B. DeMille.

89. Dempsey, David, with Raymond P. Baldwin. *The Triumphs and Trials of Lotta Crabtree.* New York: William Morrow, 1968. viii, 341 pp.

A narrative of Lotta Crabtree's life comprises over one-half of this book, with the remainder devoted to accounts of the litigation concerning her will (co-author Baldwin was on the defense team) and the appendices. The bulk of the biography pertains to the 1861-1910 period. Brief comments on other actors, for example Adah Isaacs Menken, John T. Raymond, and Edwin Adams, are included. The book is, apparently, well-researched, but poorly documented.

Illustrations. Seventeen, mostly photographs of Lotta Crabtree.

Features. Table of contents; list of illustrations; documentation: some sources of quotations are identified by author or title; bibliography (Appendix C); Appendix A: chronology of Lotta Crabtree's life (specific dates are indicated); Appendix B: undated, incomplete list of plays in which Lotta Crabtree appeared; index.

Actors. Lotta Crabtree.

90.   DeWolfe, Elsie [Anderson]. *After All.* New York: Harper & Brothers, 1935. x, 278 pp.

> The author supplies an autobiographical narrative, many anecdotes, and reflections on her friends, the art of interior decoration, and personal beauty. She includes comments on the period from the late 1870s to the 1930s, rarely indicating specific dates. Less than one-half of the book pertains to the pre-1911 period, and little information is provided on the author's experiences as an actress from 1891 to 1900.

> *Illustrations.* Twenty-eight, mostly photographs of the author, her friends and associates, furniture, rooms, and buildings.

> *Features.* Table of contents; list of illustrations.

> *Actors.* Elsie DeWolfe.

91.   Dier, Mary Caroline [Lawrence]. *The Lady of the Gardens: Mary Elitch Long.* Foreword by Burns Mantle. Hollywood: Hollycrofters, 1932. 305 pp.

Ibid. Lost Angeles: Saturday Night Publishing, 1932. vii, 139 pp.

> *Hollycrofters ed.:* Approximately one-half of this book consists of the author's brief appreciation of Mary Elitch Long and Mrs. Long's reminiscent narrative of Elitch's Gardens from 1890 through 1915. This amusement park in Denver, Colorado, housed summer theatrical performances. Mrs. Long provides brief recollections of many actors, including Frank Mayo, Blanche Walsh, Henrietta Crosman, and David Warfield. Photographs from Elitch's Gardens comprise the remainder of the book.

> *Saturday Night Publishing ed.:* The text of this edition, aside from omitting the author's note, varies only slightly from that of the Hollycrofters edition. The illustrations in this edition are interspersed throughout the text.

Illustrations. Hollycrofters ed.: eighty, mostly photographs of people and scenes associated with Elitch's Gardens.
Saturday Night Publishing ed.: seventy-nine, mostly photographs of people and scenes associated with Elitch's Gardens.

Features. Hollycrofters ed.: Author's note; foreword by Burns Mantle; index [list] of illustrations; documentation: sources of quotations are indicated by author and/or title and/or date; alphabetical lists of actors who performed at Elitch's Gardens, 1897-1932.
Saturday Night Publishing ed.: Same, except author's note is omitted.

Actors. General.

92. Dithmar, Edward A[ugustus]. *John Drew.* New York: Frederick A. Stokes, ©1900. vi, 137 pp.

A fairly straight-forward narrative, this volume traces John Drew II's career from his New York debut in 1875 through the 1899/1900 season. Brief descriptions of plays and roles in which Drew appeared, slight indications of the author's opinions of Drew's performances, and a few anecdotes and specific dates are included. The author rarely refers to his subject's offstage life.

Illustrations. Twenty-five, mostly photographs of John Drew II in several roles.

Features. List of illustrations.

Actors. John Drew II, Ada Rehan.

93. [Dithmar, Edward Augustus]. *Memories of Daly's Theatres, with Passing Recollections of Others, Including a Record of Plays and Actors at the Fifth Avenue Theatre and Daly's Theatre, 1869-95.* New York: Privately printed [copyright held by Augustin Daly, 1896],

1897. 143 pp.

With much of the information in this volume based on the author's earlier *Memories of One Theatre*. . .(see 94), this book traces the activities of Augustin Daly's theatrical companies. Following a narrative of Daly's Fifth Avenue Theatres (1869-77), the author summarizes the activities of Daly's Theatre (1879-95) and of the European tours by Daly's company. A chronological listing of plays performed at Daly's New York theatres (1869-93), including dates of openings and partial cast lists, and an appreciation of Daly by John Talbot Smith complete the work. The author's brief critical and reminiscent comments on several actors, most notably Ada Rehan, are included along with three reviews of Miss Rehan's London performance of Rosalind in 1890.

Illustrations. Seventy-two photographs, engravings, drawings, and paintings of Augustin Daly, actors, theatres, playbills, and fanciful scenes from plays.

Features. Introduction; "To Ada Rehan," a poem by Justin Huntley McCarthy; list of Shakespearean plays and of "old comedies produced by Daly, 1869-95; chronological list of productions at Daly's New York theatres, 1869-93 (includes dates of openings and partial cast lists).

Actors. Ada Rehan.

94.   Dithmar, Edward A[ugustus]. *Memories of One Theatre, with Passing Recollections of Many Others, including a Record of Plays and Actors at the Fifth Avenue Theatre, 1869-1877.* n.p.: n.n., 1891 [the date is probably a misprint: Dithmar's introduction is dated "October, 1893"; also, Dithmar includes information on events which occurred later than 1891]. Unnumbered.

The chapters in this book "were written in various moods, at odd times and with no particular plan in view. The idea of arranging them so as to form in some sort a connected, if not a complete, record of the public career of Augustin Daly. . .was an after-thought." The book does sketch the career of Daly, paying special attention to the activities of his theatre companies. The 1868-77 period is considered in a careful, chronological narrative, and the later period is summarized. Included are some factual materials and the author's critical recollections of several Daly actors.

Illustrations. None.

Features. Introduction; lists of plays performed at Daly's Fifth Avenue Theatres, 1869-77 (includes dates of openings and partial cast lists).

Actors. John Drew II, Ada Rehan.

95. Dodge, John Mason, as told to William H. Holcomb. *"Jack" Dodge (John Mason Dodge), the Friend of Every Man: His Life and His Times.* Los Angeles: Sherman Danby, 1937. 179 pp.

Jack Dodge was a railroad man, theatrical manager, politician, and sometime actor. This book contains selections from his rambling reminiscences, linked by Holcomb's florid tributes. Having managed theatres in San Diego for the half-century following 1880, Dodge includes anecdotes based on his experiences with several visiting star actors.

Illustrations. One photograph of the author.

Features. Table of contents.

Actors. Jack Dodge.

96. Dole, Nathan Haskell. *Joseph Jefferson at Home.* Boston: Estes and Lauriat, 1898. 110 pp.

This anecdotal narrative of Joseph Jefferson III's life,

emphasizing the 1829-1880 period, is heavily indebted to Jefferson's *Autobiography* (see 177), with some material drawn from Winter's *Life and Art of Joseph Jefferson* (see 347). Only a few generalized comments on the actor and his Buzzard Bay home are independent of these sources.

Illustrations. Sixteen photographs of Joseph Jefferson III, his Buzzard Bay home, and his paintings.

Features. List of illustrations.

Actors. Joseph Jefferson III.

97.　Donohue, Joseph W., Jr. (ed.). *The Theatrical Manager in England and America, Player of a Perilous Game: Philip Henslowe, Tate Wilkinson, Stephen Price, Edwin Booth, Charles Wyndham.* Princeton, New Jersey: Princeton University Press, 1971. xii, 216 pp.

The essays in this volume, originally presented as lectures at Princeton University during the 1969-70 academic year, examine the practices, personalities, and contributions of five English and American theatrical managers. The subjects and authors of the essays are: Henslowe by Bernard Beckerman, Wilkinson by Charles Beecher Hogan, Price by Barnard Hewitt, Booth by Charles Shattuck, and Wyndham by George Rowell. The Booth essay, emphasizing his association with Booth's Theatre, utilizes data from account books, excerpts from letters, and other materials. Brief indications of the "success" at Booth's Theatre of several actors, for example John Sleeper Clarke, Joseph Jefferson III, and Lawrence Barrett, are included.

Illustrations. Twenty-one photographs, engravings, and facsimile reproductions of the subjects of the essays, playbills, diary entries, etc. (two pertain to Edwin Booth).

Features. Foreword and introduction by Joseph W. Donohue, Jr.; table of contents; list of illustrations; extensive documentation; notes on the contributors.

Actors. Edwin Booth.

98. Dressler, Marie. *The Eminent American Comedienne Marie Dressler in The Life Story of an Ugly Duckling: An Autobiographical Fragment in Seven Parts, Illustrated with Many Pleasing Scenes from Former Triumps and from Private Life, Now for the First Time Under the Management of Robert M. McBride.* New York: Robert M. McBride, 1924. x, 234 pp.

Anecdotes, narrative, self-appraisal predominate in this volume of informal reminiscence. The author proceeds in approximate chronological order, with numerous digressions for bits of philosophy and discussions of theatrical subjects. Writing solely from memory, the author apologizes for possible errors in chronology and she includes no specific dates. Nearly one-half of the book pertains to the pre-1911 period.

Illustrations. Thirty-one photographs and cartoons, mostly of Marie Dressler.

Features. Table of contents; list of illustrations.

Actors. Marie Dressler, Lillian Russell.

99. —. *My Own Story.* As told to Mildred Harrington. Foreword by Will Rogers. Boston: Little, Brown, 1934. xii, 290 pp.

The comedienne's account of her life from chidhood in the 1870s and 1880s to her motion picture successes in the early 1930s embraces narration, anecdotes, and personal opinion, but few dates. She reminisces about her career and private life, including many stories—slightly rewritten—from her earlier *Life Story of an Ugly Duckling* (see 98). Brief comments on numerous stage and film performers are included. Approximately one-half of the book deals with the pre-1911 period.

Illustrations. Twenty-seven, mostly photographs of Marie

Dressler.

Features. Foreword by Will Rogers.

Actors. Marie Dressler, Lillian Russell.

100. Drew, John [II]. *My Years on the Stage.* Foreword by
     Booth Tarkington. New York: E. P. Dutton, 1922.
     xii, 242 pp.

> Over ninety per cent of this volume of reminiscences re-
> lates to the pre-1911 period, emphasizing the author's
> theatre-related experiences. Few specific dates and criti-
> cisms are included, but the author offers scores of anec-
> dotes and reflections concerning himself, other members
> of the Drew-Barrymore family, the Augustin Daly com-
> pany from the late 1870s to the early 1890s, and Drew's
> productions under Charles Frohman's management from
> 1892 to 1915. The author inserts cast lists of many pro-
> ductions in which he appeared.

> *Illustrations.* Fifty-eight, mostly photographs of John
>   Drew II and other actors, including many
>   scenes from productions.

> *Features.* Foreword by Booth Tarkington; list of illustra-
>   tions; documentation: most sources of quota-
>   tions are indicated by author and/or title;
>   index.

> *Actors.* John Drew II, James Lewis, Ada Rehan.

101. Drew, Mrs. John [Louisa Lane]. *Autobiographical Sketch
     of Mrs. John Drew.* Introduction by John Drew [II].
     Biographical notes by Douglas Taylor. New York:
     Charles Scribner's Sons, 1899; rpt. New York: Benja-
     min Blom, 1971. xiv, 200 pp.

> In this posthumously-published autobiography, the author
> recounts her professional career from the 1820s to the
> 1890s. Approximately one-fourth of the sketchy narra-

tive concerns the post-1860 period. She includes brief appreciations of such actors as E. L. Davenport, Edwin Booth, and Joseph Jefferson III.

Illustrations. Forty-three photographs, engravings, and drawings of the author and many of her associates.

Features. Introduction by John Drew II; list of illustrations; appended biographical notes by Douglas Taylor (brief sketches of twenty-six persons mentioned by Mrs. Drew, mainly pre-Civil War actors).

Actors. Mrs. John Drew.

102. Eaton, Walter Prichard. *The Actor's Heritage: Scenes from the Theatre of Yesterday and the Day Before.* Boston: Atlantic Monthly Press, © 1924; rpt. Freeport, New York: Books for Libraries, 1970. 294 pp.

This book is a collection of miscellaneous essays on theatrical subjects. Among the topics discussed are Thomas Holcroft, the character of Shylock, conventionalized gesture, and the behavior of theatre audiences. A chapter on Weber and Fields includes an appreciation of their burlesques and brief descriptions of business in some of their productions. An essay entitled "Legs in Grandpa's Day" contains lengthy quotations from Olive Logan's *Apropos of Women and Theatres* (see 193).

Illustrations. Forty-one photographs, engravings, drawings, paintings, and facsimiles, mostly of actors, theatres, and playbills.

Features. Prefatory note; table of contents; list of illustrations; documentation: sources of quotations are identified by author and/or title and/or date; index.

Actors. Olive Logan.

103. —. *The American Stage of To-Day.* Boston: Small, Maynard, 1908. 338 pp.

> This volume collects several of the author's essays on various aspects of theatre. The essays were written during the 1906-08 period and many of them were published previous to their collection in this book. Several production reviews are included. The author is mainly concerned with the drama, preferring the "new" realistic style, but he also comments on specific acting performances and generalizes on the merits of several actors. In addition to those actors noted below, the author evaluates the work of Henry Miller, Mrs. Fiske, Russ Whytal, Otis Skinner, Robert B. Mantell, and others.

> *Illustrations.* None.

> *Features.* Prefatory note; table of contents.

> *Actors.* David Belasco, George M. Cohan, Alla Nazimova, E. H. Sothern.

104. —. *At the New Theatre and Others. The American Stage: Its Problems and Performances, 1908-1910.* Boston: Small, Maynard, © 1910. x, 359 pp.

> This volume is divided into three parts: reviews and a summary of the first season of the New Theatre (1909-10), other reviews from the 1909-10 season, and miscellaneous essays on theatrical subjects (e.g., operetta, Clyde Fitch, William Winter, the Drama League of America, etc.). Although primarily concerned with the drama, the author also includes brief but perceptive comments on several actors, such as William Faversham, Otis Skinner, Ethel Barrymore, Mrs. Fiske, and Alla Nazimova.

> *Illustrations.* None.

> *Features.* Prefatory note; introduction: "The Theatrical Syndicate"; table of contents.

> *Actors.* General.

105. Edgett, Edwin Francis (ed.). *Edward Loomis Davenport: A Biography.* New York: Dunlap Society, 1901; rpt. New York: Burt Franklin, 1970. x, 145 pp.

> This narrative traces E. L. Davenport's theatrical career from his debut in 1836 to his death in 1877. Approximately one-third of the text concerns the 1861-77 period. Several letters written by Davenport, lengthy reviews and appreciations of his acting, some cast lists, and passing mentions of other actors are included. Many specific dates are indicated. The volume concludes with brief biographical comments on Davenport's wife and children.

> *Illustrations.* Ten photographs, mostly of E. L. Davenport.

> *Features.* Preface; documentation: sources of some quotations are partially identified; index.

> *Actors.* E. L. Davenport.

106. Edwards, Herbert J., and Julie A. Herne. *James A. Herne: The Rise of Realism in the American Drama.* Orono, Maine: University of Maine Press, 1964. vi, 182 pp.

> This book, based on Julie A. Herne's unpublished biography of her father, chronicles James A. Herne's life and career from his youth in the 1850s to his death in 1901. The book places major emphasis on Herne's plays, but also contains information concerning his acting, directing, theatre management, and personal life. Many contemporary evaluations, specific dates, and brief comments on Herne's fellow-actors, such as Lucille and Helen Western, David Belasco, and John Drew II, are included.

> *Illustrations.* Thirteen photographs, mostly of James A. Herne and his family.

> *Features.* Preface; table of contents; documentation: sources of quotations are indicated by author, title, and/or date; bibliography; explanatory "Notes"; chronological list of plays by James

A. Herne (includes source, if an adaptation, theatre, and specific date of premiere); index.

Actors. James A. Herne, Katherine Corcoran Herne.

107. Ellsler, John A[dam]. *The Stage Memories of John A. Ellsler.* Ed. by Effie Ellsler Weston. Foreword by Willis Thornton. Cleveland, Ohio: The Rowfant Club, 1950. 159 pp.

These memories, "called up by John Ellsler in his old age and gathered and edited by his daughter," concern Ellsler's stage career from the late 1930s to 1886. As an actor and manager, primarily in Cleveland, the author was acquainted with many of the most famous performers of his day. Along with recollections of his own career, the author includes anecdotes and personal evaluations of such actors as Junius Brutus, Edwin, and John Wilkes Booth, Macready, Forrest, and E. L. Davenport. Approximately three-fourths of the book concerns the pre-Civil War period.

Illustrations. Two photographs, one each of John A. Ellsler and Effie Ellsler Weston.

Features. Foreword by Willis Thornton; table of contents.

Actors. Edwin Booth, John Wilkes Booth, John A. Ellsler.

108. Elwood, Muriel. *Pauline Frederick: On and Off the Stage.* Chicago: A. Kroch, 1940. 225 pp.

This uncritical, anecdotal narrative commences with Pauline Frederick's stage debut in 1902 and continues until her death in 1938. The author provides information on Miss Frederick's stage and film (silents beginning in 1914 and "talkies" beginning in 1928) careers, her five marriages, and her personal character. Some laudatory reviews of her performances, but no descriptions of her acting and few specific dates, are included. Less than one-fourth of the book concerns the period before 1911.

Illustrations. Ten photographs, mostly of Pauline Fredrick.

Features. Table of contents; documentation: sources of quotations are identified by author and/or title; list of "Stage and Screen Appearances of Pauline Frederick" (titles only); index.

Actors. Pauline Frederick.

109. Ernst, Alice Henson. *Trouping in the Oregon Country: A History of Frontier Theatre.* Introd. by Stewart Holbrook. Portland, Oregon: Oregon Historical Society, © 1961. xviii, 197 pp.

This history of theatrical entertainments in Oregon surveys the period from the 1940s to the 1920s, with the bulk of the material concerning the Civil War-World I era. Brief comments on theatres, managers, audiences, and actors are included. Among the actors mentioned are Lotta Crabtree, Julia Dean Hayne, James A. Herne, and David Belasco. Few specific dates are indicated.

Illustrations. Nineteen photographs and engravings of performers, managers, theatres, and theatre bills.

Features. Acknowledgements; introduction by Stewart Holbrook; table of contents; documentation: some sources of materials are identified by author and/or title and/or date; selected bibliography; index.

Actors. General.

110. Everett, Marshall. *The Great Chicago Theater Disaster: The Complete Story Told by the Survivors, Presenting a Vivid Picture, Both by Pen and Camera, of One of*

*the Greatest Fire Horrors of Modern Times, Embracing
a Flash-Light Sketch of the Holocaust, Detailed Narratives
by Participants in the Horror, Heroic Work of
Rescuers, Reports of the Building Experts at to the Responsibility
for the Wholesale Slaughter of Women and
Children, Memorable Fires of the Past, etc., etc.* n.p.:
Publishers Union of America, © 1904. 368 pp.

Accounts of the Iroquois Theatre fire during a performance
of *Mr. Bluebeard, Jr.* on December 30, 1903, and
of the aftermath of that catastrophe comprise this volume.
Composed largely of eyewitness accounts and inquest
testimony, the book also includes the author's
narration of events and comments by the author and by
others concerning theatre safety and the effects of the
Iroquois fire. The testimonies of several members of the
Mr. Bluebeard, Jr. company are quoted. The book contains
a list of the people who died in the fire.

Illustrations. Seventy-nine photographs and drawings of
the Iroquois Theatre before, during, and
after the fire, of victims of the fire, and of
people associated with the theatre or with
the inquiry following the fire.

Features. Author's preface; publisher's preface; table of
contents; documentation: most sources of quotations
are identified by author and/or title
and/or date: "Memorial Prayer" by the Rt.
Rev. Samuel Fallows; "Memorial Hymn";
"Have a Thought," poem by Walter Bissinger.

Actors. Eddie Foy.

111. Eytinge, Rose. *The Memories of Rose Eytinge: Being
Recollections and Observations of Men, Women, and
Events, During Half a Century.* New York: Frederick
A. Stokes, © 1905. xiii, 311 pp. Illus.

The author reminisces about her life during the second
half of the nineteenth century, emphasizing the 1860s
and 1870s. Approximately two-thirds of the book deals

with her theatrical experiences, with the remainder concerning her nonprofessional sojourns abroad, especially in Egypt. Through the use of charming anecdotes, brief evaluations, and occasional descriptions, she presents an interesting picture of herself, theatrical conditions, and many of her fellow actors, for example Charles R. Thorne, Lester Wallack, and Mrs. John Drew.

Illustrations. Eight portrait photographs of the author and other theatrical personalities.

Features. Table of contents; list of illustrations.

Actors. E. L. Davenport, Rose Eytinge, Steele MacKaye, James W. Wallack, Jr.

112. Farjeon, Eleanor. *Portrait of a Family.* New York: Frederick A. Stokes, 1936. xiv, 456 pp.

An anecdotal biography of the Farjeon and Jefferson families comprises this book. Although emphasizing the Farjeon family, including herself, her father (Benjamin L. Farjeon), and her mother (Margaret Jefferson Farjeon), the author includes some material on her grandfather—Joseph Jefferson III. Some letters from and anecdotes concerning her grandfather are contained in the book.

Illustrations. Twenty-seven photographs of Farjeons and Jeffersons.

Features. Foreword; table of contents; list of illustrations; documentation: some quotations are identified by author.

Actors. Joseph Jefferson III.

113. Farrar, J. Maurice. *Mary Anderson: The Story of Her Life and Professional Career.* New York: N. L. Munro 1885. 83 pp.

The London-based author presents a well-written biographical account of Mary Anderson, with much of his information apparently gathered from personal conversations with the actress. Factual and some anecdotal materials are included in the narrative of her youth, early career, successes, and British appearances. Of special worth are the inclusion of some American reviews and over twenty pages of British reviews of her performances. The author attempts to correct some rumors concerning Miss Anderson and provides his personal evaluation of her acting.

Illustrations. One portrait engraving of Mary Anderson.

Features. Preface; table of contents; documentation: sources of quotations are identified by title and, rarely, date.

Actors. Mary Anderson.

114. Felheim, Marvin. *The Theatre of Augustin Daly: An Account of the Late Nineteenth Century American Stage.* Cambridge, Massachusetts: Harvard University Press, 1956; rpt. New York: Greenwood, 1969. ix, 329 pp.

The author surveys practices in the American theatre from the Civil War to 1900 by examining the career of Augustin Daly. He investigates Daly's managerial efforts, his work as an original playwright, dramatizer of novels, and adaptor of European plays, and his activities as an adaptor/producer of Shakespearean plays and old comedies. Many quotations from reviews, memoirs, and letters, especially the correspondence between Augustin and Joseph Francis Daly, are included. In addition to Miss Rehan, the author comments briefly on many other actors associated with Daly's companies, such as John Drew II, James Lewis, and Mrs. G. H. Gilbert.

Illustrations. Five, mostly photographs of Augustin Daly and actors.

Features. Preface; table of contents; list of illustrations; documentation: sources of quotations are identified by author and/or title; index.

Actors. Ada Rehan.

115. Field, Kate. *Charles Albert Fechter.* Boston: James R. Osgood, 1882; rpt. New York: Benjamin Blom, 1969. 205 pp.

> This book contains an anecdotal biography of Charles Fechter, descriptions of six of his characterizations, and several reviews and appreciations of him and his performances. The biography, comprising nearly one-half of the text, emphasizes his professional activities in Europe, England, and America. The author, who knew Fechter in America, indicates her opinion of his work. The descriptions, which comment most fully upon his Hamlet and Claude Melnotte, suggest his interpretations and describe parts of his performances. Reviews excerpted from several London newspapers and appreciations by Wilkie Collins, Edmund Yates, Herman Vezin, and Charles Dickens contain some descriptions of his portrayals.

> *Illustrations.* Five, mostly engravings of Charles Fechter.

> *Features.* Table of contents; list of illustrations; documentation: some quotations are identified by author and/or title and/or date; index.

Actors. Charles Fechter.

116. Fiske, Harrison Grey (ed.). *The New York Mirror Annual and Directory of the Theatrical Profession for 1888.* New York: New York Mirror, © 1888. vi, 208 pp.

> Attempting to provide a "reliable and compendious yearly chronicle" of the stage, this volume was *The New York Mirror's* first and only annual. The first of the six main divisions is a "Chronological Dramatic Record, 1887," which records notable theatrical events in England, France, Germany, and, especially, America in a day-by-day manner for 1887. This section includes original cast

lists for new productions and some plot synopses, as well as title, author, place of production, and miscellaneous information. Next is the "Necrology for 1887," which includes brief identifications of the deceased. The "Dramatic Bibliography" lists books and periodical articles published in America, England, France, and Germany during 1887. The next section quotes in its entirety and briefly comments upon the "Inter-State Commerce Law" of 1887. The fifth section alphabetically lists "Stars, Combinations, and Stock Companies [for the] Season 1887-88." The final section, "Directory of the Theatrical Profession in America," is a listing of active professionals in the American theatre, including managers, agents, actors, technicians, opera singers, instrumentalists, specialty performers, critics, etc. The directory is arranged according to lines of business—as supplied by the subjects—and includes each person's mailing address and, when pertinent, company or theatre affiliation. Although extensive, the directory is incomplete: John Drew II, Ada Rehan, James O'Neill, and Richard Mansfield are among those actors omitted. The index does not include references to the "Stars. . ." and "Directory. . ." sections and is incomplete in its coverage of the chronology.

Illustrations. Six engravings, mostly of performers.

Features. Introduction; table of contents; index.

Actors. General.

117. Fiske, Minnie Maddern [Davey]. *Mrs. Fiske, Her Views on Actors, Acting, and the Problems of Production.* Recorded by Alexander Woollcott. New York: Century, 1917. 229 pp. Illus.

Ibid. Rpt. as *Mrs. Fiske: Her Views on the Stage.* New York: Benjamin Blom, 1968. 229 pp. Illus.

Deciding to "summon his memories of casual and incautious conversations, to chronicle her table-talk, faintly, but faithfully," Woollcott recorded these conversations with Mrs. Fiske in 1916. The actress comments on a variety of theatrical subjects, including the actor's preparation for a role, the "science" of acting, the harmfulness of repertory theatre, the popularity and greatness of Ibsen's plays, and the struggle for the "Perfect" production. Speaking primarily in generalities, with some brief references to her contemporaries (e.g., Duse, Belasco, and Ellen Terry) and to specific Fiske productions, the actress is shown to be a highly idealistic, modest, and iconoclastic woman "*of* the theatre." In a postscript, Woollcott includes a lengthy letter from Mrs. Fiske in which she praises his memory and adds some afterthoughts. Woollcott contributes a sketch of Mrs. Fiske's life, prepared without her aid, and a fairly complete listing of her roles through 1916, giving the year of her first performances of those roles played 1893 and after.

Illustrations. Twenty-five, mostly photographs of Minnie Maddern Fiske.

Features. Table of contents; list of illustrations; biographical sketch of Minnie Maddern Fiske (including lists of most of her roles) by Alexander Woollcott.

Actors. Minnie Maddern Fiske.

118. Forbes-Robertson, Diana. *My Aunt Maxine: The Story of Maxine Elliott.* New York: The Viking Press, © 1964. xii, 306 pp. Illus.

This chronicle of Maxine Elliott's life and career was written by her niece, a daughter of Sir Johnstone and Gertrude (Elliott) Forbes-Robertson. The author, who knew "Aunt Dettie" during the 1920s and 1930s, reconstructs Miss Elliott's story with the full use of family papers, as well as other historical materials. Approximately two-thirds of the book concerns the pre-1911 period and includes substantial information on Maxine's, Gertrude's, and Nat C. Goodwin's acting careers (Goodwin was Miss Elliott's second husband). The anecdotal narrative contains much information on Miss Elliott's personality and social activities, as well as her theatrical career. Some specific dates, but few contemporary evaluations or descriptions of Miss Elliott's acting, are included.

Illustrations. Fifty-seven, mostly photographs of Maxine Elliott and members of her family.

Features. Acknowledgements; table of contents; list of illustrations; documentation: sources of quotations are identified by author and/or title and/or date; "Theatrical Chronology of Maxine Elliott" (include specific dates); index.

Actors. Gertrude Elliott, Maxine Elliott, Nat C. Goodwin.

119. Ford, James L[auren]. *Forty-Odd Years in the Literary Shop.* New York: E. P. Dutton, © 1921. vii, 362 pp. Illus.

This book of reminiscences covers the author's life from the mid-1800s to the time of publication. A long-time journalist and contributor of theatrical articles to many periodicals, the author presents miscellaneous anecdotes and tidbits of information. Among the many actors mentioned are Edwin Booth, Mary Anderson, Mrs. Leslie Carter, Geroge Arliss, and Francis Starr.

Illustrations. Fifty-five, mostly photographs of the author's acquaintances.

Features. List of illustrations.

Actors. General.

120. Forrester, Izola [Louise]. *This One Mad Act: The Unknown Story of John Wilkes Booth and His Family, by his Granddaughter.* Boston: Hale, Cushman & Flint, 1937. xii, 500 pp. Illus.

The author sets down her recollections of her grandmother, mother, and Uncle Harry—respectively, the secret wife, daughter, and son of John Wilkes Booth—as well as a record of her own search for information concerning Wilkes Booth. Utilizing family records and oral tradition, interviews, published materials, and conjecture, the author arrives at three major conclusions: 1) that Wilkes Booth married in 1859 and produced two children with his wife Izola; 2) that Booth's assassination of Lincoln was instigated by "men high in the order of the Knights of the Golden Circle, said to have been a branch of Freemasonry"; and 3) that Wilkes Booth actually died in 1879, probably in Bombay, India. The author inserts many quotations, but, unfortunately, inadequately documents her sources.

Illustrations. Twenty-seven, mostly photographs of John Wilkes Booth and his "descendants," and of items and people relating to his life.

Features. Preface; table of contents; list of illustrations; documentation: some sources of quotations are partially identified; index.

Actors. Edwin Booth, John Wilkes Booth, Ogarita Rosalie Booth (Rita Booth, Rita Henderson).

121. Fowler, Gene. *Good Night, Sweet Prince: The Life and Times of John Barrymore.* New York: Viking, 1944. xvii, 477 pp. Illus.

Ibid. Philadelphia: Blakiston, © 1944. vii, 474 pp. Illus.

Ibid. New York: Editions for the Armed Services, © 1944. 509 pp. Illus.

Ibid. New York: Ballantine, 1971. 525 pp. Illus.

The author, a personal friend of his subject for over twenty years, presents a fond biography of John Barrymore. Drawing upon personal observations, upon conversations with John and Lionel Barrymore and with friends of the Barrymores, and upon published materials, he includes information on most theatrical members of the Drew-Barrymore family. Most of the material is anecdotal, with little description or evaluation of performance. Slightly less than one-third of the book concerns the pre-1911 period.

Illustrations. Sixteen, mostly photographs of John Barrymore.

Features. "Overture"; table of contents; list of illustrations; documentation: most sources of quotations are identified by author and/or title; index.

Actors. Ethel Barrymore, John Barrymore, Lionel Barrymore, Maurice Barrymore, William Collier, John Drew II, Mrs. John Drew.

122. Foy, Eddie, and Alvin F. Harlow. *Clowning Through Life.* New York: E. P. Dutton, © 1928. 331 pp. Illus.

This volume of personal and professional memories covers the period from Eddie Foy's childhood in Civil War America to the time of publication, emphasizing the pre-1911 period. Dominated by anecdotes and narration, with few specific dates, the book contains material on the author's career in honkytonks, extravaganza, musical comedy, and vaudeville, as well as brief references to such actors as Nat C. Goodwin and Edwin Booth. Foy includes his eyewitness account of the disastrous Iroquois Theatre fire in 1903.

Illustrations. Twenty-two photographs, mostly of Eddie Foy, his family and friends, and scenes connected with his life.

Features. List of illustrations.

Actors. Eddie Foy.

123. French, C[harles] E[lwell] (ed.). *Six Years at the Castle*

Square Theatre, with Portraits of the Members of the Company and Complete Programs of All Plays Produced: May 3, 1897-May 3, 1903. Boston: Charles Elwell French, 1903. 406 pp. Illus.

This "remembrance" volume is divided into two parts. The initial one-third of the book consists of photographs and brief, popularly-written biographical sketches of most of the regular members of the Castle Square Theatre Company, Boston, from its founding in 1897 through May 3, 1903. The remainder of the work is a chronological record of playbills of all productions at that theatre during the same period.

Illustrations. Fifty-nine portrait photographs of members of the Castle Square Theatre Company.

Features. Index.

Actors. General.

124. Frohman, Daniel. *Daniel Frohman Presents: An Autobiography.* New York: C. Kendall & W. Sharp, © 1935; New York: Lee Furman, © 1935 [Furman ed. published in 1937]. xv, 317 pp. Illus.

Primarily a volume of reminiscences, this book concerns the period from the 1850s to 1935, emphasizing the pre-1911 era. Materials pertaining to the author's youth, career in theatrical management, and experiences with the film industry are included. The author utilizes personal recollection, hearsay, and some, mostly unnamed, published sources. The author inserts brief, anecdotal comments on many actors, including DeWolf Hopper, Joseph Jefferson III, Charlotte Cushman, Richard Mansfield, Robert B. Mantell, and many others. Some of the text is derived, nearly verbatim, from the author's earlier *Memories of a Manager* (see 126).

Illustrations. Sixty-four, mostly photographs of the author's friends.

Features. Table of contents; list of illustrations; index.

Actors. Edwin Booth, William Gillette, Helena Modjeska, E. H. Sothern.

125. —. *Encore.* New York: Lee Furman, © 1937; rpt. Freeport, New York: Books for Libraries, 1970. xii, 295 pp. Illus.

This book contains some of the author's personal reminiscences, although the bulk of the text is composed of anecdotes and biographical materials on theatre people from the time of Richard Burbage to that of W. C. Macready, with some miscellaneous reflections and anecdotes. The information concerning Booth and Boucicault is mostly anecdotal.

Illustrations. Thirty-seven engravings, photographs, and paintings, mostly of actors from the seventeenth through the nineteenth centuries.

Features. Introduction; table of contents; list of illustrations; documentation: most sources of quotations are identified by author and/or title and/or date; bibliography; index.

Actors. Edwin Booth, Dion Boucicault.

126. —. *Memories of a Manager: Reminiscences of the Old Lyceum and of Some of the Players of the Last Quarter Century.* Garden City, New York: Doubleday, Page, 1911. xvii, 235 pp. Illus.

This book contains the author's recollections of and reflections on theatrical matters of the 1880-1910 period. He writes on playwriting technique, English dramatic taste, his managerial activities, playwrights, and actors. Anecdotes, brief descriptions, and capsule evaluations concerning dozens of actors are included. In addition to those actors noted below, the author comments briefly on W. J. LeMoyne, William Faversham, James K. Hackett,

William Gillette, Richard Mansfield, and many others.

Illustrations. Thirty-six, mostly photographs of actors and scenes from productions.

Features. Preface; table of contents; list of illustrations; appendices: "History of the Lyceum Theatre by Dates of the Productions of Plays" (1885-1902), "Daly's Theatre Under Daniel Frohman's Management" (dates and plays, 1899-1905), "Casts of Famous First Nights" (playbill copy from five Lyceum Theatre productions).

Actors. Dion Boucicault, Helena Modjeska, E. H. Sothern.

127. Fuller, Edward (ed.). *The Dramatic Year (1887-88): Brief Criticisms of Important Theatrical Events in the United States, with a Sketch of the Season in London by William Archer.* Boston: Ticknor, 1889. viii, 268 pp.

The book is a "critical review" of selected aspects of the 1887-88 theatrical season. With the exception of Archer's review of the London season, the contents pertain to the American, mainly New York and Boston, theatre. Among the essays contained in this volume are surveys of various theatres—such as Daly's, Wallack's, Palmer's Madison Square, and the Boston Museum—and reviews of individual productions—such as *Paul Kauvar,* the Wallack testimonial *Hamlet,* and *La Tosca.* Several of the essays pay particular attention to specific actors, for example E. H. Sothern, Frederick Warde, Clara Morris, and Richard Mansfield. The contributors are the editor, George Edgar Montgomery, J. Ranken Towse, C. T. Copeland, Howard Malcolm Ticknor, Lyman H. Weeks, B. E. Woolf, and Archer.

Illustrations. None.

Features. Editor's note; table of contents.

Actors. Lawrence Barrett, Edwin Booth, Fanny Janauschek, Helena Modjeska.

128. Gagey, Edmond M[cAdoo]. *The San Francisco Stage: A
  History. Based on Annals Compiled by the Research
  Department of the San Francisco Federal Theatre.*
  New York: Columbia University Press, 1950; rpt.
  Westport, Connecticut: Greenwood, 1970. xv, 264
  pp. Illus.

  Based on the unpublished 1937 annals compiled by the
  San Francisco Federal Theatre, supplemented by the
  author's additional research, this book traces San Francisco theatrical activity from Gold Rush days to the early
  years of the twentieth century. The main emphasis is
  on the last half of the nineteenth century; approximately
  one-tenth of the text covers the 1900-34 period and provides the summary. The author includes some contemporary newspaper criticisms and descriptions of actors,
  brief biographical sketches of many actors, and some
  anecdotal material. Although rarely providing specific
  dates of incidents, the author usually indicates the season
  in which major, and some minor, engagements occurred.
  Hardly a complete record of the San Francisco stage, the
  book is a useful summary of nineteenth-century theatrical
  activity in that city.

  Illustrations. Forty-two photographs of performers, thea-
    tres, and programs.

  Features. Preface; table of contents; list of illustrations;
    little documentation; selected bibliography;
    index.

  Actors. General.

129. Gallegly, Joseph [S.]. *Footlights on the Border: The Galveston and Houston Stage Before 1900.* New York:
  Humanities Press, 1962. 262 pp. Illus.

  This well-documented study chronicles professional

theatrical activity in Galveston and Houston from the 1838-39 season through the 1899-1900 season. Approximately two-thirds of the text concerns the post-Civil War period. Commenting on theatres, managers, and, especially, performers, the author includes many specific dates and contemporary criticisms in the narrative. Among the many actors receiving brief comment are Edwin Booth, Lawrence Barrett, Joseph Jefferson III, Louis James, Richard Mansfield, Clara Morris, and James O'Neill.

Illustrations. Fifty-three photographs and engravings of performers, managers, theatres, and programs.

Features. Preface; introduction; table of contents; extensive documentation; bibliography; appendix: "The Houston and Galveston Stage, 1838-1900. List of Attractions" (includes city, theatre, date, title, name of stars/companies/combinations, and, in many cases, number of performances); index.

Actors. General.

130. Gard, Robert E., and David Semmes. *America's Players.* New York: Seabury Press, 1967. viii, 152 pp. Illus.

"This book is entended to acquaint younger readers with some of the highlights in the history of the American stage, to introduce them to a selected number of America's actresses and actors and theatre personalities, and, hopefully, to awaken an awareness of the pleasures and benefits inherent in the world of the theatre." Anecdotes and biographical data are included in the several chapters related to actors.

Illustrations. Numerous drawings of fanciful scenes and of actors (most having remarkably little resemblance to the actor named).

Features. Introduction; table of contents; brief bibliogra-

phy; list of plays, with brief comments, referred
to in the text.

Actors. David Belasco, Edwin Booth, Lotta Crabtree,
Charlotte Cushman, William Gillette, Joseph Jefferson III, Richard Mansfield, Helena Modjeska.

131. Garland, Hamlin. *Companions on the Trail: A Literary
Chronicle.* New York: Macmillan, 1931. vi, 539 pp.

This sequel to *Roadside Meetings* (see 132) covers the
period 1899-1914. It is closely based on the author's
daily diaries for those years. Among the literary and personal reminiscences are brief comments on the actors
Henry Miller, Arnold Daly, Helena Modjeska, and Richard
Mansfield.

Illustrations. One drawing of the author.

Features. Introduction; table of contents; "Concluding
Word."

Actors. General.

132. —. *Roadside Meetings.* New York: Macmillan, 1930. viii,
474 pp.

This "loosely strung series of literary and artistic portraits" is based on the author's memories and notebooks
of the 1884-99 period. Most of the subjects of his reminiscences are literary figures, such as Howells, Crane,
Whitman, and Joaquin Miller. The author also comments
on some actors, especially Edwin Booth and James A.
Herne, with briefer statements concerning such players
as Katherine Corcoran Herne, Mary Shaw, and William
Gillette. Brief evaluations of performances, anecdotes,
and texts of letters from Booth and Mr. Herne are included.

Illustrations. One drawing of the author.

Features. Prefatory note; table of contents.

Actors. Edwin Booth, James A. Herne.

132a. Gelb, Arthur and Barbara. *O'Neill.* Harper and Brothers. © 1962. xx, 970 pp.

Ibid. New York: Harper and Row, © 1973. xx, 990 pp.

This superb study traces Eugene O'Neill's life and career from his birth in 1888 to his funeral in 1953. The author utilize interviews with over four hundred people, as well as O'Neill's personal papers and published sources, to compile this detailed portrait containing historical data, anecdotes, and critical quotations. The early portion of the volume contains considerable biographical and professional description of James O'Neill's colleagues, such as Joseph Jefferson and Edwin Booth.

1973 ed.: This edition reprints the earlier work with minor alterations and adds an epilogue which is mainly concerned with Carlotta Monterey O'Neill's life from 1953 to her death in 1970.

Illustrations. 1962 ed.: Seventy-three, mainly photographs of O'Neill, his family, and scenes from his plays (both editions).

Features. Acknowledgments; introduction; table of contents; documentation: some quotations are identified by author and/or title and/or date; bibliography included in acknowledgments; "Chronological Table of O'Neill's Published Plays;" index.
1973 ed.: Same, plus epilogue.

Actors. James O'Neill (both editions).

133. [Gerson, Noel Bertram], Paul Lewis [pseud.]. *Queen of the Plaza: A Biography of Adah Isaacs Menken.* New

York: Funk & Wagnals, ©1964. 307 pp.

The author utilizes his subject's diary, autobiographical prose fragment, letters, and papers, as well as published materials by various authors. The narrative contains many anecdotes, selections from Miss Menken's writings, some evaluations of her personality and acting, and a few dates. Over two-thirds of the book concerns the years 1861-68. Brief comments on such actors as Edwin Booth, James Murdoch, and Charles Fechter are included.

Illustrations. None.

Features. Table of contents; documentation: sources of quotations are indicated by author and/or title and/or date; bibliography; index.

Actors. Adah Isaacs Menken.

134. Gilbert, Mrs. [Anne Hartley]. *The Stage Reminiscences of Mrs. Gilbert.* Ed., with an introd., by Charlotte M. Martin. New York: Charles Scribner's Sons, 1901. xiii, 248 pp.

In this volume of reminiscences, the author sketches her life, emphasizing her theatrical career. Approximately one-half of the text concerns her years with Augustin Daly's theatrical company (1869-99), containing much comment on Daly. Brief comments and anecdotes concerning various actors, including Edwin Forrest, John Drew II, and James Lewis, are included.

Illustrations. Thirty-five, mostly photographs of the author and other actors.

Features. Introduction by Charlotte M. Martin; list of illustrations; documentation: the source of the one quotation is identified.

Actors. Mrs. G. H. Gilbert.

135. Gillette, William [Hooker]. *The Illusion of the First Time in Acting.* Introd. by George Arliss. Notes by [James] Brander Matthews. New York: Printed for the Dramatic Museum of Columbia University, 1915. 58 pp.

> Three sections comprise this volume: Arliss' introduction, Gillett's address (originally delivered in 1913), and Matthews' notes. Gillette reflects on the nature of drama and a few of the requirements and pitfalls of acting. A-mong the topics he includes are the "illusion of the first time," the danger of behaving "correctly" onstage (i.e., according to "authorities" on etiquette, elocution, etc.), and the value of individual personality to the actor. Arliss addresses his comments primarily to the subjects of personality and the illusion of the first time. Matthews' notes support four of Gillette's main points through quotations and paraphrases of comments by Goethe, Joseph Jefferson III, Fanny Kemble, and others.

> *Illustrations.* None.

> *Features.* Introduction by George Arliss; table of contents; documentation: partial identification of sources quoted in Matthews' notes; notes by [James] Brander Matthews.

> *Actors.* George Arliss, William Gillette.

136. Gladding, W. J. *A Group of Theatrical Caricatures.* Introd. and biographical sketches by Louis Evan Shipman. New York: Dunlap Society, 1897. viii, 78 pp.

> The twelve caricatures of theatrical figures were drawn in 1868 by Gladding. The introduction and brief biographical sketches of each of Gladding's subjects were prepared by Shipman especially for this publication. The biographies contain factual data, anecdotes, and appreciations of each subject's personal and professional qualities. The information in the sketches concerns both pre- and post-Civil War years. In addition to the actors noted below, caricatures and biographies of Dan Bryant, Charles T.

White, and Tony Pastor are included.

Illustrations. Twelve caricatures of theatre workers.

Features. Introduction by Louis Evan Shipman; documentation: sources of quotations are identified by author and/or title.

Actors. Edwin Booth, John Brougham, Francis Chanfrau,
William J. Florence, Edwin Forrest, George L.
Fox, John E. Owens, Lester Wallack, William
Wheatley.

137. Glover, Lyman B. *The Story of a Theatre.* Chicago: R. R.
Donnelley, n.d. 129 pp.

This book is a souvenir of Power's Theatre, formerly
known as Hooley's Theatre, in Chicago. Included are: a
brief narrative of the theatre's activities, including some
mention of actors who performed there and their relative
successes; the texts of numerous short letters from performers, containing anecdotes and other materials relating
to Hooley's Theatre and/or congratulations to Henry J.
Powers upon his assumption of ownership of the theatre;
paragraphs, including factual data, on all Chicago theatres
up to 1898; a record of the bookings at Hooley's Theatre,
1877-97; and sundry information on the theatre building.

Illustrations. Numerous engravings of actors, critics, and
views of Hooley's/Power's Theatre; several
facsimile reproductions of letters from
actors.

Features. Introductory note; list of bookings at Hooley's
Theatre, 1877-97 (includes dates and names of
stars and/or companies and/or plays).

Actors. General.

138. Golden, John, and Viola Brothers Shore. *Stage-Struck
John Golden.* Foreword by Irvin S. Cobb. New York

and Los Angeles: Samuel French, 1930. xvi, 323 pp.

Over one-third of this book of recollections relates to the period from the late 1880s to 1911. Included in this section are some reminiscences of Golden's brief career as an actor. Anecdotes concerning his work as a song-writer, playwright, and producer of plays and films predominate.

Illustrations. Forty-one, mostly photographs, of John Golden and associates.

Features. Foreword by Irvin S. Cobb; brief appreciations of John Golden by Ring Lardner, George Ade, and Rupert Hughes; index.

Actors. John Golden.

139. Goldsmith, B[erthold] H. *Arnold Daly.* New York: James T. White, © 1927. 57 pp.

The greater portion of this brief work is a chronicle of Arnold Daly's theatrical career. Some anecdotal material, excerpts from reviews, and selections from Daly's writings are interspersed with the factual data. The volume concludes with the author's personal sketch of Daly and selections from four appreciations of the actor. This essay is most useful as a general indication of the types of and locations of Daly's theatrical endeavors.

Illustrations. Four photographs of Arnold Daly.

Features. Publisher's note; documentation: some sources of quotations are partially identified; "Chronology: Plays and Roles in which Arnold Daly appeared during his thirty-five years on the stage" (incomplete).

Actors. Arnold Daly.

140. Goodale, Katherine (Kitty Molony). *Behind the Scenes with Edwin Booth.* Foreword by Minnie Maddern

Fiske. Boston and New York: Houghton Mifflin, 1931; rpt. New York: Benjamin Blom, 1969. xiv, 328 pp.

The author recollects her 1886-87 season with Edwin Booth's theatrical company and her friendship with the star—her hero. These charming memoires emphasize the offstage life of Booth's company, but also contain many descriptions and personal evaluations of onstage occurrences. The author affords an unusual view of Booth as a private man and an interesting picture of touring with a major theatrical company in the 1880s.

Illustrations. Twelve photographs of Edwin Booth, the author, and others.

Features. Preface; foreword by Minnie Maddern Fiske; table of contents; list of illustrations; index.

Actors. Lawrence Barrett, Edwin Booth, Kitty Molony (later Katerine Goodale), Ida Rock, Emma Vaders.

141. Goodwin, Nat[haniel] C[arl]. *Nat Goodwin's Book.* Boston: Richard G. Badger, ©1914. xv, 366 pp.

The author, writing "purely from memory's tablets," interweaves autobiographical narration with reminiscences of fellow theatre-workers and comments on a variety of theatrical and non-theatrical subjects. The book is mainly composed of anecdotes and the author's personal opinions of the professional and personal merits of himself and his acquaintances. In addition to the actors noted below, the book contains comments on John McCullough, Maude Adams, Wilton Lackaye, James A. Herne, and many other performers.

Illustrations. Forty-eight photographs, drawings, and engravings of the author and his acquaintances.

Features. Preface; table of contents; list of illustrations; index.

Actors. Maxine Elliott, Nat C. Goodwin, Joseph Jefferson III, Richard Mansfield, Stuart Robson, Sol Smith Russell, Charles R. Thorne, Jr., Eliza Weathersby.

142. Grau, Robert. *Forty Years Observation of Music and the Drama.* New York and Baltimore: Broadway Publishing, 1909. vi, 370 pp.

This book consists of miscellaneous reminiscences of people associated with the dramatic, variety, operatic, and musical professions from the 1860s to the time of publication. Brief anecdotal, evaluative, and biographical comments on hundreds of performers, managers, press agents, writers, etc., are included. Among the actors mentioned are Fanny Janauschek, Mrs. John Drew, Alla Nazimova, George L. Fox, Francis Wilson, and scores of others. Few specific dates are indicated.

Illustrations. Two hundred, mostly photographs, of people associated with various branches of the theatre during the last half of the nineteenth century and the beginning of the twentieth.

Features. Prefatory note; table of contents.

Actors. General.

142a. Grebanier, Bernard. *Then Came Each Actor: Shakespearean Actors, Great and Otherwise, Including Players and Princes, Rogues, Vagabonds and Actors Motley, from Will Kempe to Olivier and Gielgud and After.* New York: David McKay, © 1975.

This work is an interesting but highly uneven chronicle of Shakespearean acting from the 1600s to 1970s. The author includes anecdotes, biographical data, critical quotations, brief suggestions of the players' styles, and some interpretations of the plays. His enthusiastic effort to combine substantive content with entertaining material sometimes slips to trivia, but he has inserted a wealth of information. While the work focuses primarily on major English actors, such as Quin, Garrick, Keen, Beerbohm Tree, etc., there is one chapter on Edwin Booth. Two chapters are comprised of brief biographical notes on scores of nineteenth and twentieth century English, American, and European actors, such as Forrest, Modjeska, McCullough, and E. L. Davenport.

Illustrations. One hundred and five photographs, engravings, paintings, etc., mainly of English and American actors in Shakespearean roles.

Features. Preface; table of contents; adequate documentation; bibliography; index.

Actors. Edwin Booth.

143. *The Green Room Book, or Who's Who on the Stage: An Annual Biographical Record of the Dramatic, Musical, and Variety World, 1906.* Ed. by Bampton Hunt. New York: Frederick Warne, 1906. 452 pp.

This book is primarily composed of an alphabetically-arranged collection of hundreds of brief biographical sketches of living persons associated with the theatre. The emphasis is overwhelmingly British, but some American and continental performers and managers are included. Most entries contain the following information: name; role in the theatre (e.g., actor, critic, etc.); place and/or date of birth; information on education, marriage, and debut; selected chronology; address; and some miscellaneous information (e.g., hobbies, clubs, etc.).

Illustrations. Forty-six portrait photographs of some of the subjects of the biographies.

Features. Table of contents; "Addenda to Biographies"; "Players in the Peerage"; "Famous Stage Families: Genealogical Tables"; "London and Provincial Productions During 1905..."; "Theatrical Happenings in 1905"; "The Stage in the Law Courts, 1905"; "The Licensing of the

London Theatres"; "Sunday Concerts in Theatres"; "The Sketch Question"; "List of London and Suburban Theatres and Music Halls. . ."; "Provincial Theatres and Music Halls"; "Theatrical Clubs, Charities, and Allied Associations"; "Players Who Have Passed—Obituary Notices of 1905."

Actors. General.

144. Griffith, Frank Carlos. *Mrs. Fiske.* New York: Neale, 1912. 146 pp.

The author of this volume was Mrs. Fiske's "acting manager" from 1897 to 1910. He provides some biographical material and brief appreciations of some of the actress' successful roles, but no careful description or criticism of her acting. The bulk of the book consists of anecdotal reminiscences touching on Mrs. Fiske's offstage characteristics. Included is the text of Mrs. Fiske's address to the National Alliance for the Protection of Stage Children, delivered on February 9, 1912.

Illustrations. Seveneen photographs of Mrs. Fiske and of scenes from her productions.

Features. Table of contents; list of illustrations.

Actors. Minnie Maddern Fiske.

145. Gronowicz, Antoni. *Modjeska: Her Life and Loves.* New York: Thomas Yoseloff, © 1956. 256 pp.

This book purports to be a biography of Helena Modjeska from her childhood to her death, "based on twenty years of research, interviews, and travel throughout Europe and America getting material on [her] life." Dealing primarily with her private life, the author constructs lengthy dialogues "conceived from the Polish notes of Modjeska, together with conversations held by the author with those who lived with the actress and worked with her." He also includes occasional quotations from published sources and extracts from Mme. Modjeska's diary of her 1889-90 tour with Edwin Booth. An emphasis on sensationalism, the questionable dialogues, and gross factual errors make this book of dubious worth.

Illustrations. Twenty, mostly photographs of Helena Modjeska and other actors.

Features. Author's note; table of contents; list of illustrations.

Actors. Edwin Booth, Helena Modjeska.

146. Gustafson, Zadel Barnes. *Genevieve Ward: A Biographical Sketch from Original Material Derived from Her Family and Friends.* Boston: James R. Osgood, 1882. xv, 261 pp.

The author, mainly utilizing material provided by Genevieve Ward and Miss Ward's mother, traces Miss Ward's life and career to the spring of 1881. The book contains information on the subject's youth, operatic experiences, and, from 1873, dramatic career. Narration, anecdotes, excerpts from English, French, and American reviews, and many letters to or concerning Miss Ward are included. Brief evaluations and descriptions of the actress' performances and, after 1873, some specific dates are contained in the volume.

Illustrations. One photograph of Genevieve Ward.

Features. Preface; documentation: sources of quotations are identified by author and/or title and, rarely, date; appendix: affadavits and exhibits from Genevieve Ward's suit for injunction against the Wallack and Moss Production of *Forget Me Not* (1880; includes several reviews of Miss Ward's performance in the play); "Index of Names of Families that have Intermarried with the Ward Family and Its Descendents. . . ."

Actors. Genevieve Ward.

147. Hall, Lillian Arvilla. *Catalogue of Dramatic Portraits in the Theatre Collection of the Harvard College Library.* 4 vols. Cambridge, Massachusetts: Harvard University Press, 1930. Vol. I: vii, 438 pp.; Vol. II: 427 pp.; Vol. III: 456 pp.; Vol. IV: 357 pp.

"It is the purpose of this catalogue to provide a descriptive index to the engraved dramatic portraits in the Theatre Collection at Harvard College. The prints, approximately forty thousand in number, which are considered in this present work consist of portraits of individuals, chiefly British and American, whose names are associated with the past and present history of the Drama. In addition to portraits of public performers and exhibitors of many varieties, the catalogue includes dramatists, composers, theatrical managers, critics, and even occasionally such minor figures as scene-painters and costumers. . . . The prints are arranged alphabetically according to names. In the cases of actors, personal portraits are placed first in order, and followed by portraits in character, which are arranged alphabetically according to roles." Each entry indicates its subject's professional specialty (e.g., actor, singer, etc.), and most dates of birth, death, and/or professional debut. Vol. I: A-E; Vol. II: F-K; Vol. III: L-R; Vol. IV: S-Z.

Illustrations. None.

Features. Preface (Vol. I); list of abbreviations (each vol.); indices of artists and engravers (each vol.); "Corrections" (Vol. IV for Vols. I-III).

Actors. General.

148. Hall, [William T.] "Biff." *The Turnover Club. Tales Told at the Meetings of the Turnover Club, About Actors and Actresses.* Chicago and New York: Rand, McNally, 1890. 234 pp.

This book is composed of dozens of anecdotes, mostly about the theatre and theatre-folk, many about actors. The author, a reporter for the *Chicago Sunday Herald,* preserves the anonymity of his sources for these humorous, and possibly apocryphal, stories.

Illustrations. None.

Features. Table of contents.

Actors. General.

149. Hamm, Margherita Arlina. *Eminent Actors in Their Homes: Personal Descriptions and Interviews.* New York: James Pott, 1902. xii, 336 pp.

Each of the twenty-four chapters in this book records a visit to the home(s) of an American actor. The author describes the grounds and the homes, often room-by-room. She pays particular attention to special collections (e.g., books, china, theatrical memorabilia) possessed by her subjects. Comments by the players concerning their hobbies, life-style, and/or profession are included. Although written in an admiring, fan-magazine-type style, these home-life articles afford interesting and often informative glimpses at the private personalities of these public figures.

Illustrations. Twenty photographs of actors at home and of rooms in the actors' houses.

Features. Preface; introduction; table of contents; list of illustrations; index.

Actors. Viola Allen, Mary Anderson, Marie Bates, Amelia Bingham, Beatrice Cameron, William H. Crane, Elsie de Wolfe, Robert Edeson, Maxine Elliott, Minnie Maddern Fiske, Nat C. Goodwin, James K. Hackett, Virginia Harned, Edward Harrigan, Joseph Jefferson III, Burr McIntosh, Mary Mannering, Richard Mansfield, Julia Marlowe, Chauncey Olcott, Annie O'Neill, May Robson,

Annie Russell, Otis Skinner, E. H. Sothern, Annie Ward Tiffany, David Warfield, Francis Wilson.

150. Hancock, Ralph, and Letitia Fairbanks. *Douglas Fairbanks: The Fourth Musketeer.* New York: Henry Holt, ©1953. 276 pp.

This book traces Douglas Fairbanks' life, 1883-1939. Composed of anecdotes, personal evaluation, narration, and some specific dates, the volume includes information concerning Fairbanks' stage career from 1900 to 1915. Approximately one-third of the book concerns the pre-1911 period.

Illustrations. Twenty-seven photographs of Douglas Fairbanks, his family and associates, and Pickfair.

Features. Acknowledgements.

Actors. Douglas Fairbanks.

151. Hapgood, Norman. *The Stage in America: 1897-1900.* New York: Macmillan, 1901. viii, 408 pp.

This book was "designed to describe, in what can be seen on the American stage to-day, those things of most importance to a thinking observer of the drama. . . ." To this end, the author collects diverse essays on playwrights, productions, and dramatic genres. Criticism and description of individual dramas and performances predominate. Among the topics essayed are "The Drama of Ideas," "Broad American Humor," New York German theatre, recent Shakespearian productions, and imported dramas. Included are criticisms of many actors, including brief comments on such players as May Irwin, Maude Adams, Julia Arthur, William Faversham, and Louis James.

Illustrations. None.

Features. Author's note; introduction; table of contents;
documentation: sources of quotations are
identified by author and/or title and/or date;
index.

Actors. Richard Mansfield, Ada Rehan, E. H. Sothern.

152. Harrison, Gabriel. *Edwin Forrest: The Actor and the
Man. Critical and Reminiscent.* Brooklyn, New York:
The Press of the Brooklyn Eagle Book Printing Depart-
ment, 1889. 210 pp.

The author, having seen Forrest act "over one hundred
times" and having been a long-time friend of his subject,
records his impressions of Forrest onstage and off. Included in this adulatory work are detailed descriptions of
Forrest's portrayals of Virginius, Metamora, Othello, and
King Lear, as well as a briefer description of his Damon.
The author recounts his visit with Forrest on Thanksgiving
Day, 1872, and provides information on the actor's elocution, his last appearance as an actor, and his severe illness,
death, and funeral. Substantial space is devoted to the
author's discussions of subjects only tangentially related
to Forrest. Some of Forrest's letters and recollections by
some of his friends are included.

Illustrations. Eleven photographs, engravings, and water-
colors, mostly of Edwin Forrest.

Features. Preface; table of contents; list of illustrations;
documentation: some sources of quotations
are partially identified.

Actors. Edwin Forrest.

153. Hart, William S[urrey]. *My Life East and West.* Boston
and New York: Houghton Mifflin, 1929; rpt. New
York: Benjamin Blom, 1968. viii, 363 pp.

The author, chronicling his life during the last third of
the nineteenth century and the first quarter of the twen-

tieth, reminisces about his youth, stage career, and silent film activities. He includes anecdotes, narration, reflections on many subjects, and comments on scores of friends and associates. Over one-half of the book pertains to the pre-1911 period; approximately half of this section concerns the author's stage career. Among the actors mentioned briefly are Lawrence Barrett, and Julia Arthur.

Illustrations. Twenty-five, mostly photographs of the author.

Features. Table of contents; list of illustrations; documentation: most sources of quotations are identified by author and/or title; index.

Actors. William S. Hart.

154. Henderson, Myrtle E. *A History of the Theatre in Salt Lake City from 1850 to 1870.* Evanston, Illinois: n.n., 1934. 161 pp.

This published master's thesis traces theatrical activity in Salt Lake City under the aegis of the Latter-Day Saints from 1850 to 1870. Although largely composed of information on theatre buildings, dramatic associations, and rules and regulations, the author includes data concerning stock company rosters, visiting stars, and dates of performances, along with a few contemporary reviews.

Illustrations. Thirteen engravings and photographs of buildings, playbills, properties, and actors.

Features. Introduction; table of contents; list of illustrations; documentation: sources of quotations are identified; bibliography; lists of productions, 1865-68 and 1888-96 (include dates, titles, authors, and partial cast lists).

Actors. General.

155. Henry, David D[odds]. *William Vaughn Moody: A Study.*

Boston: Bruce Humphries, ©1934. 276 pp.

In this scholarly volume "the objective facts of biography have been used extensively in the interpretation of Moody's achievement in literature." Biographical data and personal appraisal of Moody, as well as critical evaluations of his critical, poetic, and dramatic works, are included. The sections on *The Great Divide* and *The Faith Healer* contain material on the productions of those plays, with information on Moody's relationships with Henry Miller and Margaret Anglin.

Illustrations. None.

Features. Foreword; table of contents; documentation: extensive; bibliography; "Appendix A—Twenty New Letters"; "Appendix B—Early Poems"; index.

Actors. Margaret Anglin, Henry Miller.

156. Hines, Dixie, and Harry Prescott Hanaford (ed.). *Who's Who in Music and Drama: An Encyclopaedia of Biography of Notable Men and Women in Music and the Drama, 1914.* New York: H. P. Hanaford, 1914. 556 pp.

Hundreds of factual biographical sketches of living persons associated with music and drama comprise the bulk of this volume. The majority of the entries are for American performers, although the selection is not limited by nationality or to performers. A typical entry contains information on the subject's birth, education, career, and address. Career information for actors includes important engagements and/or roles, with dates and theatres for the major appearances. Some major figures were omitted due to their lack of cooperation with the editors.

Illustrations. Thirty-six portrait photographs of subjects of the biographies.

Features. "Proem"; table of contents; list of illustrations;

cast lists, 1910-13, for the Boston Grand Opera, Chicago Grand Opera, Metropolitan Grand Opera, and Metropolitan Opera (Philadelphia) companies; "Index to Players."

Actors. General.

157. Hogan, Robert [Goode] . *Dion Boucicault.* New York: Twayne, ©1969. 146 pp.

Approximately one-half of this survey of Boucicault's life and work is a critical examination of his major plays; nearly one-third comprises a biography of him; and the remainder consists of comments on his influence in the areas of acting, directing, theatre management, and play-writing. One-third of the biographical sketch relates to the post-1861 years, including many specific dates.

Illustrations. None.

Features. Preface; table of contents; documentation: extensive; bibliography; chronology of Dion Doucicault's life; index.

Actors. Dion Boucicault.

158. *Holland Memorial. Sketch of the Life of George Holland, the Veteran Comedian, with Dramatic Reminiscences, Anecdotes, &c.* New York: T. H. Morrell, 1871. 124 pp.

This memorial volume, possibly written by T. H. Morrell, eulogizes George Holland, who died on December 20, 1870, and comments on related events following his death. Included are a biographical sketch of the actor, a discussion of the religious controversy touched off by his funeral, a tribute to the Church of the Transfiguration ("the little church around the corner"), and the program of the extensive Holland Testimonial performances. Factual data, anecdotes, letters to and from the actor, and lengthy quotations from contemporary newspapers are utilized in this discursive work.

Illustrations. One engraving of George Holland and one facsimile reproduction of a letter from Holland to Augustin Daly.

Features. Documentation: sources of quotations are identified.

Actors. George Holland.

159. Hooper, DeWolf, in collaboration with Wesley Winans Stout. *Once a Clown, Always a Clown: Reminiscences of DeWolf Hopper.* Boston: Little, Brown, 1927. x, 238 pp.

Ibid. *Reminiscences of DeWolf Hopper: Once a Clown, Always a Clown.* Garden City, New York: Garden City Publishing, 1932. x, 238 pp.

Reminiscing about his experiences in the theatre, silent films, and the Lambs Club, the author devotes over one-half of this book to the last quarter of the nineteenth century and the first decade of the twentieth. Anecdotes and relfections concerning himself, film and stage acting, and other actors, such as Louis James, Mrs. John Drew, and Maurice Barrymore, are included. Few dates are specified and performance description is rare in this book.

Illustrations. Twelve photographs, mostly of the author and other actors.

Features. Table of contents; documentation: sources of quotations are identified by author.

Actors. Harry Davenport, DeWolf Hopper, Joseph Jefferson III.

160. Horton, Judge [William Ellis] . *About Stage Folks.* Introd. by George P. Goodale. Detroit, Michigan: Free Press Printing, 1902. 160 pp.

Short chapters containing miscellaneous information on the theatre, vaudeville, and the circus comprise this book. Brief anecdotes and comments on stage practices are included, along with random listings of such items as actors' birthplaces, burial places, birthdates, summer homes, and associations with volunteer fire departments.

Illustrations. Seventeen portrait photographs, mostly of variety performers.

Features. Introduction by George P. Goodale; table of contents.

Actors. General.

161. —. *Driftwood of the Stage.* Detroit, Michigan: Press of Winn & Hammond, 1904. 383 pp.

These wide-ranging chapters contain miscellaneous information concerning all manner of theatrical activity, some gleaned from the author's personal acquaintance with theatre-folk. Factual data and anecdotes are included. Among the materials on actors are chapters concerning actors' debuts, farewells, and burial sites, famous testimonial and benefit performances, occasions of actors being hissed when they were sick, and patriotic activities by theatre people. Most of the information relates to the last quarter of the nineteenth century. Some of the material is taken from the author's *About Stage Folks* (see 160).

Illustrations. Nineteen portrait photographs of actors.

Features. Preface; table of contents; list of illustrations; index.

Actors. General.

162. Howe, M[ark] A[ntony] DeWolfe. *Memories of a Hostess: A Chronicle of Eminent Friendships, Drawn Chiefly from the Diaries of Mrs. James T. Fields.* Bos-

ton: The Atlantic Monthly Press, ©1922. 312 pp.

Along with the author's linking commentaries, this book consists of entries selected from Mrs. James T. Fields personal journals from 1860 to 1913, emphasizing the 1860s and 1870s. The entries are arranged according to the person with whom they are primarily concerned, including such friends and visitors of the Fields as Oliver Wendell Holmes, Longfellow, Mark Twain, and Charles Dickens. Among the actors mentioned are Edwin Booth, Joseph Jefferson III, Charlotte Cushman, and Charles Fechter.

Illustrations. Forty-seven, mostly photographs of friends of the Fields family and facsimiles of letters.

Features. Table of contents; list of illustrations; documentation: entries are dated.

Actors. General.

162a. Hubert, Philip G., Jr. *The Stage as a Career: A Sketch of the Actor's Life, Its Requirements, Hardships, and Rewards.* New York: G. P. Putnam's Sons, 1900. vii, 192 pp.

This volume contains comments by the author and by several American and English actors and actresses concerning acting as a profession: its artistic demands, social status, qualifications, means of training, etc. Offered as a guide to the serious acting prospect and as a deterrent to the non-serious, the author includes theoretical views and practical advice by such performers as Maggie Mitchell, Boucicault, Modieska, McCullough, Lawrence Barrett, Mary Anderson, Clara Morris, and Georgia Cayvan. Most of the American actors are quoted from articles originally published in the *North American Review.*

Illustrations. None.

Features. Preface; table of contents; documentation: sources of quotations are identified by author, index.

Actors. General.

163. Huneker, James Gibbons. *Steeplejack.* 2 vols. New York: Charles Scribner's Sons, 1920. Vol. I: 320 pp.; Vol. II: 327 pp.

Ibid. 2 vols. in 1. New York: Charles Scribner's Sons, 1922.

These rambling and enthusiastic memoires by the noted newspaperman and critic are composed primarily of anecdotes from his life and opinions and memories concerning scores of his acquaintances, including George Brandes, Bernard Shaw, and Joseph Conrad. Most of the author's references to actors are brief, but, frequently, interesting. He includes a letter from Richard Mansfield concerning that actor's production of *Peer Gynt.* The author's comments on his fellow critics, especially William Winter and John Ranken Towse ("Mr. Towse is the sounder critic of the two") are sometimes illuminating.

Illustrations. Vol. I: Five photographs of the author and his family.
Vol. II: Two photographs of the author and his family.

Features. "Apology" (Vol. I); table of contents (Vol. I for both volumes); list of illustrations (Vol. I for both volumes); index (Vol. II for both volumes).

Actors. Richard Mansfield, E. A. Sothern.

164. Hunter, Alexander, and J[oseph] H. Polkinhorn. *New National Theatre, Washington, D.C.: A Record of Fifty Years.* Washington, D.C.: R. O. Polkinhorn & Son, 1885. 101 pp.

A souvenir of the 1885 opening of the rebuilt New National Theatre, this volume traces the various manifestations of the (New) National Theatre for 1835 to 1885. The chronological narrative notes major engagements for each season, often indicating specific dates. Some playbills and occasional brief descriptions and criticisms of actors, excerpted from periodicals or provided by the authors, are included. Over one-half of the book concerns the post-1860 period.

Illustrations. Thirteen drawings, mostly of fixtures and decorations in the New National Theatre.

Features. Introduction; appended materials concerning the 1885 reopening of the theatre include: playbill, opening address by Edward Crapsey, and lists of builders, contractors, and officials.

Actors. General.

165. Hutton, Laurence. *Curiosities of the American Stage* New York: Harper & Brothers, 1891; rpt. St. Clair Shores, Michigan: Scholarly Press, 1969. xv, 347 pp.

Chapters on various aspects of American drama and theatre from the mid-eighteenth century to late in the nineteenth century comprise this volume. The major categories discussed are: "The Native American Drama" (with such subdivisions as "The Indian Drama," "The Revolutionary and War Drama," and "The Society Drama"), "The American Stage Negro," "The American Burlesque," "Infant Phenomena of America," and "A Century of American Hamlets." Although mainly an historical survey of its subjects, the book contains some scattered description and evaluation of actors. Among the actors mentioned briefly are Charles Fechter, Lawrence Barrett, E. L. Davenport, and Frank Mayo.

Illustrations. Eighty-five engravings, mostly of American actors.

Features. Preface; table of contents, list of illustrations; documentation: sources of a few quotations are indicated by author and title; indices of people and places.

Actors. Edwin Booth, George L. Fox.

166. —. *Edwin Booth.* New York: Harper & Brothers, 1893. 59 pp.

The author, a friend of Booth's for two decades, offers a brief, personal appreciation of the actor followed by a straight-forward biographical sketch. The biography emphasizes unusual events in Booth's career and gives scant attention to the last several years of Booth's life. A few anecdotes and a reminiscence of Junius Brutus Booth written by Edwin are included.

Illustrations. Seven photographs and engravings, mostly of Edwin Booth offstage.

Features. List of illustrations.

Actors. Edwin Booth.

167. —. *Plays and Players.* New York: Hurd and Houghton, 1875. vii, 276 pp.

This volume of miscellaneous papers on plays, players, and playhouses is composed mainly of historical materials relating to the nineteenth-century American stage. The author includes biographical data on actors, cast lists and dates of many notable performances, and some anecdotes, descriptions, and appreciations of players. Although most of the material pertains to the pre-1861 period, some information on later times is included. Among the actors mentioned briefly are Julia Dean Hayne, Mary Gannon, Laura Keene, Joseph Jefferson III, and Charlotte Cushman.

Illustrations. None.

Features. Table of contents; indices of persons, plays, and theatres.

Actors. General.

168. —. *Talks in a Library with Laurence Hutton.* Recorded by Isabel Moore. Introductory note by G. H. P[utnam]. New York: G. P. Putnam's Sons, 1905. xvii, 458 pp.

> The author recollects his friends and experiences during the last half of the nineteenth century. Included are anecdotes and discussions of scores of acquaintances. Among the actors mentioned briefly are Mary Anderson, Joseph Jefferson III, Lester Wallack, and William J. Florence.

> *Illustrations.* Sixty-six photographs, drawings, facsimiles, etc., of the author's friends, autographs, death masks, etc.

> *Features.* Introductory note by G. H. P[utnam]; introduction; note by Isabel Moore; table of contents; list of illustrations; index.

> *Actors.* Lawrence Barrett, Edwin Booth.

169. *The Illustrated American Stage: A Pictorial Review of the Most Notable Recent Theatrical Successes, Together with Many Drawings and Portraits of Celebraed Players.* New York: R. H. Russell, 1901. Unnumbered.

> This book is a collection of pictorial souvenirs published by R. H. Russell during 1900-01, with some additional illustrations added. In most cases, between fifteen and twenty-five illustrations are included for a single production. Emphasis is placed on the star performer for each production (only the star is named and most of the illustrations for each production are of the star in a group or alone). The stage setting is retouched or washed out in most of the photographs.

> *Illustrations.* Numerous photographs and some drawings of actors in roles and of scenes from productions.

> *Features.* None.

Actors. Maude Adams, John Drew II, William Gillette, Mary Mannering, Julia Marlowe, Annie Russell.

170. *In Memory of John McCullough.* New York: At the DeVinne Press, [1889]. 66 pp.

> This volume contains a brief "Life of McCullough" by William Winter and several tributes to the actor. Winter's life includes a fairly straightforward narrative of McCullough's life and career, a "list of the parts and plays that were included in McCullough's [starring] repertory," and an appreciation of the actor's personal and professional qualities. The tributes are mainly addresses and poems for the McCullough Monument. Among the contributors are Winter, Steele Mackaye, Henry Edwards, and William F. Johnson. Primarily tributes to McCullough's personal character, thre is little information on McCullough's acting that is of a descriptive or critical nature.

> *Illustrations.* Two photographs, one each of John McCullough and of the McCullough Monument.

> *Features.* Table of contents; list of roles and plays in John McCullough's starring repertory.

> *Actors.* John McCullough.

171. *Index to the Portraits in Odell's "Annals of the New York Stage": Transcribed from the File in the Theatre Collection.* Foreword by Alan S. Downer. n.p.: The American Society for Theatre Research, ©1963. iv, 179 pp.

> An index to the illustrations in the fifteen volumes of George C. D. Odell's *Annals of the New York Stage* (see 238) comprises this volume. Names of people, theatres, and plays are included in a single alphabetical listing, with references to the volume and page numbers where illustrations are located in Odell's *Annals.* When an illustration of a play specifies individual performers, the index entry for the play lists those performers. References to production portraits are also indicated in the entry for each per-

former identified.

Illustrations. None.

Features. Foreword by Alan S. Downer.

Actors. General.

172. Isaacs, Edith J[uliet] R. *The Negro in the American Theatre.* New York: Theatre Arts, 1947; rpt. College Park, Maryland: McGrath, 1968. 143 pp.

> This volume is a short history of Negro contributions to the American theatre from 1821 to 1946 and an exhortation for future progress. Slightly more than one-sixth of the book concerns the pre-1911 period, primarily dealing with minstrel and musical entertainments. Brief comments on such performers as George Walker and Bob Cole are given, along with a more substantial section on Bert Williams.

> *Illustrations.* Fifty-eight, mostly photographs of Negro performers and productions.

> *Features.* Introduction; table of contents; list of illustrations; documentation: sources of most quotations are identified by author.

> *Actors.* Bert Williams.

173. Isman, Felix. *Weber and Fields: Their Tribulations, Triumphs and Their Associates.* New York: Boni and Liveright, 1924. xii, 345 pp.

> This book, written by a long-time Weber and Fields business associate, traces the partnership of the famous pair from their childhood in the 1870s through their tremendous popularity at the turn of the century and culminating in their reunion in 1912. The author apparently gathered his information mainly through his observation of and acquaintance with his subjects. Included are

anecdotes and reconstructed conversations concerning the comedians' theatrical careers and associates, descriptions of their variety shows and travesties, and numerous fragments of stage dialogue. Few specific dates and critical reactions are contained in the book.

Illustrations. Thirty-four photographs and drawings of Weber and Fields and other performers.

Features. Introduction; list of illustrations; music and lyrics for eight songs from Weber and Fields' shows.

Actors. Lou Fields, DeWolf Hopper, Louis Mann, Lillian Russell, David Warfield, Joe Weber.

174. Izard, Forrest. *Heroines of the Modern Stage.* New York: Sturgis & Walton, 1915. ix, 390 pp.

This book is composed of chapters on Bernhardt, Rejane, Duse, Ellen Terry, and the six American actresses noted below, with an additional chapter commenting briefly on several other American actresses—such as Margaret Anglin, Ethel Barrymore, and Alla Nazimova. The essays include various combinations of biographical data (usually omitting specific dates), critical comment (usually laudatory) and personal description.

Illustrations. Ten portraits of actresses.

Features. Preface; table of contents; list of illustrations; documentation: sources of quotations are usually identified by author and title; bibliography; appendix: "The First English Actresses, and the Change in the Actor's Social Status"; index.

Actors. Maude Adams, Mary Anderson, Minnie Maddern Fiske, Julia Marlowe, Helena Modjeska, Ada Rehan.

175. Janis, Elsie. *So Far, So Good!* New York: E. P. Dutton, 1932. 344 pp.

> Drawing upon her memories, diaries, and family lore, the author recounts her life from her birth in 1889 until 1931. She writes about her stage, screen, and social life. Her theatrical memories more frequently concern events surrounding a production than the production itself. Anecdotes, personal opinions, and passing references to fellow performers abound, but few specific dates or descriptions of performances are included. Slightly less than one-third of the book concerns the author's life and career through 1910.

> *Illustrations.* Thirty-six photographs of the author, her family and friends, and scenes from her life.

> *Features.* List of illustrations.

> *Actors.* Elsie Janis.

176. Jefferson, Eugenie Paul. *Intimate Recollections of Joseph Jefferson.* New York: Dodd, Mead, 1909. xiv, 366 pp.

> Joseph Jefferson III's daughter-in-law collects in this volume, along with her own remembrances, a miscellany of materials relating to the actor and his homes, hobbies, friends, family, art, and memorials. She includes copious quotations from Joseph Jefferson, several of his letters, biographical data concerning the Jefferson family, and numerous, often lengthy, reminiscences of and tributes to the actor by many of his acquaintances. Among the comments by the subject are considerations of acting and other arts. This volume is primarily a warm tribute to the personal man and contains no descriptions or criticisms of his acting.

> *Illustrations.* Seventy, in various media, of Joseph Jefferson III, his family and friends, and some places and objects.

Features. Table of contents; list of illustrations; documentation: some sources of quotations are partially identified.

Actors. Edwin Booth, Charles Burke Jefferson, Joseph Jefferson III, Thomas Jefferson.

177. Jefferson Joseph [III]. *The Autobiography of Joseph Jefferson.* New York: Century, 1890. xv, 501 pp.

Ibid. *"Rip Van Winkle": The Autobiography of Joseph Jefferson.* Foreword by Eleanor Farjeon. New York: Appleton-Century-Crofts, 1950. xxxii, 375 pp.

Ibid. *The Autobiography of Joseph Jefferson.* Ed. by Alan S. Downer. Cambridge, Massachusetts: The Belknap Press of Harvard University Press, 1964. xxv, pp.

1890 ed.: The author charmingly writes about his experiences, friends, and art from the 1830s through the 1880s, including narration, anecdotes, and reflections. Nearly one-half of the text concerns the pre-1861 period and is rich in theatrical anecdotes. The later portion of the book, covering the period of the author's greatest success, concentrates more on his offstage life. This section contains many of his thoughts on the nature of acting and presents a fine personal portrait of him. He indicates few specific dates, but he offers brief recollections of many of his fellow actors, mostly deceased, including John Brougham, Dion Boucicault, Charlotte Cushman, and Francis Chanfrau.

1950 ed.: The text is the same as that of the 1890 edition. Eleanor Farjeon contributes a foreword comprising a brief memoir of her relationship with her grandfather—the author.

1964 ed.: "The present edition reprints the text of the first edition without change other than the silent correction of a few printer's errors. Jefferson's annotation has been marked with his name; the other footnotes [mostly definitions of terms and identifications of persons and plays mentioned by Jefferson] have been added by the editor." In the introduction, the editor comments on the *Autobiography* and provides a biographical sketch, with specific dates, covering the whole of Jefferson's life.

Illustrations. 1890 ed.: Seventy-seven photographs, engravings, and paintings, mostly of the author and other actors.

1950 ed.: Same as the 1890 edition.

1964 ed.: Forty illustrations (thirty-six selected from the 1890 edition and four additional photographs of the author).

Features. 1890 ed.: Preface, table of contents; list of illustrations; index.

1950 ed.: Foreword by Eleanor Farjeon; preface; table of contents; list of illustrations; index.

1964 ed.: Introduction by Alan S. Downer; note on the text by Alan S. Downer; preface; table of contents; list of illustrations; documentation: Downer's introduction is thoroughly documented; index.

Actors. Joseph Jefferson III, William Warren, Jr.

178. Jennings, John J[oseph]. *Theatrical and Circus Life; or, Secrets of the Green-Room and Sawdust Arena. Embracing a History of the Theatre from Shakespeare's Time to the Present Day, and Abounding in Anecdotes Concerning the Most Prominent Actors and Actresses Before the Public; also, a Complete Exposition of the Mysteries of the Stage, Showing the Manner in Which Wonderful Scenic and Other Effects are Produced; the Origin and Growth of Negro Minstrelsy; the Most Astonishing Tricks of Modern Magicians, and a History of the Hippodrome, etc., etc.* New and rev. ed. St. Louis, Missouri: Sun Publishing, 1882; Chicago: Laird & Lee, 1893. 608 pp.

This collection of diverse information touches on such

subjects as actors, opera singers, stage illusions, circus life, magicians' tricks, etc. The materials on actors include some biographical sketches of living players, numerous anecdotes, and miscellaneous information (such as the superstitions of and the methods of receiving an inter- viewer of several stars). The material on actors comprises only a fraction of the book and is scattered throughout the volume.

Illustrations. Over one hundred and fifty engravings of actors, fanciful scenes, and sundry subjects.

Features. Preface; table of contents.

Actors. General.

179. Kahn, E[ly] J[acques], Jr. *The Merry Partners: The Age and Stage of Harrigan and Hart.* New York: Random House, ©1955. xiii, 302 pp.

The first third of this book is an entertaining, jumbled account of the rowdier aspects of the action in Edward Harrigan's plays and of life in New York City during the last half of the nineteenth century. The remainder of the work consists of biographies of Harrigan and of Tony Hart, emphasizing their partnership of the 1870s and 1880s. Anecdotes, personal data, and information on their theatrical activities abound, but little specific de- scription or evaluation of their acting is included. Few specific dates are indicated.

Illustrations. Forty-six photographs, engravings, and draw- ings, mostly of Edward Harrigan and Tony Hart.

Features. Author's note; table of contents; list of illustra- tions; documentation: sources of some quota- tions are identified by author and/or title.

Actors. Edward Harrigan, Tony Hart.

180. Keese, William L[inn]. *A Group of Comedians.* New York: Dunlap Society, 1901; rpt. New York: Burt Franklin, 1970. 91 pp.

> The short biographies of Henry Placide, William Rufus Blake, John Brougham, George Holland, and Charles Fisher contained in this volume emphasize the subjects' lives prior to the Civil War, but they contain some information on later years. The essays take the form of chronological narratives, with evaluations of the subjects' general performance characteristics and of some of their characterizations interspersed. Many specific dates and cast lists are included. The author had seen each of his subjects perform.

> *Illustrations.* Six photographs, two of Henry Placide and one of each of the other subjects of the biographies.

> *Features.* Preface; documentation: sources of quotations are usually identified by author.

> *Actors.* William R. Blake, John Brougham, Charles Fisher, George Holland, Henry Placide.

181. Kendall, John S[mith]. *The Golden Age of the New Orleans Theater.* Baton Rouge, Louisiana: Louisiana State University Press, ©1952; rpt. New York: Greenwood, 1968. viii, 624 pp.

> The author presents a history of English-language activity on the New Orleans stage from the beginning of the nineteenth century to the first decade of the twentieth, with approximately one-third of the text concerning the post-Civil War era. He draws upon published materials (mainly newspapers), personal experience (as a New Orleans journalist at the end of the nineteenth century), and oral tradition (derived from conversations with veteran theatre workers). The narrative contains many specific dates of engagements and prominent performances, indications of relative successes (sometimes with financial statements), and biographical data. The book includes brief comments

on scores of major and minor actors, for example the
Booths, Joseph Jefferson III, John Lewis Baker, and
Charles W. Couldock.

Illustrations. Thirteen drawings, engravings, and photographs of managers and theatres.

Features. Preface; table of contents; list of illustrations;
documentation: sources of quotations are
usually identified by author and/or title and/or
date; bibliographical notes; index.

Actors. Ben DeBar, John E. Owens.

182. Kimmel, Stanley [Preston]. *The Mad Booths of Maryland.*
Indianapolis and New York: Bobbs-Merrill, ©1940.
400 pp.

Ibid. 2nd rev. and enl. ed. New York: Dover, ©1969.
418 pp.

1940 ed.: This, generally, chronological biography of the
Booth family is concerned primarily with Junius Brutus
Booth and his three actor-sons—Junius, Jr., Edwin, and
John Wilkes (especially the latter two). The author utilizes published materials, previously unpublished letters,
and federal archives, and he includes factual data (including many specific dates), anecdotes, narration, and brief
performance evaluations. Little description of the acting
of the subjects is contained in the book. Nealy one-half
of the text deals with the pre-1861 period and approximately one-sixth concerns Wilkes Booth's assassination
of Lincoln. The "Comments" section includes citations
for numerous sources of material, discursive notes, and
quotations from many letters and documents.

1969 ed.: In the form of "corrections and revisions of the
text, new evidence [has been added] concerning John
Wilkes Booth's common-law wife and children, and other
information from heretofore unpublished documents and
family letters. Six new Supplements, including excerpts
from articles by the present writer which appeared during

the intervening years, add to the information in the previous work." With the exception of one brief section on
"The Feud Between Asia and Edwin Booth," the supplements deal exclusively with Wilkes Booth.

Illustrations. 1940 ed.: Eleven photographs, mostly of
members of the Booth family.
1969 ed.: Eighty-three mostly photographs,
mainly of members of the Booth family and
of people and places associated with the Lincoln conspiracy.

Features. 1940 ed.: Foreword; table of contents; list of
illustrations; documentation: sources of most
of the materials are identified in the "Comments"; index.
1969 ed.: Foreword to the Dover edition; foreword; table of contents; list of illustrations;
documentation: sources of most of the materials are identified in the "Comments"; six
supplements (mostly concerning John Wilkes
Booth); index (does not include references to
the supplements).

Actors. Edwin Booth, John Wilkes Booth, Junius Brutus
Booth, Jr., John Sleeper Clarke.

183. Kobbe, Gustav. *Famous Actors & Actresses and Their
Homes.* Boston: Little, Brown, 1903. ix, 360 pp.

This collection of popularly-written articles affords offstage glimpses of famous performers. The author includes
his own views of his subjects, descriptions of their homes
and hobbies, bits of biography, and quotations from the
subjects or their friends in these sketches. Although the
articles focus primarily on each subject's character and
activities away from the stage, some indication of professional attitudes and methods are included. Anecdotal and
descriptive chapters concerning The Lambs and The Players clubs are added to the articles on performers.

Illustrations. Sixty-three photographs of the subjects and their homes.

Features. Table of contents; list of illustrations.

Actors. Maude Adams, Ethel Barrymore, John Drew II, William Gillette, Virginia Harned, Richard Mansfield, Julia Marlowe, Annie Russell, E. H. Sothern, Francis Wilson.

184. —. *Famous Actors and Their Homes.* Boston: Little, Brown, 1905. x, 222 pp.

This volume is composed of seven articles originally included in the author's *Famous Actors & Actresses and Their Homes* (see 183). The chapters on The Lambs and The Players clubs are included in this book.

Illustrations. Thirty-eight photographs of the subjects and their homes.

Features. Table of contents; list of illustrations.

Actors. John Drew II, William Gillette, Virginia Harned, Richard Mansfield, E. H. Sothern, Francis Wilson.

185. —. *Famous Actresses and Their Homes.* Boston: Little, Brown, 1905. x, 243 pp.

Utilizing the same approach as in *Famous Actors & Actresses and Their Homes* (see 183), the author reprints the articles on the Misses Adams, Barrymore, Marlowe, and Russell from the earlier book and adds chapters on Mrs. Fiske, "The Actress's Home Behind the Scenes," "The Actress's Christmas," and "Some Actresses in Summer." The later three articles contain anecdotes and description of various actresses.

Illustrations. Thirty-six photographs of actresses and their homes.

Features. Table of contents; list of illustrations.

Actors. Maude Adams, Ethel Barrymore, Mrs. Leslie Carter, Dorothy Donnelly, Maxine Elliott, Mary Mannering, Julia Marlowe, Eleanor Robson, Annie Russell.

186. Leach, Joseph. *Bright Particular Star: The Life & Times of Charlotte Cushman.* New Haven, Connecticut: Yale University Press, 1970. xvi, 453 pp.

This narrative of Charlotte Cushman's life is extensively documented with quotations from periodical articles, books, and Cushman correspondence. The volume contains numerous appreciations of her as a person, as an actress, and in her characterizations. Descriptions of parts of her performances are included, primarily in reference to her early assumptions of various roles. Approximately one-fourth of the text relates to the post-1860 period of her life. Brief comments, often Miss Cushman's, on many other players—such as Edwin Booth, Edwin Forrest, and E. L. Davenport—are included.

Illustrations. Ten photographs, engravings, drawings, and sculptures of Charlotte Cushman.

Features. Preface; acknowledgements; table of contents; list of illustrations; documentation: extensive endnotes (quotations in the text are not footnoted; endnotes contain references to page numbers in the text, key phrase identifications of passages, and full bibliographic citations for the sources of those passages); bibliographical note; index.

Actors. Charlotte Cushman.

187. Leavitt, M[ichael] B[ennett]. *Fifty Years in Theatrical Management.* New York: Broadway, ©1912. xxiv, 735 pp.

This lengthy volume comprises the author's recollections of his career as a theatrical promoter and manager in America and abroad during the 1859-1909 period. He discusses many types of entertainments, from the circus to grand opera and including some material on legitimate drama. Variety entertainments are emphasized. He includes bits of biography, theatre history (with some specific dates), comments on various genres of theatrical entertainment, anecdotes, and brief sketches and/or evaluations of hundreds of theatre managers, performers, press agents, etc.

Illustrations. Over five hundred photographs of people, places, and contracts associated with the theatre.

Features. Introduction; table of contents; list of pages of illustrations; index.

Actors. General.

188. Leman, Walter M[oore]. *Memoires of an Old Actor.* San Francisco: A. Roman, 1886; rpt. New York: Benjamin Blom, 1969; rpt. St. Clair Shores, Michigan: Scholarly Press, [1969?]. xv, 406 pp.

This volume of chronologically-arranged reminiscences traces the author's life, emphasizing his theatrical career, from the 1920s to 1885. Memories, descriptions, and evaluations of scores of actors, from Thomas Abthorpe Cooper to John McCullough, are included. During the years following the mid-1850s, most of the author's activities were centered in California. Nearly one-third of the book concerns the period after 1860.

Illustrations. One engraving of the author.

Features. Table of contents; documentation: most sources of quotations are identified by author and/or title.

Actors. Walter M. Leman.

189. Lesser, Allen. *Enchanting Rebel (The Secret of Adah Isaacs Menken).* New York: Beechhurst, ©1947. 284 pp.

This anecdotal narrative chronicles Adah Isaacs Menken's personal and theatrical activities from 1856 to 1868, the years of her theatrical career. Many selections from letters, mostly written by the actress, and brief excerpts from published sources, principally newspapers, are included. The concluding chapter questions the veracity of some previous biographies of Miss Menken. The appended autobiographical "Notes on My Life" by Miss Menken was delivered to Augustin Daly in 1862 and, in Daly's words, as quoted by Lesser, this essay was "made as salable as possible by the introduction of some innocent romancing."

Illustrations. Seventeen, mostly photographs and engravings of Adah Issacs Menken.

Features. Preface; table of contents; documentation: sources of most quotations are identified by author and/or title and/or date; bibliography; Appendix I: "Notes on My Life" by Adah Isaacs Menken; Appendix II: "The Poems and Essays of Adah Isaacs Menken in Order of Publication"; index.

Actors. Adah Isaacs Menken.

189a. Lewis, Philip C. *Trouping: How the Show Came to Town.* New York: Harper and Row, ©1973. x, 266 pp.

This informal history of theatrical touring in America, written by a former "trouper," presents a picture of the road by focusing on theatre conditions and practices in different periods from the Hallams to silent movies. Humorous and informative anecdotes, descriptions of productions and touring life, semi-fictional passages, and road statistics are utilized to construct an entertaining picture of the subject. The author discusses actors, plays, genres, producers, and theatres. Among the actors mentioned briefly are Dustin Farnum, William S. Hart, and Lotta Crabtree. Among the interesting aspects is a schedule, with travel times, for Edwin Booth's tour for the 1887-88 season.

Illustrations. Twenty-three, mostly photographs and engravings of actors.

Features. Acknowledgments; table of contents; list of illustrations; adequate documentation; index of towns and cities; index of plays and musicals; index of songs; general index.

Actors. Edwin Booth, Joseph Jefferson III, James O'Neill, Denman Thompson.

190. Lindsay, John S[hanks]. *The Mormons and the Theatre, or, The History of Theatricals in Utah, with Reminiscences and Comments Humorous and Critical.* Salt Lake City, Utah: Century Printing, 1905. 178 pp.

This narrative of theatrical activity in Salt Lake City from 1850 to 1882 focuses primarily on the Salt Lake Theatre from its founding in 1862 until the disbanding of its stock company in 1882. Factual data, including many specific dates, and numerous anecdotes concerning the stock company and visiting stars are contained in the book. Much of the information comes from the author's personal experiences and acquaintances: he first acted in the Salt Lake Theatre stock company in 1863 and, with a few absences, long continued his association with theatre in Salt Lake City.

Illustrations. One portrait photograph of the author.

Features. Documentation: many sources of quotations are identified by author and/or title and/or date.

Actors. Julia Dean Hayne, John S. Lindsay.

191. Lockridge, Richard. *Darling of Misfortune: Edwin Booth: 1883-1893.* New York: Century, ©1932; rpt. New York: Benjamin Blom, 1971. xi, 358 pp.

> This useful volume contains an anecdotal narrative of the life and career of Edwin Booth, preceded by a biographical sketch of Junius Brutus Booth and followed by an appreciation of Edwin's acting. The author includes numerous selections from criticisms of Booth's acting, from descriptions and evaluations of him, and from letters by, to, and concerning him. Many specific dates are indicated. Approximately one-fourth of the book relates to the pre-1861 period.

> *Illustrations.* Eight photographs and paintings of members of the Booth family.

> *Features.* Table of contents; list of illustrations; documentation: sources of some quotations are partially identified; index.

> *Actors.* Lawrence Barrett, Edwin Booth, John Wilkes Booth.

192. Logan, Olive. *Apropos of Women and Theatres. With a Paper or Two on Parisian Topics.* New York: Carleton, 1869. 240 pp.

> This volume contains anecdotes and the author's opinions on a variety of topics, including the woman's place in life (the author was an early suffragette), long-run plays, "nudity" in the theatre, and life in Paris. Some of the materials are autobiographical, but no dates are provided.

> *Illustrations.* None.

> *Features.* Note; preface; table of contents; documentation: sources of quotations are identified by periodical title and/or date.

> *Actors.* Olive Logan.

193. —. *Before the Footlights and Behind the Scenes: A Book about "the Show Business" in All Its Branches: from Puppet Shows to Grand Opera; from Mountebanks to Menageries; from Learned Pigs to Lecturers; from Burlesque Blondes to Actors and Actresses: with Some Observations and Reflections (Original and Reflected) on Morality and Immorality in Amusements: Thus Exhibiting the "Show World" as Seen from Within, through the Eyes of the Former Actress, as Well as from Without, through the Eyes of the Present Lecturer and Author.* Philadelphia, Cincinnati, Middletown, Connecticut: Parmalee, 1870; San Francisco: H. H. Bancroft, 1870. vi, 612 pp.

Ibid. *The Mimic World, and Public Exhibitions: Their History, Their Morals, and Effects.* Philadelphia: New-World Publishing, 1871; Middletown, Connecticut: Parmalee, 1871; Burlington, Iowa: R. T. Root, 1871. 590 pp.

Before the Footlights: The actress-author reminisces about her career and includes her observations and opinions concerning theatre, ballet, opera, circuses, menageries, etc. The numerous descriptions and anecdotes illustrative of theatrical practices of the mid-nineteenth century are interesting and informative, but there are only brief references to specific performers or dates. The author includes an attack on the "leg business" of the *Black Crook* and the "British Blondes" variety.

The Mimic World: This edition omits the first chapter of the earlier edition. Otherwise, the texts are the same.

Illustrations. Before the Footlights: Fifty-five engravings of actors, theatres, and fanciful scenes.
   The Mimic World: Twenty-one engravings of actors, theatres, and fanciful scenes (mostly selected from *Before the Footlights*).

Features. Preface; table of contents; list of illustrations (both editions).

Actors. Olive Logan.

194. MacAdam, George. *The Little Church Around the Corner.*
New York: G. P. Putnam's Sons, 1925. x, 347 pp.

This volume is an anecdotal history of the Church of the
Transfiguration in New York City from the mid-1800s
to 1923, along with biographies of the Reverend Drs.
George Hendric Houghton and George Clarke Houghton,
the church's only two rectors during that period. The
book contains information on the controversy surrounding the funeral of George Holland, including quotations
from contemporary interviews and newspaper articles.
This controversy resulted in the church being nicknamed
"the Little Church Around the Corner."

Illustrations. Forty photographs, engravings, and drawings
of people and events related to the Church
of the Transfiguration, including portraits of
several actors.

Features. Prologue; table of contents; list of illustrations;
documentation: sources of some quotations
are partially identified.

Actors. George Holland.

195. McKay, Frederic Edward, and Charles E[dgar] L[ewis]
Wingate (eds.). *Famous American Actors of To-day.*
New York: Thomas Y. Crowell, ©1896. viii, 399 pp.

Gathering forty-one authors to contribute articles on as
many subjects, the editors note the "central idea" of this
volume as being "to bring before the reader each noted
player as he is viewed by a writer who either has known
the actor personally, or has made an especial study of his
professional work. . .the time of 'to-day' was limited (with
one exception) to the decade just closing." The style and
contents of the essays vary according to the contributors,
but most include biographical, anecdotal, and critical
materials. The criticism is not deeply technical, but, since

the contributors observed their subjects, the opinions are useful in reconstructing the actors' stage manners. Most of the articles are complimentary, but few descend to the level of "puffs." Among the contributors are Henry Austin Clapp, T. Allston Brown, Edward A. Dithmar, George Pierce Baker, Laurence Hutton, A. M. Palmer, Lewis Strang, Harrison Grey Fiske, and Edwin F. Edgett.

Illustrations. Forty photographs of the subjects of the essays (only Warren is not pictured).

Features. Preface; table of contents.

Actors. Mary Anderson, Lawrence Barrett, Maurice Barrymore, Agnes Booth, Edwin Booth, Dion Boucicault, Georgia Cayvan, Rose Coghlan, Lotta Crabtree, William H. Crane, Fanny Davenport, John Drew II, Mrs. John Drew, Charles Fisher, Minnie Maddern Fiske, Malvina Pray Florence, William J. Florence, John Gilbert, Nat C. Goodwin, Edwin Harrigan, E. M. Holland, Fanny Janauschek, Joseph Jefferson III, W. J. LeMoyne, Richard Mansfield, Julia Marlowe, Maggie Mitchell, Helena Modjeska, Clara Morris, James O'Neill, John T. Raymond, Ada Rehan, Stuart Robson, Sol Smith Russell, Alexander Salvini, E. H. Sothern, J. H. Stoddart, Denman Thompson, Charles R. Thorne, Jr., Mrs. Mary Ann Vincent, Lester Wallack, William Warren, Jr.

196. MacKaye, Percy. *Epoch—The Life of Steele MacKaye, Genius of the Theatre, in Relation to His Times & Contemporaries. A Memoir by His Son.* 2 vols. New York: Boni and Liveright, ©1927; rpt. Grosse Pointe, Michigan: Scholarly Press, 1968. Vol. I: xlvii, 489 pp.; Vol. II: cxxvi, 485 pp.

These two volumes comprise an exhaustive chronicle of the life of the brilliant and erratic Steele MacKaye. Although the tone of the work frequently approaches idolatry, the vast quantity of documents and information make this work extremely valuable to any study of MacKaye.

The author includes copious quotations from letters by, to, and about MacKaye, excerpts from contemporary periodical articles, family reminiscences, excerpts from MacKaye's notebooks, etc. Much of the information concerns MacKaye's personal life, professional associations, playwriting, and work on the Spectatorium, but there is also material on his acting, his relationship with Francois Delsarte, and his teaching of acting. There is no close examination of his acting theories, acting style, or teaching methods. A valuable biography, this is not a critical work.

Illustrations. Vol. I: Fifty-eight half-tone plates (most comprised of two or more illustrations) and thirteen illustrations in the text, including photographs, drawings, woodcuts, paintings, and engravings of Steele MacKaye, his family, other theatre workers, other people, theatres, letters, designs, inventions, etc.
Vol. II: Forty-two half-tone plates and thirty-five illustrations in the text, of the same types and subjects as those contained in the first volume.

Features. Vol. I: Preface; table of contents; outline of *Epoch;* list of illustrations; extensive documentation: two patent office specifications.
Vol. II: Table of contents; list of illustrations; extensive documentation; brief bibliography; chronological lists of the dramatic works of and the roles acted by Steele MacKaye; an epitomized list of Steele MacKaye's stage inventions; a list of some actors and actresses who played in dramas by Steele MacKaye; "Some Innovations of Steele MacKaye"; "Some Commentators on Steele MacKaye and His Works"; "Biographer's Note"; "Biographical and Historical Records" (relates to subjects dealt with in both volumes; includes letters, stories, etc.); comments on artistic work by Steele MacKaye's grandchildren; seven patent office specifications; postscript; index (to both volumes).

Actors. Steele MacKaye.

197. Mahoney, Ella V. *Sketches of Tudor Hall and the Booth Family.* Belair, Maryland: Tudor Hall, 1925. 59 pp.

The author of this informal volume was a long-time resident of Tudor Hall, the former Booth-family estate, and a daughter of a childhood companion of John Wilkes Booth. The book contains descriptions of the estate and brief sketches of Junius Brutus, Edwin, and John Wilkes Booth. The biographies contain factual data (including some errors), anecdotes, and previously published appreciations of the subjects. The material on Wilkes Booth is aimed mainly at refuting the rumors of his escape after the assassination of Lincoln.

Illustrations. Five photographs of Booths and the Tudor Hall estate.

Features. Author's note; table of contents; documentation: sources of quotations are identified by author and/or title and/or date; bibliography: partial listing of sources in the author's note.

Actors. Edwin Booth, John Wilkes Booth.

198. Malvern, Gladys. *Good Troupers All: The Story of Joseph Jefferson.* Philadelphia: Macrae, Smith, 1945. 287 pp.

This popularly-written account of the life of Joseph Jefferson III draws heavily upon the actor's *Autobiography* (see 177) and, like that work, emphasizes Jefferson's career up to his London premiere of *Rip Van Winkle*. Approximately one-fifth of this book concerns Jefferson's life after 1860. Anecdotes, fictionalized conversations (some of which are "remembered" in the *Autobiography*), and some factual materials are included. Of little value to the specialist, this book is a readable introduction to the famous comedian for general and juvenile readers.

Illustrations. Twenty-four photographs, engravings, and

paintings of Joseph Jefferson III, other actors, theatres, and theatre programs.

Features. Table of contents; list of illustrations; bibliography.

Actors. Joseph Jefferson III.

199. Mantle, Burns, and Garrison P. Sherwood (eds.). *The Best Plays of 1899-1909 and the Year Book of the Drama in America.* New York: Dodd, Mead, 1944. ix, 624 pp.

This volume consists of condensed versions of ten plays, one each for the seasons 1899/1900-1908/09, and a listing of plays produced in New York City from 1899 through 1909. Mantle contributes the play digests and short introductions containing comments on each season. Sherwood compiled the "Plays Produced in New York, July 12, 1899-June 14, 1909" section. The latter portion of the book is divided according to theatrical season, with plays listed chronologically by dates of first performances. The following information is provided for most entries in this section: title of the play, number of performances, genre (e.g., melodrama, extravaganza, etc.), producer, theatre, date of opening, and cast. Names of characters played by specific actors, information on revivals, and other comments are included for some entries.

Illustrations. Eight photographs, one scene from each of the following plays: *Barbara Frietchie, The Darling of the Gods, The County Chairman, Leah Kleschna, The Squaw Man, The Great Divide,* and *The Witching Hour.*

Features. Introduction; table of contents; list of illustrations; brief biographical sketches of the authors of the plays; list of prominent theatre workers who died, 1899-1909 (includes year of birth and date of death); list of Pulitzer Prize-winning plays, 1917/18-1941/42; list of previous volumes of the "Best Plays" series (in-

cludes list of plays condensed in each volume);
index.

Actors. General.

200. —. *The Best Plays of 1909-1919 and the Year Book of the Drama in America.* New York: Dodd, Mead, 1933. x, 702 pp.

> The format in this work is the same as that which is followed in the volume for 1899-1909 (see 199). Sherwood's record is of "Plays Produced in New York, June 15, 1909-June 15, 1919."

> > *Illustrations.* Ten photographs, one scene from each of the following: *Disraeli, The Easiest Way, Mrs. Bumpstead-Leigh, Romance, Seven Keys to Baldpate, On Trial, The Unchastened Woman, Good Gracious Annabelle, Why Marry?,* and *John Ferguson.*

> > *Features.* Introduction, table of contents; list of illustrations; list of prominent theatre workers who died, 1909-1919 (includes year of birth and date of death); list of Pulitzer Prize-winning plays, 1917/18-1931/32; list of previous volumes in the "Best Plays" series (includes list of plays condensed in each volume); index.

> *Actors.* General.

201. Marbury, Elisabeth. *My Crystal Ball: Reminiscences.* New York: Boni and Liveright, ©1923. 355 pp.

> The author sets down anecdotes and reflections on her life from the mid-nineteenth century to the time of publication. Some recollections of her career as an author's agent are included, along with brief comments on a few actors, such as Elsie DeWolfe, Richard Mansfield, and William Gillette.

Illustrations. Twenty, mostly photographs of the author, her friends, and her residences.

Features. Preface; list of illustrations.

Actors. General.

202. Marcosson, Isaac F[rederick], and Daniel Frohman. *Charles Frohman: Manager and Man.* Appreciation by James M. Barrie. New York: Harper & Brothers, 1916. 439 pp.

> This friendly biography charts Charles Frohman's life from his childhood in the 1960s to his death in 1915, emphasizing his theatrical career. The book contains much information and scores of anecdotes concerning Frohman's personal character and professional practices. In addition to those players noted below, comments are included on many actors associated with Frohman, for example Henry Miller, William Faversham, Billie Burke, and William H. Crane.

> *Illustrations.* Thirty-eight mostly portrait photographs of people associated with Charles Frohman.

> *Features.* Appreciation by James M. Barrie; table of contents; list of illustrations; documentation: sources of quotations are indicated by author; Appendix A: "The Letters of Charles Frohman" (includes few dates); Appendix B: "Complete Chronological List of the Frohman Productions" (includes title, date, and theatre; 1883-1916; America, England, and France).

> *Actors.* Maude Adams, Ethel Barrymore, John Drew II, William Gillette.

203. Marinacci, Barbara. *Leading Leadies: A Gallery of Famous Actresses.* New York: Dodd, Mead, 1961. xiii, 306 pp.

This book consists of popularly-written chapters on May Betterton, Peg Woffington, Mrs. Siddons, Charlotte Cushman, Ellen Terry, Sarah Bernhardt, Eleanora Duse, Mrs. Fiske, Ethel Barrymore, Laurette Taylor, and Gertrude Lawrence. Each article contains a narrative of the subject's life interspersed with comments on her personality and acting. Brief excerpts from reviews, tributes, and autobiographical writings are included. The chapter on Ethel Barrymore contains scattered references to other members of the Drew-Barrymore family.

Illustrations. Twenty photographs, engravings, and paintings of the subjects.

Features. Table of contents; list of illustrations; selected bibliography; index.

Actors. Ethel Barrymore, Charlotte Cushman, Minnie Maddern Fiske, Laurette Taylor.

203a. Marker, Lise-Lone. *David Belasco: Naturalism in the American Theatre.* Princeton, New Jersey: Princeton University Press, ©1975. xiv, 248 pp.

This well-documented study aims to provide "a stylistic analysis of the scenic art of one of the American theatre's most fascinating practitioners (and) to synthesize the aims, methods, and techniques inherent in the naturalistic production style which Belasco evolved." While presenting some biographical data and a brief description of late nineteenth-century theatre practice, the author concentrates on Belasco's theatrical theories and practices. The author provides extensive descriptions of Belasco's productions of *Sweet Kitty Bellairs, The Girl of the Golden West, The Easiest Way,* and *The Merchant of Venice.* Source materials include Belasco's promptbooks, correspondence, and other personal papers, as well as contemporary criticism. In addition to discussion of the subject's approaches to acting and directing, there are brief comments on numerous actors, such as David Warfield, Mrs. Leslie Carter, Cushman, Belasco, and Edwin Booth.

Illustrations. Sixteen, mostly photographs of Belasco productions.

Features. Foreword; introduction; table of contents; list of illustrations; thorough documentation; extensive bibliography; chronology: "New York Productions of David Belasco's Major Plays and Adaptations;" index.

Actors. David Belasco.

204. Marshall, Thomas Frederic. *A History of the Philadelphia Theatre, 1878-1890: (An Essential Portion of) a Doctoral Dissertation in English.* Philadelphia: University of Pennsylvania, 1943. 54 pp.

This published excerpt from a doctoral dissertation at the University of Pennsylvania is divided into three sections: a commentary on the theatrical events in Philadelphia during 1878 and 1879, a "Day-Book" for Philadelphia theatre during 1878 and 1879, and a "Check List of Plays Now to Philadelphia, 1878-1890." The commentary includes brief summaries of theatrical affairs under the following headings: theatres, plays, and actors. The actors section is essentially a selective listing of star and stock actors appearing in Philadelphia. The "Day-Book" is divided into sections for 1878 and for 1879; under each year, the major legitimate theatres are arranged alphabetically, and a day-by-day listing of productions is provided; cast lists are given for plays presented in Philadelphia for the first time. The "Check List" comprises an alphabetical list of plays presented in Philadelphia for the first time during the period 1878-90; the type of production (e.g., burlesque, melodrama, etc.) and, when possible, the name of the author are indicated.

Illustrations. None.

Features. Introduction.

Actors. General.

205. Marston, [John] Westland. *Our Recent Actors: Being Recollections Critical, and, in Many Cases, Personal, of Late Distinguished Performers of Both Sexes.* With Some Incidental Notices of Living Actors. 2 vols. in I. Boston: Roberts, 1881.

> This reminiscent work concerning actors deals with the English theatre, emphasizing the period from the late 1930s through the 1860s. The author draws mainly upon his personal experiences (he knew many of the actors) in writing these anecdotal and critical memoirs. Brief descriptions of performances, critical appraisals, and offstage evaluations are included. An interesting chapter on Charlotte Cushman relates to her visit to London in the mid-1840s.

> *Illustrations.* None.

> *Features.* Preface (Vol. I); tables of contents (each volume for that volume).

> *Actors. Vol. II:* Charles Fechter, E. A. Sothern.

206. Mason, Hamilton. *French Theatre in New York: A List of Plays, 1899-1939.* New York: Columbia University Press, 1940. viii, 422 pp.

> "This work is intended to be an exhaustive [chronologically arranged] listing of first-run and second-run [professional] productions of French plays in French and in English in Manhattan. By first-run productions is meant original Broadway productions; by second-run productions, productions by established stock companies or repertory groups. This is also thought to be a complete listing of French plays given in the Bronx." Operas, light operas, and dance dramas are omitted; pantomimes are included. When relevant, entries include: English title, French title, author, adaptor, composer, producer, theater, date of opening, number of performances, cast list (role assignments are usually indicated), and a brief note concerning plot, original Paris production, and/or other information.

Illustrations. None.

Features. Preface; introduction; table of contents; bibliography; index.

Actors. General.

207. Matthews, [James] Brander, and Laurence Hutton (eds.). *Actors and Actresses of Great Britain and the United States.* 5 vols. Boston: L. C. Page, ©1886; New York: Cassell, ©1886. Vol. I ("David Garrick and His Contemporaries"): x, 279 pp.; Vol. II ("The Kembles and Their Contemporaries"): 329 pp.; Vol. III ("Kean and Booth and Their Contemporaries"): 313 pp.; Vol. IV ("Macready and Forrest and Their Contemporaries"): 319 pp.; Vol. V ("Edwin Booth and His Contemporaries"): 317 pp.

This work contains biographical sketches of seventy-eight English and American actors who performed during the period from the early eighteenth through the late nineteenth century. Each essay is supplemented by "a variety of extracts from all sources, from contemporary criticism, from the later biographies and memoirs, from the collections of correspondence, from the files of newspapers and magazines, and even, in a few cases, from more recent writers who have selected with skill rambling anecdotes and concisely summed up scattered criticisms." Anecdotes, specific biographical data, criticisms, and appreciations are included. Among the authors of the biographies are the following actors: Edwin Booth (on Edmund Kean and Junius Brutus Booth), Lawrence Barrett (on Edwin Booth), and William J. Florence (on E. A. Sothern).

Illustrations. Vol. I: Sixteen engravings of actors.
   Vol. II: Sixteen engravings of actors.
   Vol. III: Fifteen engravings and photographs of actors.
   Vol. IV: Fifteen engravings and photographs of actors.
   Vol. V: Seventeen photographs of actors.

Features. Introduction (Vol. I); table of contents (each volume for that volume); list of illustrations (each volume for that volume); documentation: sources of quotations are identified by author, title, date (for periodicals), and, sometimes, page or chapter numbers; indices (each volume for that volume).

Actors. (Volume number in parentheses). Mary Anderson (V), Lawrence Barrett (V), Edwin Booth (V), Dion Boucicault (V), John Brougham (III), John Sleeper Clarke (V), Charlotte Cushman (IV), E. L. Davenport (IV), Charles Fechter (IV), Malvina Pray Florence (V), William J. Florence (V), Edwin Forrest (IV), Matilda Heron (IV), Joseph Jefferson III (V), John McCullough (V), Helena Modjeska (V), Clara Morris (V), John T. Raymond (V), Agnes Robertson (V), E. A. Sothern (IV), Lester Wallack (V).

208. Matthews, [James] Brander (ed.). *Papers on Acting.* Preface by Henry W. Wells. New York: Hill and Wang, ©1958. viii, 303 pp.

This volume collects essays, introductions, and notes concerned with the theory and practice of acting which had previously been published by the Dramatic Museum of Columbia University and edited by Matthews. Most of the essays and introductions were written by practicing American, English, and European actors. The editor contributes the notes.

Illustrations. None.

Features. Preface by Henry W. Wells; table of conents; documentation: sources of quotations are identified by author and/or title and/or date; list of publications of the Dramatic Museum of Columbia University; index.

Actors. George Arliss, Edwin Booth, Dion Boucicault, William Gillette, Otis Skinner.

209. —. *Principles of Playmaking and Other Discussions of the Drama.* New York: Charles Scribner's Sons, 1919; rpt. Freeport, New York: Books for Libraries, 1970. vii, 306 pp.

The papers on theatrical topics which are collected in this volume were written during the period 1911-19. Including criticism, theatre history, biography, and reminiscence, the essays deal with such subjects as "How to Write a Play," "Irish Plays and Irish Playwrights," "Matthew Arnold and the Theatre," and "The Simplification of Stage Scenery." The paper on "Shakespearian Stage-Traditions" contains brief descriptions of stage business of such actors as Ada Rehan, Fechter, Irving, and Salvini. "Memories of Edwin Booth" comprises the author's personal recollections of that actor.

Illustrations. None.

Features. Table of contents.

Actors. Edwin Booth.

210. —. *Rip Van Winkle Goes to the Play and Other Essays on Plays and Players.* New York: Charles Scribner's Sons, 1926; rpt. Port Washington, New York: Kennikat, 1967. 256 pp.

Eleven essays on theatrical subjects compose this book. The author is primarily concerned with dramatic writing, but he includes a consideration of the art of acting and a chapter of reminiscences concerning several actresses. Brief evaluations and some descriptions of the actresses noted below and Helena Modjeska, Mrs. G. H. Gilbert, and Mrs. John Drew are included.

Illustrations. None.

Features. Table of contents.

Actors. Clara Morris, Ada Rehan.

211. —. *These Many Years: Recollections of a New Yorker.* New York: Charles Scribner's Sons, 1917. 463 pp.

In this volume of reminiscences, the author has "set down . . .only the pleasanter memories of [his] journey through life." Covering the last half of the nineteenth century and the early years of the twentieth, the author emphasizes his educational, literary, and dramatic experiences and acquaintances in America, France, and England. He includes brief anecdotes and appreciations of many actors, including John Gilbert, Edwin Booth, Joseph Jefferson III, William H. Crane, and Lester Wallack.

Illustrations. None.

Features. Table of contents.

Actors. General.

212. Maughan, Ila Fisher. *Pioneer Theatre in the Desert.* Foreword by C. Lowell Lees. Salt Lake City, Utah: Deseret, 1961. xii, 172 pp.

This book surveys theatrical entertainments given under the auspices of the Church of Jesus Christ of Latter-Day Saints in Salt Lake City from 1852 until 1869. During the 1860s, professional actors, including such notables as E. L. Davenport and Charlotte Cushman, began appearing with the resident stock company of Salt Lake City residents. Although little information on actors is included, the book contains some indication of who played in Salt Lake City, when they played there, and what roles they performed.

Illustrations. Twenty-six photographs and drawings of actors, buildings, etc.

Features. Preface; foreword by C. Lowell Lees; table of contents; documentation: sources of some quotations are identified; bibliography; appended lists of members of the Deseret Dramatic Association from 1852 through May 9, 1869;

list of supernumeraries and "bit" part players
at the Salt Lake Theatre, 1862-69; list of children who acted at the Salt Lake Theatre,
1862-69; list of references for the list of members of the Deseret Dramatic Association.

Actors. Julia Dean Hayne.

213. Meade, Edwards Hoag. *Doubling Back: Autobiography of
an Actor, Serio-Comical.* Chicago: Hammond Press,
W. B. Conkey, ©1916. 180 pp.

This autobiography chronicles the author's life from his
birth in 1863 until the time of writing in 1914. Along
with many anecdotes and original verses, the author includes information on his theatrical ventures in the western United States during the 1890-1912 period.

Illustrations. Ten photographs of the author and people
and places associated with his life.

Features. Preface.

Actors. Ed Meade.

214. *Memorial Celebration of the Sixtieth Anniversary of the
Birth of Edwin Booth. Held in the Madison Square
Garden Concert Hall, November the Thirteenth,
MDCCCXCIII, by The Players.* New York: The Gilliss
Press, n.d. 60 pp.

This volume is composed mainly of addresses by Joseph
Jefferson III, Parke Godwin, Tommaso Salvini (and a
translation of Salvini's speech), and Henry Irving, and an
elegy by George E. Woodberry, all of which were delivered at the memorial celebration. Although some
biographical and anecdotal material are included, particu-
larly in Godwin's speech, the addresses are primarily personal tributes to Booth.

Illustrations. One half-tone reproduction of the John S.

Sargent painting of Edwin Booth.

Features. List of committee members for the memorial celebration; the admission ticket; the pro- gramme of events.

Actors. Edwin Booth.

215. Middleton, George. *These Things are Mine: The Auto- biography of Journeyman Playwright.* New York: Macmillan, 1947. xv, 448 pp.

In this volume of reminiscence, anecdote, and reflection, the author traces his life from the 1880s to the 1940s. Materials on his personal life and on his career as a play- wright are included. In the slightly more than one-fifth of the book which concerns the pre-1911 period, the author comments briefly on such actors as Richard Mansfield, Ada Rehan, Julia Marlowe, and Fola LaFollette (later Mrs. Middleton).

Illustrations. Thirty-six photographs of the author, his family, and his acquaintances.

Features. Preface; table of contents; list of illustrations; documentation: sources of quotations are identified by author and/or title; index.

Actors. General.

216. Modjeska, Helena. *Memories and Impressions of Helena Modjeska: An Autobiography.* New York: Macmil- lan, 1910; rpt. New York: Benjamin Blom, 1969. ix, 571 pp.

Mme. Modjeska reminisces about her life from her child- hood in the 1940s to shortly before her death in 1909. Including narration, reflections, anecdotes, letters, and diary entries, she recounts her personal and professional experiences, comments on many of her friends and acquaintances, and discusses many topics of theatrical interest. Expecting letters and diary entries, few dates are specified. Her brief comments on fellow actors are mostly laudatory and include some description and evaluation. Among the many players whom she mentions are Clara Morris, Dion Boucicault, Eleanora Duse, Henry Irving and Ellen Terry, Lotta Crabtree, John McCullough, and Tommaso Salvini.

Illustrations. One hundred and five, mostly photographs of the author, her friends, acquaintances, and homes.

Features. Introduction; list of illustrations; index.

Actors. Edwin Booth, Helena Modjeska.

217. Moody, Richard. *Edwin Forrest: First Star of the American Stage.* New York: Alfred A. Knopf, 1960. xii, 416, i-xi pp.

This fine biography of Edwin Forrest contains information on the actor's personal and professional lives. The anecdotal narrative is liberally sprinkled with specific dates, financial reports, and excerpts from Forrest's letters and diaries. Approximately one-tenth of the volume concerns Forrest's life after 1861, but material relating to the disposition of his estate and to the Edwin Forrest home and an excellent summary chapter are included.

Illustrations. Twenty-eight photographs, engravings, and paintings, mostly of Edwin Forrest.

Features. Foreword; table of contents; list of illustrations; documentation: sources of most quotations are identified by author and/or title; bibliography: "Notes on Sources," includes a selected bibliography; index.

Actors. Edwin Forrest.

218. Moody, William Vaughn. *Letters to Harriet.* Ed., with an introd. and a conclusion, by Percy MacKaye. Boston and New York: Houghton Mifflin, 1935. x, 458 pp.

These letters from the noted poet-playwright to Harriet Converse Tilden span the period from shortly after their first encounter in 1901 to slightly before their marriage in 1909. The letters contain much information on Moody's personal and professional feelings and activities. Many comments on early twentieth-century theatre and actors, primarily Henry Miller and Margaret Anglin, but also including such players as E. H. Sothern, Ethel Barrymore, and William Faversham, are contained in the letters. MacKaye's lengthy introduction, conclusion, and notes include biographical data and personal appraisals of Moody.

Illustrations. One photograph of the author and one painting of Harriet Moody.

Features. Introduction by Percy MacKaye; table of contents; documentation: adequate; conclusion by Percy MacKaye; bibliography; biographical data on William Vaughn Moody and Harriet Moody; index.

Actors. Margaret Anglin, Henry Miller.

219. Moore, Lester L. *Outside Broadway: A History of the Professional Theater in Newark, New Jersey from the Beginnings to 1867.* Metuchen, New Jersey: Scarecrow Press, 1970. x, 182 pp.

This selective narrative traces professional theatre activity in Newark, N.J., from the first recorded professional performance in 1799 to 1867. The data was gathered from extant periodicals, theatre playbills, and broadsides. Noting the "fugitive and dissembling nature" of his materials, the author concludes that "one must assume this story of the Newark theatre to be obviously incomplete." Over one-third of the text concerns the post-1860 period.

Illustrations. None.

Features. Foreword; table of contents; thorough documentation; afterword; selective bibliography;

Appendix A: alphabetical list of plays performed in Newark, 1799-1867, with dates of performances; Appendix B: alphabetical list of actors who performed in Newark, with dates of performances and references to the plays performed.

Actors. General.

220. Morehouse, Ward. *George M. Cohan: Prince of the American Theater.* Philadelphia and New York: J. B. Lippincott, ©1943. 240 pp.

Following a brief summary of Cohan's life, this book is a chronological narrative of the actor's life and career from his birth on July 3, 1878, to his death in 1942. The author's acquaintance with his subject for twenty years, information from Cohan's associates, and published materials are utilized in the biography. Many anecdotes and specific dates are included, along with some reviews, appreciations, and Cohan's autobiographical statements. The author briefly mentions other performers, such as John Barrymore, Fay Templeton, and other Cohans. Approximately forty per cent of the book concerns the pre-1911 period.

Illustrations. Eighteen photographs of George M. Cohan.

Features. Foreword; table of contents; list of illustrations; documentation: most sources of quotations are identified by author and title; appendix: "Important dates in the life of George M. Cohan arranged chronologically"(1901-42).

Actors. George M. Cohan.

221. Morell, [Alfred] Parker. *Diamond Jim: The Life and Times of James Buchanan Brady.* New York: Simon and Schuster, ©1934; rpt. New York: AMS Press, 1970. 286 pp.

This book is an anecdotal "informal chronicle" of the life of "Diamond Jim" Brady (1856-1917). Some information on Brady's friendship with Lillian Russell, as well as passing references to other performers, are included:

Illustrations. Twenty-two photographs of "Diamond Jim" Brady, his friends, and scenes and objects associated with him.

Features. Table of contents; list of illustrations; appendix concerning the evaluation and fate of Brady's jewels after his death; index.

Actors. Lillian Russell.

222. —. *Lilliam Russell: The Era of the Plush.* New York: Random House, ©1940; Garden City, New York: Garden City Publishing, [1943]. 319 pp.

This popularly-written account of Lillian Russell's life chronicles the years from her debut at Tony Pastor's theatre in 1880 to her death in 1922. Her life as a performer, fashion-plate, gourmand, journalist, feminist, and patriot is discussed utilizing many quotations from contemporary periodicals and from the actress' writings. Anecdotal, factual, and critical materials concerning Miss Russell are included, along with much informtion pertaining to the excesses of "the era of the plush" in which she lived.

Illustrations. Eighteen photographs, primarily of Lillian Russell and her associates.

Features. Table of contents; list of illustrations; documentation: sources of quotations are identified by author and/or title; index.

Actors. Lou Fields, Lillian Russell, Joe Weber.

223. Morris, Clara. *The Life of a Star.* New York: McClure, Phillips, 1906. 363 pp.

This book of recollections concerns, mainly, the 1870s and 1880s and contains comments on the author's theatrical activities and reminiscences of people associated with the stage. Anecdotes and brief descriptions of performances are included. No specific dates are indicated.

Illustrations. None.

Features. Preface; table of contents.

Actors. Dion Boucicault, Clara Morris, Alexander Salvini.

224. —. *Life on the Stage: My Personal Experiences and Recollections.* New York: McClure, Phillips, 1901. 399 pp.

This volume of reminiscences concerns the author's life from the middle of the nineteenth century to the mid-1870s. Her early years in stock companies and her successes with Augustin Daly's company receive most prominent notice. Although emphasizing backstage life, many comments on theatrical practices, descriptions of stage business, and evaluations of fellow players are included. In addition to those noted below, the author comments on such actors as Edwin Adams, Dan Setchall, James Murdoch, and Fanny Davenport. Considerable attention is given to Daly's personality and practices.

Illustrations. One photograph of the author.

Features. Table of contents.

Actors. Daniel Bandmann, Lawrence Barrett, John Wilkes Booth, Charles W. Couldock, E. L. Davenport, John A. Ellsler, Robert E. J. Miles, Clara Morris, John E. Owens.

225. —. *Stage Confidences: Talks About Players and Play Acting.* Boston: Lothrop, ©1902. 316 pp.

This volume is composed of anecdotes and the author's

reflections on, mainly, theatrical subjects. She discusses the requirements of an actress and gives advice to people seeking theatrical careers. Most of the anecdotal material derives from her experiences during the 1870s and 1880s. The only actor, aside from herself, upon whom she comments at length is Tommaso Salvini.

Illustrations. Nineteen photographs, mostly of Clara Morris.

Features. Prefatory note; table of contents; list of illustrations.

Actors. Clara Morris.

226. Morris, Felix. *Reminiscences.* Introd. by George P. Goodale. New York: International Telegram, [1892]. vii, 175 pp.

This book contains the author's chronological narrative of his acting career. The book concerns the period from the author's first arrival in America (c. 1870) and his early struggles to his first great success on a visit to England in the mid-1880s. Anecdotes, the author's brief comments on other actors, and other actors' comments on the author are included. Specific dates are not indicated.

Illustrations. Four photographs of the author.

Features. Introduction by George P. Goodale.

Actors. Felix Morris.

227. Morrissey, James W. *Noted Men and Women, Containing the Humor, Wit, Sentiment, and Diplomacy in the Social, Artistic, and Business Lives of the People Herein Set Forth.* n.p.: The Klebold Press, ©1910. 262 pp.

This book consists of a series of informally-written anecdotes derived from the author's career as a theatrical manager. The anecdotes concern many theatrical and musical personalities, as well as people in other professions.

Illustrations. Thirty-eight portrait photographs of many of the subjects of the anecdotes.

Features. Table of contents (includes no page numbers); list of illustrations.

Actors. Mary Anderson, Rose Coghlan, Owen Fawcett, Joseph Jefferson III, Richard Mansfield.

228. Morse, Frank P[hilip]. *Backstage with Henry Miller.* Introd. by George M. Cohan. New York: E. P. Dutton, 1938. 288 pp.

This biography of Henry Miller as director, producer, and actor contains information on Miller's entire life, but it emphasizes the period 1906-26, during which time the author was acquainted with and, frequently, employed by his subject. Most of the materials, primarily anecdotes, were apparently derived from the author's observation of Miller, from recollections of Miller's co-workers, and from the actor-manager's own reminiscences. Some specific dates, descriptions of Miller's directing practices, and numerous illustrations of his personal character and temperament are included, but few descriptions of his acting are contained in the book.

Illustrations. Twenty photographs, mostly of Henry Miller and other performers.

Features. Introduction, "An Appreciation of Henry Miller: Actor, Producer, Director," by George M. Cohan; table of contents; list of illustrations; index.

Actors. Margaret Anglin, Walter Hampden, Bijou Heron, Henry Miller, Alla Nazimova.

229. Moses, Montrose J[onas], and John Mason Brown (eds.).

The American Theatre as Seen by Its Critics, 1752-1934. New York: W. W. Norton, ©1934; rpt. New York: Cooper Square, 1967. 391 pp.

This potpourri of American dramatic and theatrical criticism includes one hundred and four articles spanning the years from 1752 to 1934. Approximately one-third of the text concerns the 1861-1910 period. Most of the authors were professional critic-reviewers. The articles were chosen "not only on the basis of what is characteristic of the critics whose writings we have included but also on the basis of what happens to have been typical of the theatre about which they have written." The concerns of the individual selections vary widely, including considerations of dramatic genres and of individual actors, playwrights, and productions. The comments on actors include evaluation and some description. Among the actors discussed are Edwin Booth, Richard Mansfield, Joseph Jefferson III, Mrs. Fiske, Edwin Forrest, Helena Modjeska, and many others.

Illustrations. None.

Features. Introduction by John Mason Brown; table of contents; documentation: the source of each selection is identified by author, title, and date; appendices: "Acknowledgements," "Contents Arranged Chronologically," and brief biographical sketches on many of the subjects of the sketches and on the critics.

Actors. General.

230. Moses, Montrose J[onas], and Virginia Gerson. *Clyde Fitch and His Letters.* Boston: Little, Brown, 1924. xx, 406 pp.

This volume contains an appreciation of Clyde Fitch by Moses, hundreds of chronologically-arranged letters dating from the 1874-1909 period, and commentary on Fitch's life by Moses and Gerson. Although the majority of the letters were written by Fitch, many were addressed to him and some concern him but were not intended for his perusal. The letters touch on myriad personal and professional matters and include comments by, to, and about many actors of Fitch's acquaintance, including Maude Adams, Otis Skinner, Nat C. Goodwin, Clara Bloodgood, and Amelia Bingham.

Illustrations. Thirty-one, mostly photographs of Clyde Fitch and his associates.

Features. Introduction by Montrose J. Moses; table of contents; list of illustrations; documentation: date and place of authorship provided for the letters, other quoted material is usually identified by author; "List of Plays by Clyde Fitch, Giving the Theatre, Date, Leading Players"; index.

Actors. General.

231. Moses, Montrose J[onas]. *The Fabulous Forrest: The Record of an American Actor.* Boston: Little, Brown, 1929; rpt. New York: Benjamin Blom, 1969. xxi, 369 pp.

This narrative of Edwin Forrest's life contains biographical data (with many specific dates), quotations from previously published sources, excerpts from Forrest's letters and diaries, and anecdotes. The author adds reflections on the social and political forces which helped shape Forrest's personality and somewhat antagonistic interpretations of the actor's character. Slight attention is paid to the post-1861 period.

Illustrations. Twenty-two engravings, drawings, and photographs of Edwin Forrest, other actors, managers, and theatres.

Features. Preface; table of contents; list of illustrations; documentation: sources of materials are identified by author and/or title and/or date; bibliography; index.

Actors. Edwin Forrest.

232. —. *Famous Actor-Families in America.* New York: Thomas Y. Crowell, 1906; rpt. New York: Greenwood, 1968; rpt. New York: Benjamin Blom, 1968. viii, 341 pp.

Chapters concerning famous nineteenth-century theatrical families comprise this volume. The families are: the Booths, the Jeffersons, the Sotherns, the Boucicaults, the Hacketts, the Drews and the Barrymores, the Wallacks, the Davenports, the Hollands, and the Powers. Biographical narrative, including many specific dates, composes the bulk of the volume. Personal and professional evaluations and descriptions, both by the author and from other sources, is also included. Much of the information pertains to the pre-1861 period. In addition to the players noted below, brief mention is made of many actors, such as John Wilkes Booth, Ethel Barrymore, and Virginia Harned.

Illustrations. Sixty photographs and engravings, mostly of subjects of the chapter.

Features. Foreword; table of contents; list of illustrations; documentation: sources of quotations are identified by author and/or title; bibliography; genealogical tables for each family.

Actors. Maurice Barrymore, Edwin Booth, Dion Boucicault, E. L. Davenport, Fanny Davenport, John Drew II, Mrs. John Drew, James K. Hackett, E. M. Holland, Joseph Holland, Joseph Jefferson III, Tyrone Power II, Agnes Robertson, E. A. Sothern, E. H. Sothern, Lester Wallack.

233. Murdoch, James E[dward]. *Analytic Elocution, Containing Studies, Theoretical and Practical, of Expressive Speech.* New York and Cincinnati: Van Antwerp, Bragg, ©1884. ix, 504 pp.

This book was written as a practical companion to the author's earlier *A Plea for the Spoken Language* (see 234). Brief discussions of elements of the vocal mechanism and of the variable and expressive potentialities of the voice are followed by hundreds of exercises aimed toward the cultivation of vocal skills. The volume concludes with selected practice readings from prose, drama, and poetry.

Illustrations. None.

Features. Preface; table of contents; index of extracts from prose and poetical works.

Actors. James E. Murdoch.

234. —. *A Plea for the Spoken Language. An Essay upon Comparative Elocution, Condensed from Lectures Delivered Throughout the United States.* New York and Cincinnati: Van Antwerp, Bragg, ©1883. viii, 320 pp.

The author attempts "to demonstrate, through an historic and comparative treatment of the subject of elocution, its claims as a scientific study, and its possibilities as a disciplined art; and thence to show how a thorough universal system of instruction may be attained. . . ." The author acknowledges his heavy debt to Dr. James Rush for many of the ideas in this primarily theoretical and historical essay. Appended are Dr. Berber's "Essay on Rhythms" (1823) and Aaron Hill's "An Essay on the Dramatic Passions. . ." (1779).

Illustrations. None.

Features. Preface; introduction; table of contents; documentation: sources of most quotations are identified by author and, occasionally, title; appendices: "The Principles of Rhythms," "Essay on Rhythms" by Dr. Barber, "Selections Scored for Illustration," "An Essay on the Dramatic Passions. . ." by Aaron Hill.

Actors. James E. Murdoch.

235. —. *The Stage, or, Recollections of Actors and Acting from an Experience of Fifty Years: A Series of Dramatic Sketches.* Philadelphia: J. M. Stoddart, 1880; rpt. New York: Benjamin Blom, 1969. 510 pp.

This book contains a series of reflections on the art of acting and descriptions and anecdotes concerning prominent players—from Garrick to Edwin Forrest—gleaned from the author's observations and reading. Although all dated references are to pre-Civil War days, the author stresses his ideas on stage speaking and elocution, which remained influential following the war. The main portion of the text is preceded by J. Bunting's biographical sketch of the author.

Illustrations. One engraving of the author.

Features. Preface; table of contents; documentation: sources of quotations are identified by author and, usually, title; biographical sketch of the author by J. Bunting; several appendices relating mainly to eighteenth-century theatre (notably David Garrick); index.

Actors. James E. Murdoch.

236. [Navarro], Mary Anderson [de]. *A Few Memories.* New York: Harper & Brothers, 1896. 262 pp.

The author reminisces about her life and theatrical career from her childhood in the 1860s to her marriage in 1890. She includes numerous anecdotes and brief comments on other actors, such as Lawrence Barrett, John McCullough, Clara Morris, and Charlotte Cushman, but she indicates few specific dates. In addition, the author reflects on many topics and friends, for example the stock company system, French theatre, audiences, Tennyson, and Longfellow. The volume contains several letters to Miss Anderson and two reviews of her theatrical debut.

Illustrations. Seven, mostly photographs, sketches, and paintings of Mary Anderson.

Features. List of illustrations; documentation: sources
of most quotations are identified by author and
title; index of names.

Actors. Mary Anderson, Edwin Booth.

236a. Newman, Shirlee Petkin. *Ethel Barrymore: Girl Actress.*
Indianapolis, Indiana: Bobbs-Merrill, ©1966. 200 pp.

A part of the "Childhood of Famous Americans" series,
this heavily fictionalized account of Ethel Barrymore's
life to her stage debut at age fourteen contains much
imagined "coversation." Among the characters are Mrs.
John Drew, Georgiana Drew Barrymore, Maurice and
Lionel Barrymore, and Joseph Jefferson. The volume
contains a brief summary of Miss Barrymore's stage
career.

Illustrations. Ten full-page and several smaller sketches.

Features. Table of contents; list of illustrations; no documentation; brief chronology relating Ethel
Barrymore's life to other events; study projects
for children; theatre vocabulary for children.

Actors. Ethel Barrymore.

237. [O'Connor, Richard], John Burke [pseud.]. *Duet in Dia-
monds: The Flamboyant Saga of Lillian Russell and
Diamond Jim Brady in America's Gilded Age.* New
York: G. P. Putnam's Sons, ©1972. 286 pp.

Along with chronicling the lives of Lillian Russell and
"Diamond Jim" Brady, his informal account contains
much information on the opulent society in which they
moved. Anecdotes, narration, factual data, and quotations from the subjects' acquaintances are included. Miss
Russell's offstage life is emphasized, but there is some information on her stage career.

Illustrations. Eight photographs of Lillian Russell, "Diamond Jim" Brady, and related subjects.

Features. Introduction; table of contents, documentation: sources of some materials are identified
in "Notes on Sources"; bibliography; index.

Actors. Lillian Russell.

238. Odell, George C[linton] D[ensmore] . *Annals of the New
York Stage.* 15 vols. New York: Columbia University
Press, 1927-49; rpt. New York: AMS Press, 1970.
Vol. I (to 1798): xiii, 496 pp.; Vol. II (1798-1821):
viii, 643 pp.; Vol. III (1821-34): xii, 747 pp.; Vol. IV
(1834-43): xiii, 757 pp.; Vol. V (1843-50): xiii, 655
pp.; Vol. VI (1850-57): xiii, 676 pp.; Vol. VII (1857-
65): xv, 793 pp.; Vol. VIII (1865-70): xvii, 779 pp.;
Vol. IX (1870-75): xviii, 742 pp.; Vol. X (1875-79):
xix, 884 pp.; Vol. XI (1879-82): xviii, 758 pp.; Vol.
XII (1882-85): xix, 734 pp.; Vol. XIII (1885-88):
xviii, 723 pp.; Vol. XIV (1888-91): xvi, 935 pp.; Vol.
XV (1891-94): xvii, 1010 pp.

This monumental work chronicles theatrical activity in
New York City from the beginnings through September,
1894. The author combines arrangment by theatre and
by chronology within the time period delimited by each
volume. Collecting his materials "solely from contemporary newspapers, pamphlets, diaries, letters, autobiogra-
phies. playbills, account-books, etc.," he includes specific
dates, cast lists, narration, anecdotes, advertisements,
quoted criticisms, and some personal conjecture. The
author inserts his criticisms of performances which he
saw during the 1880s and 1890s.

Illustrations. Thousands of photographs, engravings, drawings, etc., mostly of performers.

Features. Introduction (Vol. I); tables of contents (each
volume for that volume); lists of illustrations
(each volume for that volume); documentation:
sources of quotations are identified by author
and/or title and/or date; indices (each volume

for that volume.

Actors. General.

239. Ormsbee, Helen. *Backstage with Actors from the Time of Shakespeare to the Present Day.* New York: Thomas Y. Crowell, ©1938; rpt. New York: Benjamin Blom, 1969; rpt. Freeport, New York: Books for Libraries, 1970. xiv, 343 pp.

> This survey of actors focuses on a few prominent English and American players of various periods, with over one-half of the volume devoted to American actors and theatre conditions. The author rarely succeeds in her desire to penetrate the minds of her subjects, but she does provide brief biographies, paraphrased or quoted reviews, and some quotations from her subjects' writings. Anecdotes, factual data, criticisms, and some brief descriptions of performances are included. The author inserts personal recollections of some modern actors.

> *Illustrations.* Twenty-five photographs, engravings, and paintings of actors.

> *Features.* Introduction; table of contents; documentation: "Notes" provides names of books and names and dates of periodicals from which quotations are selected; index.

> *Actors.* Maude Adams, Edwin Booth, Arnold Daly, Minnie Maddern Fiske, James A. Herne, Joseph Jefferson III, Richard Mansfield.

240. [Osmun, Thomas Embley], Alfred Ayres [pseud.]. *Acting and Actors, Elocution and Elocutionists: A Book About Theatre Folk and Theatre Art.* Preface by Harrison Grey Fiske. Introd. by Edgar S. Werner. Prologue by James A. Waldron. New York: D. Appleton, 1894. 287 pp.

Ibid. 2nd ed., with supplement. New York: D. Appleton, 1894. 293 pp.

1st ed.: The author, a critic and teacher of elocution, here gathers many articles and letters by himself and a few by other hands. Most of the materials are theoretical statements or practical criticisms concerning elocution and the art of acting. The essays and letters were written during the late 1880s and early 1890s. Generalized evaluations and/or criticisms of specific line readings are provided for many actors. Among the players who are briefly discussed are Edwin Booth, Clara Morris, Charlotte Cushman, Frederick Warde, and Mrs. D. P. Bowers. A debate on the nature of acting between the author and A. C. Wheeler ("Nym Crinkle") is included.

2nd ed.: This edition reprints the whole of the first edition and adds a brief article concerning the author's approach to elocution.

Illustrations. Eight photographs and drawings of the author and other people (both editions).

Features. Preface by Harrison Grey Fiske; introduction by Edgar S. Werner; prologue by James A. Waldron; documentation: sources of quotations are identified by author and/or title and/or date; index (both editions).

Actors. Lawrence Barrett, Edwin Forrest, Ada Rehan (both editions).

241. Owens, Mrs. John E. [Mary Stephens]. *Memories of the Professional and Social Life of John E. Owens, By His Wife.* Baltimore: John Murphy, 1892. vii, 292 pp.

This narrative traces John E. Owens' life from his birth in 1823 to his death in 1886, emphasizing the period following his marriage in 1849. Fond anecdotes and appreciations of his personal and professional character abound. Many specific dates of productions and engagements are indicated, but little description of his performances is offered. Over sixty per cent of the book relates to the

1861-86 period.

Illustrations. Twenty-two photographs, paintings, and en-
    gravings, mostly of John E. Owens.

Features. Preface; table of contents; list of illustrations.

Actors. John E. Owens.

242. Pascoe, Charles Eyre (comp. and ed.). *The Dramatic List:
      A Record of the Principal Performances of Living
      Actors and Actresses of the British Stage. With Criti-
      cisms from Contemporary Journals.* Boston: Roberts
      Brothers, 1879; rpt. St. Clair Shores, Michigan: Scho-
      larly Press, 1971. vi, 358 pp.

      Ibid. *Our Actors and Actresses. The Dramatic Lists:
      A Record of the Performances of Living Actors and
      Actresses of the British Stage.* 2nd ed., rev. and enl.
      London, 1880; rpt. New York: Benjamin Blom, 1969.
      iv, 432 pp.

      1879 ed.: This work is an alphabetical listing of principal
      living players of the British stage. Entries for each actor
      contain varying amounts and types of biographical data,
      notices of major London performances by the subject,
      and criticisms selected from contemporary British periodi-
      cals.   The entries often contain extensive critical com-
      ments.

      1880 ed.: This edition follows the same format as the pre-
      vious edition, except for the following: the number of
      subjects is increased by approximately one hundred; the
      biographical information is "more complete"; and the
      quantity of critical commentary is decreased.

      Illustrations. None (both editions).

      Features. 1879 ed.: Preface; documentation: sources of
          quotations from periodicals are identified by
          titles and date.
          1880 ed.: Preface; documentation: sources of

quotations from periodicals are identified by
title and date; appendix containing biographical
sketches of principal players who had died since
the publication of the first edition; index.

Actors. Dion Boucicault, John Brougham, John Sleeper
Clarke, Charles Fechter, Joseph Jefferson III,
Agnes Robertson, E. A. Sothern, Genevieve
Ward, Mrs. John Wood (both editions).

243. Patterson, Ada. *Maude Adams: A Biography.* New York:
Meyer Bros., ©1907; rpt. New York: Benjamin Blom,
1971. 109 pp.

This book is an anecdotal biography of Maude Adams'
life to the opening of *Peter Pan.* The author describes
Miss Adams' personality, New York home, hobbies, charities, etc. She includes anecdotes, generalized appreciation, and some statements by the actress, but little critical
comment and few dates.

Illustrations. Twenty-two photographs of Maude Adams.

Features. "Complete Casts of Some of the Earlier New
York Productions in Which Miss Maude Adams
Took Part" (includes theatres, dates, and
casts for productions from 1889 through
1897).

Actors. Maude Adams.

244. Paul, Howard, and George Gebbie (eds.). *The Stage and
Its Stars, Past and Present: A Gallery of Dramatic
Illustration and Critical Biographies of Distinguished
English and American Actors from the Time of Shakespeare till To-day.* 2 vols. Philadelphia: Gebbie, n.d.
[most engravings ©1887; Vol. II of this work was published no earlier than 1889].

The major portion of the text in each volume of this work
is composed of brief biographical sketches of actors, ar-

ranged in a generally chronological manner according to birth date. The first volume contains biographies of English actors from Richard Tarleton to Charles Kean, Ellen Tree, and Samuel Phelps. The second volume contains biographies of "the Most Prominent Actors Who Have Appeared on the American Stage from Its Inauguration, 1752, till the Present Time." Factual data, including some specific dates and major roles, is included, along with occasional excerpts from criticisms, memoirs, etc. The excellent full-page photogravures are accompanied by comments on their subjects; in the cases of actors portrayed, these comments are biographical and/or critical.

Illustrations. Vol. I: Fifty-six full-page photogravure plates, accompanied by numerous smaller illustrations, and one hundred and twenty-six engravings, drawings, and photographs in the text.

Vol. II: Fifty-six full-page photogravure plates, accompanied by numerous smaller illustrations, and one hundred and forty engravings, photographs, and drawings in the text.

Features. Vol. I: Preface; introduction; list of illustrations; documentation: sources of quotations are identified by author and/or title and/or date.

Vol. II: Introduction; list of illustrations; documentation: sources of quotation are identified by author and/or title and/or date; index (for both volumes).

Actors. General.

245. Pemberton, T[homas] Edgar. *Lord Dundreary: A Memoir of Edward Askew Sothern, with a Brief Sketch of the Career of E. H. Sothern.* New York: The Knickerbocker Press, [1908?]. xii, 291 pp.

This volume reprints the author's anecdotal reminiscence of his close friend E. A. Sothern (originally published in

London in 1889) and includes a short essay on E. H. Sothern. The memoir of the elder Sothern quotes extensively from that actor's letters, published writings, and conversations. It discusses the actor off the stage, his hobbies, his practical jokes, and his theatrical activities. The book contains comments by the actor and by various critics concerning the development and portrayal of Sothern's major characters, including description and evaluation. The book concerns the period from Sothern's debut in 1849 to his death in 1881, but it emphasizes the actor's life during the 1860s and 1870s, primarily in London. Although he makes no attempt to present a chronicle, the author inserts many specific dates. Less than one-tenth of the volume concerns the stage career of E. H. Sothern.

Illustrations. Several portraits and facsimiles of writings relating to the Sotherns.

Features. Introduction; table of contents; list of illustrations; documentation: quotations are usually identified by author and occasionally, title and/or date; postscript: "A Brief Sketch of the Career of E. H. Sothern"; index.

Actors. E. A. Sothern, E. H. Sothern.

246. Phelps, Henry P[itt]. *Hamlet from the Actors' Standpoint: Its Representatives and a Comparison of Their Performances.* New York: Edgar S. Werner, 1890. x, 180 pp.

The first (of two) main portions of this book consists of brief considerations of notable Hamlets from Burbage to Ernesto Rossi. The author provides varying amounts of data concerning each actor's performance of the role and quotes liberally from contemporary criticisms. The second portion of the book is a scene-by-scene comparison of the actors' performances. This comparison is accomplished by quoting contemporary critics' descriptions of the actors' manners and stage business in each scene.

Illustrations. Ten engravings and photographs of actors in the roles of Hamlet and Ophelia.

Features. Preface; table of contents; documentation: sources of quotations are usually identified by author; bibliography; index.

Actors. Edwin Booth, Charles Fechter, Edwin Forrest.

247. Phelps, H[enry] P[itt]. *Players of a Century: A Record of the Albany Stage. Including Notices of Prominent Actors Who Have Appeared in America.* Albany, New York: Joseph McDonough, 1880. x, 424 pp.

Ibid. 2nd ed. Albany, New York: Joseph McDonough, 1880; rpt. New York: Benjamin Blom, 1972. x, 424 pp.

1st ed. (limited edition):   This work traces theatrical activity in Albany, N.Y., from its amateur origins in 1760 until approximately 1873, with a few comments on the 1873-80 period.   Many specific dates, cast lists, and financial reports are included, along with a few anecdotes, criticisms, and reminiscences.   Biographical sketches of prominent actors are provided immediately following notice of their first performances in Albany.

2nd ed.: This edition includes the same text as the first edition.

Illustrations. One portrait photograph of John W. Albaugh.

Features. Preface; table of contents; documentation: some sources of quotations are identified; "Additions and Corrections"; index.

Actors. General.

248. Phelps, William Lyon. *The Twentieth Century Theatre. Observations on the Contemporary English and Ameri-*

can Stage. New York: Macmillan, 1918; rpt. Freeport, New York: Books for Libraries, 1967; rpt. Port
Washington, New York: Kennikat, 1968. ix, 147 pp.

"This little book contains a discussion, with sufficient
corroborative figures and specific illustrations, of some of
the conditions and tendencies of the English and American stage of 1900-1918." Among the areas considered
are modern playwriting, the "little theatre" movement,
and "Shakespeare on the Modern Stage." Brief comments
on a few actors, including Richard Mansfield, Maude
Adams, Louis Calvert, and Lawrence Barrett, are included.

Illustrations. None.

Features. Preface; table of contents; index.

Actors. General.

249. Pitou, Augustus. *Masters of the Show, As Seen in Retro-
spection by One Who Has Been Associated with the
American Stage for Nearly Fifty Years.* New York:
Neale Publishing, 1914. 186 pp.

This volume of reminiscences and reflections is the pro-
duct of the author's involvement with the theatre as an
actor and a manager, beginning in the 1860s. He discusses
many topics of theatrical interest, such as acting genius,
playwriting, advertising, and vaudeville, as well as commenting on many of his personal experiences and friends.
Anecdotes, descriptions, and evaluations of many performances and performers are included in the book.
Among the actors commented upon briefly are J. B.
Roberts, Lucille Western, Edwin Adams, and John E.
Owens. Most of the reminiscences concern the period
from the late 1860s through the 1880s.

Illustrations. Thirteen, mostly photographs of actors.

Features. Preface; list of illustrations.

Actors. Mary Anderson, Edwin Booth, Edwin Forrest,

Joseph Jefferson III, Augustus Pitou.

250. Pollock, Channing. *Harvest of My Years: An Autobiography.* Indianapolis, Indiana and New York: Bobbs-Merrill, ©1943. 395 pp.

> The author, who became professionally associated with the theatre as a dramatist in the late 1890s and who later functioned as a playwright, press agent, and critic, informally recounts events in his life in a generally chronological narrative. Anecdotes and personal recollections of numerous actors, authors, journalists, and managers are included, along with comments on the production circumstances of many of the author's plays. Approximately one-half of the book concerns the pre-1911 period.

> *Illustrations.* Thirty-one, mostly photographs of the author and of miscellaneous subjects related to his life.

> *Features.* Table of contents; list of illustrations; index.

> *Actors.* General.

251. *A Portfolio of Players, with a Packet of Notes Thereon.* Notes by H. C. Brunner, E. A. Dithmar, Laurence Hutton, Brander Matthews, William Winter. New York: J. W. Boulton, 1888. 89 pp.

> This souvenir of Augustin Daly's theatrical company is composed mainly of full-page illustrations, each accompanied by a two-page, signed article. The notes are primarily tributes to the players and contain generalized comments on each actor's performance qualities. Occasionally an actor's previous roles are given brief comment.

> *Illustrations.* One engraving of John Lowin, and twenty-one photographs of members of Augustin Daly's theatrical company.

Features. Table of contents.

Actors. John Drew II, Charles Fisher, Mrs. G. H. Gilbert, James Lewis, Ada Rehan.

252. *Portraits of the American Stage, 1771-1971: An Exhibition in Celebration of the Inaugural Season of The John F. Kennedy Center for the Performing Arts.* Foreword by Marvin Sadik. Introd. by Monroe H. Fabian. Washington, D.C.: Smithsonian Institute Press for the National Portrait Gallery, 1971. 203 pp.

Portratis and brief biographical sketches of ninety-one performers from the American stage comprise this volume. Many of the artists pictured were visiting performers, but many were American actors. The biographies emphasize only major events in the subject's careers. The illustrations are of high quality.

Illustrations. Ninety-eight portraits in various media (no photographs) of "Noted actors, actresses, singers, dancers, instrumentalists, and conductors."

Features. List of "Lenders to the Exhibition"; foreword by Marvin Sadik; introduction by Monroe H. Fabian; index of main subjects.

Actors. Maude Adams, Ethel Barrymore, John Barrymore, Edwin Booth, Dion Boucicault, Charlotte Cushman, Minnie Maddern Fiske, Edwin Forrest, Joseph Jefferson III, John McCullough, Clara Fisher Maeder, Richard Mansfield, Julia Marlowe, Alla Nazimova, Otis Skinner.

253. Power-Waters, Alam [Shelley]. *John Barrymore: The Legend and the Man.* Foreword by Brooks Atkinson. New York: Julian Messner, ©1941. xiv, 282 pp.

This biography was written, with the actor's permission, by the wife of the company manager of the 1939-40 tour of *My Dear Children*—John Barrymore's last stage play. The book is a generally chronological collection of anecdotes about Barrymore's on- and offstage life, with linking narration. Some of the author's personal observations of Barrymore are included in the description of the *My Dear Children* tour. Some of the actor's comments on his attitude toward theatre are quoted. Less than one-fifth of the text concerns the pre-1911 period.

Illustrations. Fifty-two photographs of or by John Barrymore and members of his family.

Features. Foreword by Brooks Atkinson; table of contents; list of illustrations; documentation: quotations are usually identified by author only; index.

Actors. John Barrymore.

254. —. *The Story of Young Edwin Booth.* Foreword by Eva LeGallienne. New York: E. P. Dutton, ©1955. 192 pp.

This account of Edwin Booth's life from 1844 until his return to the stage following his brother's assassination of Abraham Lincoln is intended for juvenile readers. The treatment is novelistic, with dialogue, but most of the incidents are based on fact. History is occasionally altered for dramatic effect: for example, the author acknowledges her changing the time of Edwin's destruction of John Wilkes' costumes by "a year or so." In some cases events are heightened in importance for the sake of a good story.

Illustrations. Ten photographs of Edwin Booth and his family.

Features. Foreword by Eva LeGallienne; table of contents; list of illustrations.

Actors. Edwin Booth, John Wilkes Booth, Junius Brutus Booth, Jr.

255. Powers, James T. *Twinkle Little Star: Sparkling Memories of Seventy Years.* Foreword by Charles Hanson Towne. New York: G. P. Putnam's Sons, ©1939. xiv, 379 pp.

> The bulk of this volume of anecdotal reminiscences concerns the period from the author's youth in the 1870s to the first decade of the twentieth century; miscellaneous recollections from the next thirty years complete the book. The popular musical-comedy actor emphasizes his offstage experiences in America and England, but he also comments on some of his performances. The author includes brief anecdotes or estimates of many of his actor-friends, such as James K. Hackett, Richard Mansfield, and Nat C. Goodwin. Few dates are specified.

> *Illustrations.* One hundred and eighteen photographs, engravings, paintings, and drawings of James T. Powers, Rachel Booth (Powers), their friends, playbills, etc.

> *Features.* Introduction by Charles Hanson Towne; table of contents; list of illustrations; index.

> *Actors.* Rachel Booth, Willie Edouin, James T. Powers.

256. Price, W[illiam] T[hompson]. *A Life of Charlotte Cushman.* New York: Brentano's, ©1894. v, 180, I-XVIII pp.

> This book chronicles Charlotte Cushman's career and examines her major characterizations. According to the author, "dates and facts have been carefully collated from the newspapers of the day." The chapters on her major roles quote liberally from her contemporaries, including several other players, but much space is devoted to plot summaries, dialogue excerpts, and a short history of women performing male characters. Some portions of her performances are described.

> *Illustrations.* One photograph of Charlotte Cushman.

Features. Preface; table of contents; documentation: quotations are usually identified by author only; index.

Actors. Charlotte Cushman.

257. Pyper, George D[ollinger]. *The Romance of an Old Playhouse.* Salt Lake City, Utah: Seagull, 1928. 343 pp.

Ibid. Rev. ed. Salt Lake City, Utah: Deseret News Press, 1937. 406 pp.

1st ed.: The author was the manager of the Salt Lake Theatre for the last thirty years of its existence. In this book he presents a history of that theatre, 1862-1928, along with numerous anecdotes, personal recollections, and other comments in Salt Lake City. Included are many specific dates, curtain speeches, cast lists, letters, and quotations from periodicals and from books. While commenting substantially on the actors cited below, the author briefly notices many other players, including E. H. Sothern, Louis James, Frederick Warde, and Richard Mansfield.

Rev. ed.: This volume provides the same coverage as the first edition while including some corrections and minor revisions of the text.

Illustrations. Seventy-five pages with illustrations, including photographs, engravings, and drawings of performers, officers of the Salt Lake Theatre, and various scenes (both editions).

Features. Foreword; table of contents; list of illustrations; documentation: sources of quotations are usually identified by author and/or title and/or date.

Actors. Annie Adams, Maude Adams, George Chaplin, Julia Dean Hayne.

258. Quinn, Germain. *Fifty Years Back Stage: Being the Life Story of a Theatrical Stage Mechanic.* Minneapolis, Minnesota: Stage Publishing, ©1928. 204 pp.

> Having been employed full-time in various backstage capacities from 1875 to 1907, primarily in Minneapolis, the author had the opportunity to meet and to observe virtually every major American actor of the last quarter of the nineteenth century. Approximately two-thirds of the book is composed of his comments on actors. He includes his evaluations of the performers on- and off-stage, many anecdotes, some descriptions of performances, and some biographical data. The final portion of the book deals mainly with the stage employees union and miscellaneous matters.

> *Illustrations.* Seventy-seven photographs of actors.

> *Features.* Preface; introduction; "Introductory Remarks" by the Rev. G. L. Morrill.

> *Actors.* General.

259. [Ranous, Dora Knowlton Thompson]. *Diary of a Daly Debutante: Being Passages from the Journal of a Member of Augustin Daly's Famous Company of Players.* New York: Duffield, 1910; rpt. New York: Benjamin Blom, 1972. 249 pp.

> This volume consists of entries selected from the private journal which the author kept while she was one of the "young girls of good family and education" engaged for the Augustin Daly theatrical company. The entries, which are dated from September 4, 1879, through August 7, 1880, are "printed verbatim, with only such omissions as seemed expedient for personal reasons." Anecdotes, description, and personal opinion are contained in these glimpses of Daly and his actors in and out of the theatre in New York and on tour, affording insight to the practices and personalities of the Daly aggregation.

> *Illustrations.* Seventeen drawings and photographs of

people associated with Augustin Daly's 1879-80 theatrical company.

Features. Publisher's note; list of illustrations.

Actors. John Drew II, Dora Knowlton, Charles Leclerq, Catherine Lewis, Ada Rehan.

260. Rees, James (Colley Cibber [pseud.]). *The Life of Edwin Forrest, with Reminiscences and Personal Recollections.* Philadelphia: T. B. Peterson & Brothers, ©1874. 524 pp.

The author presents an admiring picture of his close friend "of nearly fifty years." He relates many of Forrest's views on theatrical and non-theatrical matters, offers personal opinions and observations, inserts his own and other contemporary criticisms and descriptions of Forrest's acting, and includes much biographical data. Although specific dates are frequently indicated, many anecdotes are not located by date. The bulk of the volume relates to the pre-Civil War period.

Illustrations. One photograph of Edwin Forrest.

Features. Author's note; introduction; table of contents; documentation: most sources of quotations are identified by author and/or title and/or date; "The Will of Edwin Forrest"; "An Act to Incorporate 'The Edwin Forrest Home'."

Actors. Edwin Forrest.

261. Rice, Edw[ard] LeRoy. *Monarchs of Minstrelsy, from "Daddy" Rice to Date.* New York: Kenny Publishing, ©1911. 366 pp.

This volume contains hundreds of brief biographical sketches of American "burnt cork heroes" who performed during the period from the early 1800s through 1910. Most of the performers were primarily minstrel entertainers, but many of the subjects were more famous in non-blackface roles, for example, Weber and Fields, Otis Skinner, Francis Wilson, and Wilton Lackaye. The biographies vary greatly in length and contents, but most are brief. Among the types of materials included are birth and/or death dates, indications of major engagements, identifications of specialities, brief descriptions or evaluations, and occasional irreverent remarks. The author generally adheres to a chronological arrangement by birth date of his subjects.

Illustrations. Hundreds, mostly photographs, of blackface entertainers, in and out of makeup.

Features. Foreword; introduction; documentation; quotations are identified by author and/or title; index; index to illustrations.

Actors. General.

262. Robertson, W[alford] Graham. *Life Was Worth Living, the Reminiscences of W. Graham Robertson.* Foreword by Sir Johnston Forbes-Robertson. New York: Harper and Brothers, [1931]. xii, 344 pp.

The author recollects many of his acquintances during the late Victorian and Edwardian periods, including such friends as Rossetti, Bernhardt, Irving, Wilde, Whistler, and Sargent. Having been a sometime friend and costume designer for Augustin Daly in the 1890s, the author includes a chapter on Daly and Ada Rehan. The author knew Miss Rehan offstage and he offers anecdotes, descriptions, and reflections on her private personality in contrast to her stage character and in relation to Daly. Brief discussion of John Drew II and of Miss Rehan's relationship with him are also included.

Illustrations. Sixteen paintings, drawings, and photographs, mostly of the author and his friends.

Features. Foreword by Sir Johnston Forbes-Robertson; preface; table of contents; list of illustrations;

documentation: authors and, sometimes, dates
of quoted correspondence are identified; index.

Actors.   Ada Rehan.

263. Rigdon, Walter (ed.). *The Biographical Encyclopedia &
      Who's Who of the American Theatre.*   Introd. by
      George Freedley.   New York: James H. Heineman,
      1966. xiv, 1101 pp.

This work contains the following main sections: 1) alphabetical list of productions presented in New York City
from January 1, 1900, through May 31, 1964 (includes
title, date, and theatre); 2) complete playbills for New
York City and "leading experimental and repertory theatre groups throughout the United States," 1959-61;
3) dates, places, and directors for premieres of American
plays in other countries, 1946-64; 4) "Complete biographies of the most important [living] persons, including
foreigners and Americans abroad, connected with each
aspect of the American theatre" (this section does include
people who died during the preparation of the manuscript; 5) "Biographies of American theatre groups, existing and extinct, including production records" (twentieth-
century groups, including theatres, clubs, unions, schools,
etc.; not comprehensive); 6) "Histories of New York
theatre buildings, complete with all previous names and
cross-indexed" (includes locations, dates of opening under
various names, and, sometimes, owners, architects, and
dates of demolition); 7) "A complete record of major
awards presented to members of the American theatre"
(1926-64); 8) a bibliography including "biographical and
autobiographical works dealing with leading persons in
the theatre, both living and dead" (includes full bibliographical data); 9) discographies of original cast record-
ing of Broadway and off-Broadway musical and spoken
theatre productions which were recorded prior to June 1,
1964; 10) necrology containing the "names, professions
[i.e., specific areas of theatrical activity] , place and date
of birth, place and date of death, and the age at death of
people who have contributed to the development of the
theatre from the beginnings of recorded time through

August 31, 1964" (approximately nine thousand entries). The biographies contain few entries for persons active on the stage prior to 1911. The necrology is a useful collection of vitae and includes many American actors of the 1861-1910 period.

Illustrations. None.

Features.   Introduction by George Freedley; preface; table of contents; index for the "Theatre Playbills" section.

Actors.   General.

264. Robbins, Phyllis. *Maude Adams: An Intimate Portrait.* New York: G. P. Putnam's Sons, ©1956. vi, 308 pp.

The author first met Maude Adams in 1900 and later became a close friend of the actress. She utilizes her personal memories, Miss Adams' writings, correspondence concerning the actress, and previously published materials in this book. The portion of the volume which deals with the pre-1900 period relies heavily on Miss Adams' autobiographical writings. The book contains anecdotes, some descriptions and evaluations of Miss Adams' acting, many of the actress' opinions concerning the theatre, and much specifically dated biographical data. Included are the subject's brief reminiscences of her work with E. H. Sothern, Henry Miller, and John Drew II. Nearly one-half of the book concerns the pre-1911 period.

Illustrations. Thirty-eight photographs, mostly of Maude Adams.

Features. Acknowledgements; documentation: sources of quotations are identified by author and/or title and/or date: "Genealogy of Maude Adams"; "Plays in Which Maude Adams Appeared" (includes roles and many dates and theatres); "Food Charts Prepared by Maude Adams"; index.

Actors. Maude Adams.

265. —. *The Young Maude Adams.* Francestown, New Hampshire: Marshall Jones, ©1959. 163 pp.

Although emphasizing Maude Adams' life prior to 1890, this book contains scattered comments about her work through the 1930s. Quotations from writings by and interviews with Miss Adams, excerpts from reviews of her performances, and anecdotes are included along with comments on her ancestry, descriptions of the mid-nineteenth century American west, and summaries of dialogue from plays in wich she appeared.

Illustrations. Twenty-one photographs, mostly of Maude Adams; eight reproductions of playbills.

Features. Acknowledgements; table of contents; list of illustrations; list of playbills reproduced; documentation: sources of a few of the quotations are partially identified.

Actors. Maude Adams.

266. Robins, Edward [Jr.]. *Twelve Great Actors.* New York: G. P. Putnam's Sons, 1900. xiv, 474 pp.

Biographical chapters on twelve American and English actors from Garrick to Edwin Booth comprise this book. Anecdotes, brief evaluations and descriptions, and biographical data are included. In addition to those actors noted below, a small portion of the essay on Edwin Forrest concerns the post-1860 period.

Illustrations. Twenty-three, mostly engravings, paintings, and drawings of actors.

Features. Preface; table of contents; list of illustrations; index.

Actors. Edwin Booth, Charles Fechter, E. A. Sothern,

Lester Wallack.

267. —. *Twelve Great Actresses.*   New York: G. P. Putnam's Sons, 1900. x, 446 pp.

> Popularly-written essays on Charlotte Cushman and eleven English and European actresses from Anne Bracegirdle to Ristori comprise this book. The chapter on Miss Cushman outlines her career, emphasizing major events. Some brief quotations from the actress, along with anecdotal material, are included.

> *Illustrations:* Twenty illustrations in various media of actresses.

> *Features.* Preface; table of contents, list of illustrations; index.

> *Actors.* Charlotte Cushman.

268. Rosenberg, Marvin.   *The Masks of King Lear.*   Berkeley and Los Angeles: University of California Press, 1972. viii, 431 pp.

> Proceeding scene-by-scene through *King Lear,* the author juxtaposes comments by literary critics, materials on various actors' stage interpretations, and his own critical insights. The information on actors includes brief descriptions of stage business, line readings, and interpretative concepts of English, American, Asian, and European players from the Restoration to the 1960s. The references to actors range widely, but some actors "are not named because, like some critics, they add nothing to earlier illuminations of the play." Among American Actors, 1861-1910, this valuable study contains information on the Lears of Booth, Forrest, John McCullough, and Robert B. Mantell.

> *Illustrations.* None.

> *Features.* Preface; table of contents; thorough documen-

tation; bibliography, appendix: "King Lear and
His Fool: A Study of the Conception and En-
actment of Dramatic Role in Relation to Self-
Conception" by Frank Barron and Marvin
Rosenberg; index.

Actors. Edwin Booth, Edwin Forrest.

269. —. *The Masks of Othello: The Search for the Identity of
Othello, Iago, and Desdemona by Three Centuries of
Actors and Critics.* Berkeley and Los Angeles: Uni-
versity of California Press, 1961. xii, 313 pp.

Emphasizing the roles of Othello, Iago, and Desdemona,
the author investigates *Othello* by utilizing critical and descriptive comments by literary critics, theatre critics,
actors, and himself. Approximately one-half of the book
is devoted to an examination of the major actors who
have played the three roles, especially Othello. This section spans the period from Jacobean times well into the
twentieth century. Descriptions of nineteenth-century
actors predominate, with considerable comment on
Edmund Kean, Macready, Irving, and Salvini, along with
Booth, Fechter, and Forrest.

Illustrations. One engraving of a Restoration production
of *Othello.*

Features. Preface; table of contents; thorough documentation; appendix: "A Kind Word for Bowdler";
index.

Actors. Edwin Booth, Charles Fechter, Edwin Forrest.

270. Rourke, Constance. *Troupers of the Gold Coast, or The
Rise of Lotta Crabtree.* New York: Harcourt, Brace,
©1928. xiii, 262 pp.

This book combines the story of early California theatre
and a life of Lotta Crabtree from the late 1840s to 1864.
From 1864 to the 1920s, the author concentrates almost

solely on Lotta. Approximately forty per cent of the text concerns the post-1860 period. Narration, anecdotes, description and evaluation of Lotta's performances, and the author's interpretation of Lotta's personality are included.

Illustrations. Twenty-eight, mostly photographs, of Lotta Crabtree, other people, and various scenes.

Features. "Salutation"; table of contents; list of illustrations; index.

Actors. Lotta Crabtree, Adah Isaacs Menken.

271. Rowland, Mabel (ed.). *Bert Williams, Son of Laughter: A Symposium of Tribute to the Man and to His Work, By His Friends and Associates.* Preface by David Belasco. New York: The English Crafters, 1923; rpt. New York: Negro Universities Press, 1969.

This volume consists of chapters on various phases of Bert Williams' theatrical career and offstage life. The editor provides a skeletal narrative of Williams' life which is supplemented by the actor's autobiographical statements and by numerous appreciations, criticisms, and recollections of him by such people as W. E. B. Dubois, W. C. Fields, Heywood Broun, and Rennold Wolf. Descriptions of some of Williams' performances and lyrics to many of his songs are included. Approximately one-half of the book concerns the pre-1911 period. Few dates are specified.

Illustrations. Ten photographs and drawings, mostly of Bert Williams, and a letter by Williams.

Features. Foreword by Mabel Rowland; preface by David Belasco; table of contents; documentation: sources of quotations are identified by author and/or title.

Actors. George Walker, Bert Williams.

272. Rowlands, Walter. *Among the Great Masters of the Drama: Scenes in the Lives of Famous Actors.* Boston: Dana Estes, 1903. 233 pp.

> This book is composed of chapters on thirty-four actors from the time of Shakespeare to the time of publication. Quotations from previously published works and the author's brief comments comprise each chapter on the American actors. Many of the quoted passages contain descriptions or evaluations of selected roles acted by the subjects. All of the quotations are favorable to their subjects. A chapter entitled "Jefferson" (i.e., Joseph Jefferson III) discusses mainly the painting and sculpting efforts of other actors.
>
> *Illustrations.* Thirty-three engravings, photographs, and paintings, mostly of actors.
>
> *Features.* Preface; table of contents; list of illustrations; documentation: sources of quotations are identified by author.
>
> *Actors.* Mary Anderson, Lawrence Barrett, Edwin Booth, Charlotte Cushman, Charles Fechter, Edwin Forrest, John McCullough, Helena Modjeska, William Warren, Jr.

273. Ruggles, Eleanor. *Prince of Players: Edwin Booth.* New York: W. W. Norton, 1953; rpt. Westport, Connecticut: Greenwood Press, 1972. 401 pp.

> After briefly sketching the life of Junius Brutus Booth, this highly readable biography traces the life and career of Edwin Booth. The anecdotal narrative contains biographical data, numerous excerpts from correspondence, and some critical and descriptive comments on performances. Over two-thirds of the books concerns Booth's life after 1860. The author includes brief comments on many actors, such as Dave Anderson, John Sleeper Clarke, Joseph Jefferson III, and Junius Brutus Booth, Jr.
>
> *Illustrations.* Seventeen, mostly photographs of Edwin

Booth and members of his family.

Features. Author's note; table of contents; list of illustrations; documentation: some sources of quotations are identified by author and/or title; bibliography; index.

Actors. Lawrence Barrett, Edwin Booth, John Wilkes Booth.

274. Russell, Charles Edward. *Julia Marlowe: Her Life and Art.* New York: D. Appleton, 1926. xxvi, 582 pp.

The author of this biography was Julia Marlowe's business advisor for over thirty ears, commencing in the late 1880s. The book is a chronological narrative of the actress' life through 1923, emphasizing her theatrical career. Over eight per cent of the volume concerns the pre-1911 period. Lengthy quotations from Miss Marlowe, excerts from previously published criticisms and descriptions, correspondence concerning the actress, examinations of her working methods and interpretations, and many specific dates are included. In addition to the actors noted below, many players are mentioned briefly, for example, Lawrence Barrett, Mrs. John Drew, and Clara Morris.

Illustrations. Twenty-nine, mostly photographs of Julia Marlowe.

Features. Introduction; table of contents; list of illustrations; documentation: sources of most quotations are identified by author and/or title and/or date; appendices: "Great Acting in English" (1907) by Arthur Symonds, "Woman's Work on the Stage" (1893) by Julia Marlowe, "Poetic Tributes to Julia Marlowe"; index.

Actors. Ada Dow, Julia Marlowe, E. H. Sothern, Robert Taber.

275. Ryan, Kate. *Old Boston Museum Days.* Boston: Little, Brown, 1915; St. Clair Shores, Michigan: Scholarly Press, 1971. xii, 264 pp.

> Calling upon memories of her association from 1872 to 1893 with the Boston Museum Stock Company, the author reminisces about her fellow actors and theatrical life. She provides autobiographical and biographical fragments, personal appreciations, and numerous on- and offstage anecdotes. She comments briefly on dozens of stars, such as Edwin Booth, Dion Boucicault, Fanny Janauschek, and Richard Mansfield, and company members in addition to those noted below.

> *Illustrations.* Thirty-two photographs, mostly of the author and other actors.

> *Features.* Foreword; table of contents; list of illustrations; index.

> *Actors.* Charles Barron, James Burrows, Annie M. Clarke, John Mason, James Nolan, James H. Ring, Kate Ryan, William Seymour, Mrs. J. R. Vincent, William Warren, Jr., George W. Wilson.

276. Sala, George Augustus. *Breakfast in Bed, or, Philosophy Between the Sheets: A Series of Indigestible Discourses.* Boston: J. Redpath, 1863. 274 pp.

> This collection of miscellaneous articles reprinted from London's *Temple Bar* magazine includes a criticism of E. A. Sothern's performance of Lord Dundreary in *Our American Cousin* as it was first presented in London. The author recognizes the adroitness of the performer, but he deplores the poor taste of some of the drollery and the mistake of audiences in seeing Dundreary as representative of a real-life type of "swell." Some description of Sothern's performance is included.

> *Illustrations.* None.

> *Features.* Table of contents.

Actors.   E. A. Sothern.

277. Salvini, Tommaso.   *Leaves from the Autobiography of Tommaso Salvini.*   New York: Century, 1893; rpt. New York: Benjamin Blom, 1971.   240 pp.

>The actor-author surveys his life from his youth in the 1840s until approximately 1890.   He comments on his own personality and attitudes, his characterizations, theatrical conditions, audiences, and so forth.   Evaluations of many actors, such as Henry Irving, Sarah Bernhardt, and Constant Coquelin, are included.   The sections concerning the author's American tours of the 1870s and 1880s contains brief comments on Edwin Booth and the author's son Alessandro (known as Alexander Salvini during his residence in America).

>*Illustrations.* Eight engravings of the author and other European performers.

>*Features.*   List of illustrations.

>*Actors.*   General.

278. *San Francisco Theatre Research: History of the San Francisco Theatre.*   20 vols.   San Francisco: Northern California Writers' Project of the Works Projects Administration, 1938-42.   Lengths of the volumes vary from 119 pp. to 397 pp.

>The purpose of this work is "to gather research data and write a series of monographs on the theatre and its people in San Francisco from 1849 to the present day [1938]."   The project provides "not only for extensive biographical treatment but also for detailed coverage of period history and significant phases and movements in the history of the drama and of opera."   This mimeographed work was compiled by a large staff of researchers and writers from scrap books, periodicals, memoirs, and "interviews with old time theatre people."   It offers an invaluable portrait of theatrical activity in San Francisco during the period

covered. Various volumes are devoted to individual actors or managers, playhouses, or special subjects (e.g., opera, foreign-language theatres, burlesque, little theatres, etc.). Through narration and quoted materials, the work provides factual data and evaluation and description of its subjects. In addition to the actors given prominent mention, scores of performers are mentioned briefly.

Illustrations. Vary from two to nineteen per volume, mostly photographs of theatres and theatre workers.

Features. Tables of contents (most volumes); lists of illustrations (some volumes); documentation varies from volume to volume (most sources of quotations are identified by author and/or title and/or date); bibliographies (all volumes); appendices vary from volume to volume (include such items as lists of roles, chronologies, lists of theatres, maps, etc.); indices (most volumes).

Actors. (Volume number in Parentheses). Edwin Booth (IV), Junius Brutus Booth, Jr. (IV), Lotta Crabtree (VI), Edwin Forrest (XI), Mrs. (Mariette Starfield) Judah (V), John McCullough (VI, XVI), Adah Isaacs Menken (V), James O'Neill (XX).

279. Schoberlin, Melvin. *From Candles to Footlights: A Biography of the Pikes Peak Theatre, 1859-1876.* Preface by Barrett H. Clark. Denver, Colorado: Fred A. Rosenstock, The Old West Publishing Company, 1941. xviii, 322 pp.

This book chronicles theatrical activities in Colorado, chiefly Denver, from the earliest performances in 1859 to the establishment of Colorado as a state in 1876. Drawing primarily upon periodicals of the period, the author presents a well-documented history, with specific dates, of the plays, players, playhouses, and managers of the territorial stage. Anecdotes, contemporary criticisms, and brief biographical sketches are included. Over eighty per cent of the volume concerns the post-1860 period.

Illustrations. Twenty, mostly photographs of people, theatres, and playbills.

Features. Preface by Barrett H. Clark; introduction; table of contents; thorough documentation; bibliography; appendix: "List of Colorado Theatres, 1859-1876" (includes locations and dates of openings).

Actors. John S. Langrishe.

280. Scott, Clement [William]. *The Drama of Yesterday & Today.* 2 vols. New York: Macmillan, 1899. Vol. I: xviii, 607 pp.; Vol. II: x, 581 pp.

The author prefaces this work by writing: "I shall be content. . .if it be acknowledged that no animosity has soiled the record of the past, and that I at least have remembered and tried to recall old scenes, old associations, old friendships, and celebrated players, with all the delightful and happy memories connected with them." The theatre reminiscences and history in this work deal with the English theatre during the period from the 1840s into the 1890s. The author includes his personal and critical recollections of many actors, including some descriptions of performances. He quotes liberally from previously published works by other authors.

Illustrations. Vol. I: Sixty-two, mostly photographs of actors.
Vol. II: Ninety-one, mostly photographs of actors.

Features. Preface (Vol. I); tables of contents (both volumes); lists of illustrations (both volumes); documentation; sources of quotations are identified by author index (Vol. II for both volumes).

> *Actors.* Dion Boucicault, John Sleeper Clarke, Charles Fechter, Joseph Jefferson III, Ada Rehan, E. A. Sothern.

281. Shattuck, Charles H[arlen]. *The Hamlet of Edwin Booth.* Urbana, Illinois, and Chicago: University of Illinois Press, ©1969. xxvii, 321 pp.

This volume traces the development of Edwin Booth's portrayal of Hamlet from 1853 to 1891, with additional comments on Booth's pesonality and other professional activities. Parts I and III survey Booth's career, emphasizing his Hamlet. Part II, the heart of the work (pp. 101-281), is a "reconstruction"—in minute detail—of Booth's performance of Hamlet at his own theatre in 1870. This reconstruction is based primarily on Charles Clarke's extraordinary and lengthy ("almost 60,000 words") description of the 1870 performance. The author utilizes a variety of published and unpublished material, including Booth's letters, promptbooks, and notebooks, in this impeccably scholarly work.

> *Illustrations.* Twenty-four, mostly scene designs for Edwin Booth's 1866 and 1870 productions of *Hamlet.*

> *Features.* Preface; introduction; table of contents; thorough documentation; index.

> *Actors.* Edwin Booth.

281a. —. *Shakespeare on the American Stage: From the Hallams to Edwin Booth.* Washington, D.C.: The Folger Shakespeare Library, ©1976. xiv, 170 pp.

Through examining major, representative actors who performed Shakespearean drama in America from the Hallams through Edwin Booth, the author illuminates the varying modes of presentation, while reconstructing the playing styles, strengths, and weaknesses of his subjects. Drawing primarily upon the actors' and their contempor-

aries' writings, this admirable volume presents performance description and evaluation for each of the subjects,
as well as including biographical information and other
historical data. Among the performers treated in the
essays are George Frederick Cooke, Kean, J. B. Booth,
Macready, and William E. Burton.

Illustrations. One hundred and six photographs, engravings, and paintings, mainly of theatre buildings and of actors in Shakespearean roles.

Features. Preface; introduction; table of contents; list
of illustrations; thorough documentation; index.

Actors. Edwin Booth, Charlotte Cushman, E. L. Davenport, Edwin Forrest, John McCullough.

282. Shaw, Dale. *Titans of the American Stage: Edwin Forrest, the Booths, the O'Neills.* Philadelphia: West-
minster Press, 1971. 160 pp.

This book contains popularly-written accounts of the lives
of Edwin Forrest, of Junius Brutus, Edwin, and John
Wilkes Booth, and of James and Eugene O'Neill. These
stories emphasize the most dramatic events in these men's
lives, but they provide little descriptive or critical material
concerning their acting or playwriting. Some excerpts
from personal letters and from contemporary newspaper
articles are included.

Illustrations. Twenty-four photographs and engravings of
theatre workers, playbills, buildings, and
newspaper clippings.

Features. Table of contents; brief bibliography; index.

Actors. Edwin Booth, John Wilkes Booth, Edwin Forrest, James O'Neill.

283. Shaw, [George] Bernard. *Dramatic Opinions and Essays,*

with an Apology. Ed., with "A Word on the Dramatic Opinions and Essays of Bernard Shaw," by James Huneker. 2 vols. New York: Brentano's, 1906. Vol. I: xxv, 449 pp.; Vol. II: vii, 470 pp.

Over one hundred selections from the author's dramatic criticisms for the London *Saturday Review,* 1895-98, comprise this work. Varying amounts of criticism concerning plays, producers, stagings, and actors are included. The first volume contains reviews of Augustin Daly's 1895 productions of *The Railroad of Love, The Two Gentlemen of Verona,* and *A Midsummer Night's Dream,* and of Mary Anderson's book *A Few Memories* (see 236). Interesting evaluations of Ada Rehan and Miss Anderson (Mme. de Navarro) are included. The second volume contains reviews of Daly's 1896 production of *The Countess Gucki* and of the 1898 production of *The Heart of Maryland,* with Mrs. Leslie Carter.

Illustrations. None.

Features. "A Word on the Dramatic Opinions and Essays of Bernard Shaw" by James Huneker (Vol. I); "The Author's Apology" (Vol. I); tables of contents (both volumes); documentation: sources of quotations are identified by author and/or title.

Actors. Ada Rehan.

284. Shaw, George Bernard. *Shaw's Dramatic Criticism (1895-98).* Selected by John F. Matthews. New York: Hill and Wang, 1959. viii, 306 pp.

Fifty-four selections from the author's *Saturday Review* articles, thirty-two of which are reprinted in entirety, comprise this book. The editor includes only a few reviews not contained in the earlier *Dramatic Opinions and Essays* (see 283), none of which expand the coverage of American actors. The reviews of Daly's productions of *A Midsummer Night's Dream* and *The Countess Gucki* and of Mrs. Carter's *The Heart of Maryland* are included.

Illustrations. None.

Features. Foreword by John F. Matthews; table of contents; index.

Actors. Ada Rehan.

284a. Sheaffer, Louis. *O'Neill: Son and Playwright.* Boston
Little, Brown, ©1968. xx, 543 pp.

Tracing Eugene O'Neill's life from his birth to 1920, this
excellent biography contains extensive factual and anecdotal material gleaned from hundreds of interviews, published materials, and private papers. The author emphasizes autobiographical material in O'Neill's plays, as well
as the playwright's relationship with his parents. The information on James O'Neill includes much biographical
data and some artistic evaluation, as well as considerable
analysis of his relationship with his son. Several other
late nineteenth-century actors are mentioned briefly.

Illustrations. Sixty-two, mainly photographs of Eugene
O'Neill, his family, and his friends.

Features. Foreword; acknowledgments; table of contents; list of illustrations; adequate documentation; bibliography; index.

Actors. James O'Neill.

285. Sherman, Robert L[owery]. *Actors and Authors, with
Composers and Managers Who Helped Make Them
Famous: A Chronological Record and Brief Biography
of Theatrical Celebrities from 1750 to 1950.* Chicago:
Robert L. Sherman, ©1951. 438 pp.

This volume contains an alphabetically-arranged collection of hundreds of brief biographical sketches. The
scope of the work is restricted to "performers who have
appeared on the stage of an American Theatre, or, [au-
thors] whose plays have been presented in such theatres,

regardless of their nativity. . .[also] composers and managers." The subjects are also limited to those who have been connected with " 'the legitimate stage.' " Not attempting to be comprehensive, the author narrows his selection to "those whose activity has helped the progress of the American theatre." Some information on numerous minor personnages is included. The sketches generally provide the barest indications of their subjects' activities. Frequently, important periods of the subjects' careers are ignored or given but slight notice.

Illustrations. None.

Features. Introduction.

Actors. General.

286. —. *Chicago Stage, Its Records and Achievements; Volume One: Gives a Complete Record of All Entertainments and, Substantially, the Cast of Every Play Presented in Chicago, On Its First Production in the City, from the Beginning of Theatricals in 1834 Down to the Last Before the Fire of 1871.* Chicago: Robert L. Sherman, ©1947. ii, 792 pp.

This book is a straightforward narrative of entertainments in Chicago, 1833-71. Cast lists for Chicago premieres are inserted in appropriate places in the record. Some brief biographical sketches of players and a few contemporary newspaper reviews are interspersed throughout the text.

Illustrations. Twenty photographs of people associated with the American theatre (small and of poor quality).

Features. Preface; list of illustrations; list of places of amusement in Chicago, 1833-71; index.

Actors. General.

287. —. *Drama Cyclopedia: A Bibliography of Plays and Play-*

ers. Chicago: The Author, ©1944. iii, 612 pp.

The bulk of this volume consists of a list of "substantially, every play produced in America by a professional company, from the first recorded in 1750, down to 1940." Only full-length, English-language plays and operas are included. The entries are arranged alphabetically (some errors) by title of play, and the following information is provided for each entry: title, author, city and year of first professional performance in America, and the name of "the principal, or at least a leading player." The total lack of documentation in this highly factual work suggests the advisability of verifying all data before utilizing it.

Illustrations. One photograph of the author.

Features. Preface.

Actors. General.

288. Skinner, Cornelia Otis. *Family Circle.* Boston: Houghton Mifflin, 1948. 310 pp.

The initial one-third of this biography of the Skinner family concerns the lives of Otis and Maud Durbin Skinner to 1902, the year when the author was born. The second third follows these three Skinners to 1911. The remainder of the book continues the narrative to the author's New York stage debut in the early 1920s. Anecdotes, letters (mostly by Otis Skinner), and the author's opinions, but few dates, are included.

Illustrations. Seven photographs and one painting of members of the Skinner family.

Features. Table of contents; list of illustrations; documentation: sources of quotations are usually identified by author.

Actors. John Drew II, Maud Durbin, Helena Modjeska, Ada Rehan, Otis Skinner.

289. Skinner, Maud [Durbin], and Otis Skinner. *One Man in His Time: The Adventures of H. Watkins, Strolling Player, 1845-1863, from His Journal.* Philadelphia: University of Pennsylvania Press, 1938. xvii, 258 pp.

This book consists of entries selected from Harry Watkins' personal journal, 1845-63, and a supplementary commentary by the Skinners. Watkins, who died in 1893, was an itinerant actor during the mid-nineteenth century. Brief comments on other actors, such as Junius Brutus Booth, Edwin Forrest, and Matilda Heron, are included in both the journal extracts and the commentary. Very little of the volume relates to Watkins' life and career after 1860.

Illustrations. Eight photographs, engravings, and paintings of various actors.

Features. Foreword by Otis Skinner; preface by Maud [Durbin] Skinner; table of contents; list of illustrations; index.

Actors. Harry Watkins.

290. Skinner, Otis. *Footlights and Spotlights: Recollections of My Life on the Stage.* Indianapolis, Indiana: Bobbs-Merrill, 1924; rpt. Westport, Connecticut: Greenwood, 1972. 367 pp.

After a brief description of his early life, the author recounts his forty-six years in the theatre (at the time of writing). From his early years as an actor in various stock companies and in support of touring stars (such as Barrett, Booth, and Mme. Modjeska) through his own development as a star actor, the author provides a richly varied and humorous look at himself, his fellow actors, and some of his non-theatrical friends. Primarily anecdotal, this volume also contains brief personal and professional evaluations of many actors. Statements by the author and by Joseph Jefferson III on the nature of acting are included. This book offers a readable and valuable description of working conditions and stage practices in the late nineteenth-century American theatre.

Illustrations. Forty-nine, mostly photographs, of the author, other actors, a few non-actors, and other subjects related to the author's life.

Features. Table of contents; list of illustrations; index.

Actors. Lawrence Barrett, Edwin Booth, Fanny Janauschek, Joseph Jefferson III, Margaret Mather, Helena Modjeska, Ada Rehan, Otis Skinner.

291. —. *The Last Tragedian: Booth Tells His Own Story.* New York: Dodd, Mead, 1939. xi, 213 pp.

Most of this book is composed of letters written by Edwin Booth, principally on business and personal matters, to Dave Anderson, Richard Henry Stoddard, Elizabeth Stoddard, and Lawrence Barrett. Several letters from Mary Devlin (Booth's first wife) to Elizabeth Stoddard and a few letters to or about Booth and written by the Stoddards. Adam Badeau, and Barrett are also included. Skinner's commentary, personal recollections, and appreciation of Booth complete the volume. The Booth letters were written between 1860 and approximately 1890. Most of the letters are dated.

Illustrations. Eleven photographs, sketches, and paintings of Edwin Booth, members of his family, and his associates.

Features. Foreword; table of contents; list of illustrations.

Actors. David C. Anderson, Lawrence Barrett, Edwin Booth.

292. Smith, Harry B[ache]. *First Nights and First Editions.* Foreword by William Lyon Phelps. Boston: Little, Brown, 1931. x, 325 pp.

These autobiographical reminiscences by the playwright-bibliophile-journalist form a roughly chronological account of his life from the Civil War to World War I. Having written over three hundred plays, mostly comic operas, the author includes material on the development and production of many of his plays and recollections of numerous performers, composers, and managers. Among the theatre personalities whom the author discusses are Francis Wilson, DeWolf Hopper, Reginald DeKoven, Victor Herbert, Charles Frohman, and Florenz Ziegfeld.

Illustrations. Nineteen photographs of the author, of his friends, and of autographed title-pages, flyleaves, etc., from works in his book and manuscript collection.

Features. Foreword by William Lyon Phelps; list of illustrations; general index; index to plays.

Actors. DeWolf Hopper, Francis Wilson.

293. Sothern, E[dward] H[ugh]. *Julia Marlowe's Story.* Ed. by Fairfax Downey. New York: Rinehart, ©1954. xiii, 237 pp.

When the author died in 1933 this biography of his wife was still in manuscript. Only after Miss Marlowe's death in 1950 did the editor prepare the work for publication. The author traces his subject's life, emphasizing her stage career, from her birth in 1865 to the cessation of their co-starring activities in 1924. Relating the story of her life "as she has so often repeated it to me," the author phrases the work in the first person, as if it were Miss Marlowe's autobiography. The editor contributes explanatory notes and an additional chapter which sketches Miss Marlowe's and the author's lives to their deaths. Narration, anecdotes, descriptions of performances, and opinions on theatrical topics are included, along with Arthur Symonds' essay "Great Acting in English." Few dates are specified. Approximately five-sixths of the book concerns the pre-1911 period.

Illustrations. Ten photographs and paintings, mostly of Julia Marlowe and the author.

Features. Dedication by Julia Marlowe Sothern; author's foreword; editor's foreword; table of contents; list of illustrations; documentation: sources of quotations are identified by author and/or title.

Actors. Ada Dow, Joseph Haworth, Julia Marlowe, E. H. Sothern.

294. Sothern, Edward H[ugh]. *The Melancholy Tale of "Me": My Remembrances.* New York: Charles Scribner's Sons, 1916. xvi, 409 pp.

In this volume of reminiscences the author offers scattered anecdotes and reflections about himself, members of his family, and some friends. Over one-half of the book concerns the years prior to the author's acting debut in 1879, and little of the information relates to the period after 1890. Most of the materials pertain to offstage life, with few dates or descriptions of stage events mentioned. Some general indications of the author's attitudes toward theatre are included, but he refrains from making specific statements about his acting. In addition to those people noted below, the author comments briefly on such actors as Charles W. Couldock, Maude Adams, Edwin Booth, and Richard Mansfield.

Illustrations. Sixty, mostly photographs of the author, members of his family, and his associates.

Features. Preface; table of contents; list of illustrations; documentation: sources of quotations are identified by author and/or title; index.

Actors. Charles P. Flockton, John McCullough, E. A. Sothern, E. H. Sothern, Mrs. J. R. Vincent.

295. Sprague, Arthur Colby. *Shakespearian Players and Performances.* Cambridge, Massachusetts: Harvard University Press, 1953. xi, 222 pp.

Ibid. Rpt., with a new preface to the Greenwood re-

print by the author. New York: Greenwood, 1969.
viii, 222 pp.

Most of this volume consists of the author's attempted reconstruction of eight "great Shakespearian performances," such as Betterton's Hamlet, Mrs. Siddons'
Lady Macbeth, and Irving's Shylock. Edwin Booth—as
Iago—is the only American actor represented. Centering
upon Booth's performance opposite Irving's Othello in
the famous 1880 production at the Lyceum Theatre, the
author utilizes British reviews of the production, Booth's
own notes on Iago, and other materials. A generalized
sketch of the performance, with some descriptions of
specific stage business, is provided. The volume concludes with an appraisal of William Poel's contributions to
Shakespearian staging and comments on various Shakespearian performances which the author had witnessed.

Illustrations. Twelve photographs, paintings, and engravings, mostly of actors in Shakespearian roles.

Features. Preface to the Greenwood reprint (1969 ed.
only); preface; introduction; table of contents;
list of illustrations; thorough documentation;
indices of Shakespearian plays and of players
and producers.

Actors. Edwin Booth.

296. Stebbins, Emma (ed.). *Charlotte Cushman: Her Letters
and Memories of Her Life, Edited by Her Friend.* Boston and New York: Houghton, Mifflin, ©1878; rpt.
New York: Benjamin Blom, 1972. viii, 308 pp.

This volume is primarily composed of a chronological
view of Charlotte Cushman's life which includes copious
quotations from the actress' autobiographical statements,
her letters, correspondence to or about her, and periodical
articles. The editor contributes a linking narrative and
comments on various subjects related to Miss Cushman,
for example, dramatic readings, the actress' illness, and
the role of Meg Merrilies. Biographical data, Miss Cush-

man's opinions on many subjects, appreciations of her acting, and occasional brief descriptions of her acting are included. Slightly less than one-half of the volume pertains to the post-1860 period.

Illustrations. Two photographs, one of Charlotte Cushman and one of a bust of Miss Cushman.

Features. Table of contents; documentation: sources of quotations are identified by author and/or title; index.

Actors. Charlotte Cushman.

297. Stedman, Edmund Clarence. *Genius and Other Essays.* New York: Moffat, Yard, 1911. vi, 288 pp.

This volume collects twenty-five essays by the author which were originally published or read during the period from 1864 to 1905. Included is an essay on Edwin Booth which was first published in 1866. In this article, the author evaluates Booth's acting, with special reference to the roles of Hamlet, Richelieu, and Iago, based on personal observation. Some descriptions of Booth's performances, along with the author's general appreciation of the actor's strengths and weaknesses, are contained in this essay.

Illustrations. None.

Features. Table of contents.

Actors. Edwin Booth.

298. Steinberg, Mollie B. *The History of the Fourteenth Street Theatre.* Introd. by Eva LeGallienne. New York: Lincoln MacVeagh, The Dial Press, 1931. xiii, 105 pp.

This sketchy history of the Fourteenth Street Theatre, also known as the Lyceum Theatre and the Civic Repertory Theatre, from its opening in 1866 to 1931 contains many specific dates of attractions, some partial cast lists, and some comments on individual actors. The sketches of actors, such as Laura Keene, Edwin Forrest, and Clara Morris, bear little relevance to the Fourteenth Street Theatre, excepting dates of engagements. The first two-thirds of the text pertains to the 1866-1911 period; the remainder concerns Eva LaGallienne's 1926-31 involvement with the Civic Repertory Theatre.

Illustrations. Sixteen, mostly photographs of actors and reproductions of playbills.

Features. Foreword; introduction by Eva LeGallienne; table of contents; list of illustrations; documentation: sources of quotations are usually identified by author and title.

Actors. Edwin Booth.

299. Stoddart, J[ames] H[enry], [Jr.]. *Recollections of a Player.* Prefatory note by William Winter. New York: Century, 1902. xxi, 255 pp.

This autobiographical narrative traces the author's life from his youth in the 1930s through the mid-1890s, emphasizing his acting career. His experiences in Britain prior to 1854 and in America after that year, principally with the Wallack and Palmer companies, are discussed. The author relates numerous anecdotes and evaluates the personal and professional qualities of himself and many of his fellow actors. Among the players mentioned briefly are Charles Coghlan, Maurice Barrymore, and Charles W. Couldock. Nearly one-half of the text relates to the post-1860 period.

Illustrations. Thirty-seven photographs of the author, other actors, and playbills.

Features. Prefatory note by William Winter; list of illustrations.

Actors. James H. Stoddart, Jr.

300. Stone, Fred [Andrew]. *Rolling Stone.* New York: Whittlesey House (McGraw-Hill), ©1945. vi, 246 pp.

> This anecdotal autobiography traces the author's life from his childhood in the 1870s to World War II. Some information is included on the author's work in the circus, variety, musical comedy, and films, as well as on his off-stage life. Some descriptions of his preparation and performance of specialty acts are included. Criticism is not provided and specific dates are not indicated.

> *Illustrations.* Eighteen photographs of the author, his family, and his friends.

> *Features.* Table of contents.

> *Actors.* Dave Montgomery, Ed Stone, Fred Stone.

301. Storms, A. D. (comp.). *The Players Blue Book.* Worcester, Massachusetts: Sutherland & Storms, ©1901. 304 pp.

> The aim of this book is to present one hundred and forty-nine "photographs and short biobraphies of those actors and actresses best known at the present time and to furnish in convenient form a souvenir of this age of the drama in America from the viewpoint of those who interpret it." The biographical sketches emphasize facts, with some specific dates and occasional anecdotes.

> *Illustrations.* One hundred and forty-nine portrait photographs of American actors.

> *Features.* Preface; index (in effect, a table of contents).

> *Actors.* General.

302. Strang, Lewis C[linton]. *Celebrated Comedians of Light Opera and Musical Comedy in America.* Boston: L. C. Page, 1901; rpt. New York: Benjamin Blom, 1971. 293 pp.

Sixteen of the nineteen chapters in this book are devoted to appreciations of individual comic actors in musical plays. Some attention is given to the subjects' performances in non-musical drama. The essays contain varying amounts of biographical data, autobiographical statements, performance descriptions, and the author's evaluations.

Illustrations. Twenty-five photographs of actors.

Features. Table of contents; list of illustrations; documentation: sources of quotations are identified by author; index.

Actors. Henry Clay Barnabee, Digby Bell, Richard Carle, Peter F. Dailey, Dan Daly, Frank Daniels, Jefferson DeAngelis, Henry E. Dixey, Richard Golden, Otis Harlan, DeWolf Hopper, Walter Jones, James T. Powers, Thomas Q. Seabrooke, Jerome Sykes, Francis Wilson.

303. —. *Famous Actors of the Day in America.* 2 series. Boston: L. C. Page, 1900-02. First Series: 354 pp.; Second Series: x, 343 pp.

First Series: " 'Famous Actors,' as a companion volume to 'Famous Actresses' [First Series], follows the general plan of that book" (see 304). Chapters on twenty-five American actors prominent at the end of the nineteenth century are included.

Second Series: This is a companion volume to the Second Series of *Famous Actresses* and follows the same general plan as that work (see 304). Chapters on the nineteen American actors noted below, as well as on John Hare, and Edward S. Willard, are included.

Illustrations. First Series: Fifteen photographs of actors. *Second Series:* Twenty-five photographs of actors.

Features. (both volumes). Preface; table of contents; list of illustrations; documentation: sources of quotations are identified by author and/or title and/or date; index.

Actors. First Series: William H. Crane, J. E. Dodson, John Drew II, William Faversham, William Gillette, Nat C. Goodwin, James K. Hackett, Joseph Haworth, James A. Herne, E. M. Holland, Joseph Jefferson III, Henry Jewett, Herbert Kelcey, Wilton Lackaye, Melbourne MacDowell, Richard Mansfield, Robert B. Mantell, John Mason, Henry Miller, James O'Neill, Roland Reed, Stuart Robson, Sol Smith Russell, Otis Skinner, E. H. Sothern.
Second Series: Maclyn Arbuckle, Edwin Arden, John Blair, William H. Crane, John Drew II, William Faversham, William Gillette, Nat C. Goodwin, James A. Herne, Henry Jewett, Louis Mann, Richard Mansfield, John Mason, Henry Miller, James O'Neill, Charles J. Richman, Stuart Robson, E. H. Sothern, Fritz Williams.

304. —. *Famous Actresses of the Day in America.* Boston: L. C. Page, 1899-1901. First Series: 361 pp.; Second Series: 340 pp.

First Series: This volume consists of essays on actresses prominent on the American stage at the end of the nineteenth century. Varying quantities of biographical data, anecdotes, and critical estimates comprise each chapter. The criticisms, either of general performance qualities or of a specific characterization, are mostly the author's, but some reviews by other critics are cited. Many chapters contain descriptions of performances or quoted comments by the subjects.

Second Series: This volume is primarily devoted to criticisms of specific performances during the 1899/1900 and 1900/01 theatrical seasons in America. Criticisms of plays and individual performances, some description of performances, and, for actresses not included in the First Series, biographical data are included. Almost all of the critical comments are the author's.

Illustrations. First Series: Fifteen photographs of actresses.

Second Series: Twenty-five photographs of actresses.

Features. (both volumes). Preface; table of contents; list of illustrations; documentation: sources of quotations are identified by author and/or title and/or date; index.

Actors. First Series: Maude Adams, Viola Allen, Margaret Anglin, Julia Arthur, Blanche Bates, Marie Burroughs, Mrs. Leslie Carter, Rose Coghlan, Ida Conquest, Elsie DeWolf, Maxine Elliott, Minnie Maddern Fiske, Virginia Harned, Isabel Irving, May Irwin, Kathryn Kidder, Lillian Lawrence, Sarah Cowell LeMoyne, Mary Mannering, Julia Marlowe, Helena Modjeska, Ada Rehan, Corona Riccardo, May Robson, Annie Russell, Effie Shannon, Mary Shaw, Odette Tyler, Blanche Walsh.

Second Series: Maude Adams, Viola Allen, Margaret Anglin, Valerie Bergere, Amelia Bingham, Mrs. Leslie Carter, Ida Conquest, Henrietta Crosman, Phoebe Davies, Maxine Elliott, Minnie Maddern Fiske, Grace George, Anna Held, Sarah Cowell LeMoyne, Mary Mannering, Julia Marlowe, Ada Rehan, Annie Russell, Mary Sanders, Mary Shaw, Elizabeth Tyree.

305. —. *Players and Plays of the Last Quarter Century: An Historical Summary of Causes and a Critical Review of Conditions as Existing in the American Theatre at the Close of the Nineteenth Century.* 2 vols. Boston: L. C. Page, 1902. Vol. I: x, 325 pp.; Vol. II: 335 pp.

The author surveys conditions in the English-speaking theatre, with special reference to America. The second volume emphasizes the last two decades of the nineteenth century; the first volume, as a preface to the second, scans

English and American drama and theatre from the Restor-ation to the 1880s. Volume I ("The Theatre of Yester-day") consists mainly of notes, usually brief, on tragic actors from Betterton to Edwin Booth and on comic actors from Samuel Foote to William Warren, Jr. These comments include biographical data, appreciations, and, occasionally, criticisms of specific characterizations. Volume II ("The Theatre of To-Day") pays particular attention to late-nineteenth-century English and American dramatists and plays, but also includes critical and descrip-tive comments on several actors.

Illustrations. Vol. I: Thirty-three, mostly photographs and engravings of actors.
Vol. II: Thirty-three, mostly photographs of actors.

Features. Preface (Vol. I); table of contents (each volume for that volume); lists of illustrations (each volume for that volume); documentation: sources of quotations are identified by author and/or title (both volumes); indices (each volume for that volume).

Actors. Vol. I: Lawrence Barrett, Edwin Booth, William Warren, Jr.
Vol. II: Henrietta Crosman, Minnie Maddern Fiske, William Gillette, Clara Morris.

305a. Taylor, Dwight. *Blood-and-Thunder.* New York: Athe-neum, 1962. xi, 232 pp.

This memoir of the relationship between the author and his father—playwright/manager Charles A. Taylor—consists mainly of the author's reminiscences and his recounting of his father's tales. The author includes some early on and off stage memories of Laurette Taylor, his mother. The volume contains few dates and no documentation. The author notes, ". . .it was my father's nature to 'adorn a tale'—a propensity which I have inherited."

Illustrations. None.

Features. Foreword; table of contents; no documentation.

Actors. Laurette Taylor.

306. Thomas, Augustus. *The Print of My Remembrance.* New
York: Charles Scribner's Sons, 1952. ix, 477 pp.

The author presents a chronological memoir of his life
from childhood memories during the Civil War into 1911,
with occasional remarks concerning later years. Recollections of friends and associates, sundry opinions, and anecdotes predominate. A substantial portion of the material
pertains to the author's theatrical, mainly playwriting,
experiences. Among the many actors mentioned briefly
are William J. Florence, Julia Marlowe, Nat C. Goodwin,
and John Mason.

Illustrations. Twenty-eight drawings and photographs of
the author and many of his friends and
associates.

Features. Dedication; table of contents; list of illustrations; appendix: chronological list of the author's plays, 1875-1921, with year and city of
premiere.

Actors. Maurice Barrymore.

307. Timberlake, Craig. *The Life and Work of David Belasco,
the Bishop of Broadway.* New York: Library Publishers, ©1954. 491 pp.

In this fine narrative and interpretation of David Belasco's
life and career the author includes specific biographical
data, letters to and from Belasco, the subject's autobiographical statements, excerpts from court transcripts,
and previously published appreciations of Belasco and his
productions. The emphasis is on Belasco's career and
methods as a producer and director, but considerable
attention is also paid too his personality. Approximately

three-quarters of the text concerns the pre-1911 period. In addition to those noted below, the author includes brief comments on dozens of actors, such as James A. Herne, James O'Neill, George Arliss, and Frances Starr.

Illustrations. Eighty-three, mostly photographs of David Belasco and actors.

Features. Acknowledgements; table of contents; list of illustrations; thorough documentation; bibliography; "Appendix A: Letters of Mrs. Leslie Carter to David Belasco"; "Appendix B: Chronology of [Belasco's] New York Productions" (includes title, playwright, producer, director, theatre, date of premiere, and number of performances); index.

Actors. Blanche Bates, David Belasco, Mrs. Leslie Carter, David Warfield.

308. Tompkins, Eugene, compiled with the assistance of Quincy Kilby. *The History of the Boston Theatre, 1854-1901.* Boston and New York: Houghton Mifflin, 1908. xvi, 551 pp.

This volume consists of a season-by-season record of the Boston Theatre from its opening in 1854 until the author's retirement from management in 1901. Lists of featured attractions, with the commencement dates of engagements and, usually, indications of repertoires, comprise the bulk of the volume. Anecdotes, narration, cast lists, and financial statements are occasionally inserted. Over eighty per cent of the book concerns the post-1860 period.

Illustrations. Hundreds, mostly photographs of performers.

Features. Preface by Eugene Tompkins; table of contents; list of illustrations; documentation: sources of quotations are identified by author and/or title and/or date; index.

Actors. General.

309. Townsend, George Alfred. *The Life, Crime, and Capture of John Wilkes Booth, with a Full Sketch of the Conspiracy of Which He Was the Leader, and the Pursuit, Trial, and Execution of His Accomplices.* New York: Dick & Fitzgerald, 1865. iv, 64 pp.

> Ibid. Reissue, containing some additional matter. New York: Dick & Fitzgerald, 1865. iv, 79 pp.

> *1st ed.:* This book contains several articles which the author originally wrote in his capacity as the Washington correspondent of the New York *World.* The articles describe events surrounding the assassination of Abraham Lincoln, including factual data, descriptions of events, and some speculation. One letter is a biographical sketch of John Wilkes Booth which, although emphasizing his "ribald" life, contains some information on his theatrical career and a brief estimate of his acting.

> *Reissue:* This edition does not alter the materials pertaining to Booth's theatrical career.

> *Illustrations.* (both editions).   One engraving of John Wilkes Booth.

> *Features.* (both editions). Preface.

> *Actors.* (both editions). John Wilkes Booth.

310. [Townsend, Margaret] , Margaret [pseud.] . *Theatrical Sketches: Here and There with Prominent Actors.* New York: Merriam, ©1894. vii, 217 pp.

> This book is composed of several anecdotal, gossipy chapters dealing with actors, singers, and theatrical incidents. Some of the materials derive from the author's experiences as a playwright. Some humorous letters and verse by Louis James are quoted.

Illustrations. Seven photographs of actors and managers.

Features. Table of contents; list of illustrations.

Actors. Kyrle Bellew, Louis James, Cora Urquhart Potter, Lester Wallack.

311. Towse, John Ranken. *Sixty Years of the Theatre: An Old Critic's Memories.* New York: Funk & Wagnalls, 1916. xvi, 464 pp.

The author, long a respected drama critic for the New York *Evening Post,* recollects players and plays he had seen during the last half of the nineteenth century and the first decade of the twentieth. Most of the author's comments are criticisms and descriptions of various actors. In addition to those noted below, brief comments on several American actors, mostly members of the theatrical companies of Lester Wallack, Augustin Daly, and A. M. Palmer, are included, along with more substantial chapters on many visiting players, such as Irving, Salvini, Tree, and Ristori.

Illustrations. Ninety-three, mostly photographs and engravings of actors.

Features. Preface; table of contents; list of illustrations.

Actors. Mary Anderson, Edwin Booth, Charles Coghlan, Charlotte Cushman, E. L. Davenport, Charles Fechter, Minnie Maddern Fiske, John Gilbert, Fanny Janauschek, Joseph Jefferson III, Richard Mansfield, Robert B. Mantell, Julia Marlowe, Helena Modjeska, Clara Morris, Ada Rehan, E. H. Sothern, Lester Wallack.

312. Truax, Sarah. *A Woman of Parts: Memories of a Life on Stage.* Foreword by Guthrie McClintic. New York: Longmans, 1949. 247 pp.

The author presents a narrative of her life, emphasizing

her years as a stock company actress from her debut in 1894 into the 1910s. Personal anecdotes and comments on theatrical conditions predominate. Some reviews and a few specific dates are included. In addition to the players listed below, the author commets briefly on such other actors as Maud Durbin Skinner, Frederick Warde, Grace George, and Edward Morgan.

Illustrations. Seventeen photographs of the author and her associates.

Features. Foreword by Guthrie McClintic; acknowledgements; table of contents; list of illustrations; documentation: sources of quotations are identified by author and/or title and/or date; appended "nearly complete" list of plays in which the author "enacted the principal feminine role"; index.

Actors. Guy Bates Post, Otis Skinner, Sarah Truax.

313. [Trumble, Alfred]. *Footlight Favorites. A Collection of Popular American and European Actresses in Various Roles in Which They Have Become Famous, with Biographical Sketches Compiled by a Well-Known Author and Journalist Expressly for This Work.* New York: at the National Police Gazette Office (by Richard K. Fox), [1881]. 56 pp.

Twenty-five engravings of women entertainers, accompanied by brief biographical sketches, comprise this book. The ladies were actresses, singers, dancers, and variety artistes who were popular at the time of publication. The biographical sketches contain anecdotes, generalized appraisal, superfluous comments, and occasional factual data. Among the performers included are Jennie Yeamans, Minnie Palmer, Pauline Markham, Adelaide Neilson, and Sarah Bernhardt.

Illustrations. Twenty-five engravings of actresses.

Features. Prefatory note.

Actors. General.

314. Trumble, Alfred. *Great Artists of the American Stage. A Portrait Gallery of the Leading Actors and Actresses in America. With Critical Biographies.* Part I. New York: Richard K. Fox, 1882. 73 pp.

> Brief factual biographies, short critical estimates, and engravings of thirty American actors comprise the bulk of this volume. Although part of a projected series of books on American actors, this was the only volume published. It provides useful information on some little-remembered actors and critical generalizations on the performers' styles and qualities. Among the actors included are Francis S. Chanfrau, Kate Claxton, Henry Crisp, and John McCullough.

> *Illustrations.* Thirty portrait engravings of actors.

> *Features.* Preface.

Actors. General.

315. Tyler, George C[rouse], in collaboration with J[oseph] C[hamberlain] Furnas. *Whatever Goes up—, The Hazardous Fortunes of a Natural Born Gambler.* Introd. by Booth Tarkington. Indianapolis, Indiana: Bobbs-Merrill, ©1934. 317 pp.

> This anecdotal narrative proceeds in generally chronological sequence from the 1870s through the 1920s, emphasizing the author's theatrical ventures—chiefly those as a producer. Over two-thirds of the book concerns the pre-1911 period, but specific dates are not indicated. The author comments on many playwrights, producers, and actors, including among the latter Charles Coghlan, James O'Neill, Viola Allen, and Dion Boucicault.

> *Illustrations.* Twenty-nine, mostly photographs of actors.

> *Features.* Introduction by Booth Tarkington; table of

contents; list of illustrations; index.

Actors. Charles Coghlan.

316. Veiller, Bayard. *Fun I've Had.* New York: Reynal & Hitchcock, ©1941. 373 pp.

The author relies upon his memory in writing this informal autobiography covering the period from the 1870s through the 1930s. Drawing from his long experience as a playwright, press agent, and screenwriter, the author reminisces about numerous theatre workers of his acquaintance, including such performers as Henry Miller, Edwin Booth, Rose Coghlan, Joseph Jefferson III, the Lunts and many more. Anecdotes and brief evaluations are included.

Illustrations. Thirteen drawings and photographs, mostly of the author's acquaintances.

Features. Index.

Actors. General.

317. Wagenknecht, Edward. *Merely Players.* Norman, Oklahoma: University of Oklahoma Press, ©1966. xiv, 270 pp.

This book is composed of eight "psychographs" of famous actors: Garrick, Edmund Kean, W. C. Macready, Henry Irving, and the four Americans noted below. Each essay includes sections devoted to its subject's biography, acting style, attitude toward theatre, and personal characteristics. The author quotes liberally from the subjects' writings and previously published material about his subjects, interjects his own evaluations, and, occasionally, makes conjectures.

Illustrations. Twenty-six photographs, engravings, paintings, and drawings of actors.

Features. Preface; table of contents; list of illustrations;
documentation: some sources of quotations
are partially identified; discursive bibliography;
index.

Actors. Edwin Booth, Edwin Forrest, Joseph Jefferson
III, Richard Mansfield.

318. —. *Seven Daughters of the Theatre: Jenny Lind, Sarah
Bernhardt, Ellen Terry, Julia Marlowe, Isadora Dun-
can, Mary Garden, Marilyn Monroe.* Norman, Oklahoma: University of Oklahoma Press, ©1964. x, 234
pp.

The essay on Julia Marlowe, originally published during
1959 in *Modern Drama,* contains biographical data, information concerning her personality, and material on her
approaches to acting and to theatre. Quotations from the
actress and anecdotes are included, but no sources of materials are indicated. The author also recounts a brief
meeting which he had with Miss Marlowe (aged eighty-
one) in 1946.

Illustrations. Thirty, mostly photographs of actresses.

Features. Foreword; table of contents; list of illustrations; little documentation; discursive bibliography; index.

Actors. Julia Marlowe.

319. Wallack, [John Johnstone] Lester. *Memories of Fifty
Years.* Ed., with an introd. and a biographical sketch,
by Laurence Hutton. New York: Charles Scribner's
Sons, 1889; rpt. New York: Benjamin Blom, 1969.
xiv, 232 pp.

In the preface, Laurence Hutton accurately describes the
contents of this volume as papers which "do not pretend
to be complete or consecutive; or even to be what is
termed literature: [they are] merely the Social and Pro-

fessional Memories of Half a Century." These reminiscences, recorded by a stenographer and arranged by Hutton "as far as possible in chronological order," are primarily anecdotes about Wallack's friends and fellow-actors. The author also describes his method for preparing a role and includes some autobiographical information. The memories pertain almost exclusively to the author's life prior to 1860. The editor's biographical sketch of the actor covers the whole of the actor's life and provides many specific dates.

Illustrations. Sixty-seven engravings, mostly of actors and theatres.

Features. Preface by Laurence Hutton; list of chapters; list of illustrations; biographical sketch of Lester Wallack by Hutton; list of characters played by Lester Wallack; index.

Actors. Lester Wallack.

320. Walsh, Townsend. *The Career of Dion Boucicault.* New York: Dunlap Society, 1915; rpt. New York: Benjamin Blom, 1967. xviii, 224 pp.

Over two-thirds of this chronicle of Dion Boucicault's life and career concerns the post-1860 period. The anecdotes, narration, and evaluations of his activities in America, England, and Ireland emphsize his playwriting and theatre management efforts. Some material on his acting, directing, and personality are included. The volume contains numerous quotations from Boucicault's autobiographical writings and letters, comments by his critics and his associates, and specific dates of his activities.

Illustrations. Nine, mostly photographs, of Dion Boucicault and of scenes from his plays.

Features. Preface; table of contents; list of illustrations; documentation: sources of quotations are identified by author and/or title and/or date; appendices: "Songs by Boucicault," "Appearances of the Boucicaults in Dublin" (chronological list including dates, theatres, and repertoire), "Quotable Extracts [from Boucicault's writings]," and "Chronological List of Boucicault's Dramatic Works."

Actors. Dion Boucicault.

321. Ward, Genevieve, and Richard Whiteing. *Both Sides of the Curtain.* New York: Cassell, 1918. 292 pp.

Aided by Whiteing, a friend of over forty years, Miss Ward provides autobiographical reminiscences of her operatic and theatrical career from the mid-nineteenth century to the time of writing. Biographical data, anecdotes, opinions on numerous professional and social acquaintances, and comments on various topics, mostly concerning England, comprise this volume. Some selections from letters and reviews are also included.

Illustrations. Twenty-six photographs and paintings, mostly of Genevieve Ward.

Features. Table of contents; list of illustrations; index.

Actors. Genevieve Ward.

322. Warde, Frederick [B.]. *Fifty Years of Make-Believe.* New York: International Press Syndicate (M. M. Marcy), 1920; Los Angeles: Times-Mirror Press, 1923. 314 pp.

Emphasizing his theatrical career, the author recounts his life from 1851 through 1919. Narration, anecdotes, evaluations, and some descriptions are included. Over two-thirds of the volume concerns the author's American experiences beginning in 1874. Most of the earlier portion relates to his acting in English provincial theatres. Among the actors whom the author discusses briefly are Charlotte Cushman, E. L. Davenport, and Mrs. D. P. Bowers.

Illustrations. Thirty-two photographs of the author and of other actors.

Features. Introduction; table of contents; list of illustrations; documentation: sources of quotations are identified by author and/or title and, rarely, date.

Actors. Lawrence Barrett, Edwin Booth, Louis James, John McCullough, Frederick Warde.

323. —. *The Fools of Shakespeare: An Interpretation of Their Wit, Wisdom, and Personalities.* New York: McBride, Nast, 1913. 214 pp.

Ibid. Los Angeles: Times-Mirror Press, 1923; rpt. Folcroft, Pennsylvania: Folcroft Library Editions, 1971. 244 pp.

Both editions: This book is devoted to the author's interpretations of Shakespeare's "fools," based on the idea that "Shakespeare, being an actor, wrote these plays to be acted," rather than to be criticized for literary quality. Included are some brief descriptions of performances, which were witnessed by the author, by such actors as Stuart Robson and James Lewis.

Illustrations. Six photographs and engravings of actors in "fool" roles.

Features. Preface; introduction; table of contents; list of illustrations.

Actors. Frederick Warde.

324. [Waters], Clara Erskine Clement. *Charlotte Cushman.* Boston: James R. Osgood, 1882. ix, 193 pp.

This volume is composed of three sections: a professional biography of Charlotte Cushman by Mrs. Waters (pp. 1-147), two letters by Miss Cushman (pp. 148-55), and a reminiscence of the actress by William Thomas Wins-borough Ball. The biography is a chronological narrative of Miss Cushman's life, emphasizing her acting career. Factual data, critical and descriptive materials, tributes, and some anecdotes are included. Numerous and, frequently, lengthy quotations are drawn from the writings and speeches of critics, friends, and fellow-actors of the great actress. One of the two letters presents advice from Miss Cushman to a neophyte actress and the other letter details Miss Cushman's religious beliefs. Ball's essay includes his critical and descriptive recollections of the actress' major characterizations.

Illustrations. Seven engravings and photographs of Charlotte Cushman and of people and things associated with her.

Features. Preface; table of contents; list of illustrations; documentation: sources of quotations are identified by author and/or title; index.

Actors. Charlotte Cushman.

325. Watson, Margaret G. *Silver Theatre: Amusements of the Mining Frontier in Early Nevada, 1850 to 1864.* Glendale, California: Arthur H. Clark, 1964. 387 pp.

Including copious quotations from contemporary sources, principally newspapers, this volume chronicles entertainment activities in early Nevada through the end of 1864, the year in which Nevada became a state. Factual and anecdotal materials on entertainments and entertainers are combined with social and economic history in this well-researched and readable work.

Illustrations. Thirty-five photographs, woodcuts, and drawings of people and things associated with early entertainments in Nevada.

Features. Preface; table of contents; list of illustrations; thorough documentation; bibliography; appended list of performances of individual plays

in Nevada, 1860-64 ("Only those plays specifically mentioned in the newspapers, handbills,
and programs are included along with the
known date given"); index.

Actors. General.

326. Whiffen, .Mrs. Thomas [Blance Galton] . *Keeping Off the
Shelf.* New York: E. P. Dutton, ©1928. viii, 203 pp.

In an anecdotal narrative, the author traces her life from
her youth in the mid-nineteenth century to 1906, as well
as offering random reminiscences and bits of philosophy.
She includes brief personal and professional comments on
numerous theatre workers, among them being such actors
as Lotta Crabtree, Helena Modjeska, Henry Miller, and
Steele Mackaye. She provides little critical or descriptive
material concerning performances and she usually dates
events only by year.

Illustrations. Twenty-two drawings, photographs, and engravings, mostly of the author and other
actors.

Features. Table of contents; list of illustrations.

Actors. Thomas Whiffen, Mrs. Thomas Whiffen.

327. Whiting, Lilian. *Kate Field: A Record.* Boston: Little,
Brown, 1900. ix, 610 pp.

This narrative of Kate Field's life (1838-96) contains
anecdotes, quotations from correspondence concerning
Miss Field, lengthy excerpts from her diaries, and brief
portions from her lectures. A short section on Miss
Field's brief career as an actress in the late 1870s and
short comments on such actors as Edwin Booth, Charles
Fechter, and Charlotte Cushman are included.

Illustrations. Six, mostly photographs of Kate Field.

Features. Table of contents; list of illustrations; documentation: sources of quotations are identified
by author, title, and, usually, date; index.

Actors. Kate Field.

328. Whitton, Joseph. *Wags of the Stage.* Philadelphia: George
H. Rigby, 1902. xi, 264 pp.

By means of humorous and eccentric anecdotes, the author shows the "waggery" of several actors, many of
whom he knew personally. The anecdotes are not dated.
The book contains some indications of the author's feelings toward his subjects, but little description or criticism
of their acting is included.

Illustrations. Sixteen photographs and engravings of the
author and of some of his subjects.

Features. Publisher's preface; author's introduction; table
of contents.

Actors. Charles M. Barras, John Brougham, William J.
Florence, Edwin Forest, Samuel Hemple, E. A.
Sothern, William Wheatley.

329. *Who's Who in the Theatre: A Biographical Record of the
Contemporary Stage.* Comp. and ed. by John Parker.
Foreword by Sir Herbert Beerbohm Tree. 2nd ed.
Boston: Small, Maynard, 1914. xxxix, 946 pp.

Ibid. 3rd ed., rev. and enl. New York: Sir Isaac Pitman & Sons, 1916. xxix, 1012, iv, 93 pp.

Ibid. 4th ed., rev. and enl. New York: Sir Isaac Pitman & Sons, 1922. xxxvi, 1217, 8 pp.

Ibid. 5th ed., rev. and enl. New York: Sir Isaac Pitman & Sons, 1925. cxxxiii, 1300, xlv pp.

Ibid. 6th ed., rev. and enl. New York: Sir Isaac Pitman & Sons, 1930. ccxi, 1469, xlv pp.

Ibid. 9th ed., rev. New York, Chicago: Pitman, 1939. vii, 1983 pp.

The editions in this series are, primarily, collections of thousands of biographical entries for living members of the theatrical profession in England, her colonies, America, and to a lesser extent, Europe. Each entry includes information on its subject's role in the theatre, birth, education, and major theatrical contributions (usually, with specific dates; sometimes a quite extensive listing). Some miscellaneous information, such as the subject's clubs, hobbies, or address, is occasionally provided. When the subject of an entry dies or remains long inactive, his sketch is removed from succeeding editions. As new members of the profession become noted, entries for them are inserted in later editions.

> *Illustrations.* Numerous diagrams of contemporary London theatres.

> *Features.* There are numerous changes in features from one edition to another; among the more valuable features which are included in all the editions are: preface; table of contents; genealogical tables of notable theatrical families; "Notable Productions and Principal Revivals of the London Stage" (from the earliest times to the present); "Theatrical and Musical Obituary" (includes name, role in the theatre, date of birth, and age at death); "Theatrical Wills: A List of a Few Well-Known Managers, Actors, and Others, Whose Wills Have Been Proved."

> *Actors.* General.

330. Wilder, Marshall [Pickney]. *The Sunny Side of the Street.* New York: Funk & Wagnalls, 1905. 359 pp.

This volume contains scores of anecdotes and remarks, mostly humorous, which were related to or observed by the author during the last quarter of the nineteenth century and the beginning of the twentieth. People from many walks of life are mentioned, from "Buffalo Bill" Cody and James Corbett to President McKinley and the Prince of Wales (later Edward VII). Less than one-fifth of the book concerns theatre workers and this portion includes stories by or about such actors as Joseph Jefferson III, Nat C. Goodwin, Ada Rehan, and Stuart Robson.

Illustrations. One photograph of the author and many small sketches illustrative of anecdotes.

Features. Preface; table of contents; index of persons.

Actors. General.

331. Willard, George O[wen]. *History of the Providence Stage, 1762-1891. Including Sketches of Many Prominent Actors Who Have Appeared in America.* Providence, Rhode Island: Rhode Island News, 1891. 298 pp.

Attempting to be as "correct and as concise as possible," the author presents a record of theatre in Providence, Rhode Island, from 1762 through 1891. The first twenty-five chapters comprise a chronological account of the professional stage in Providence, with each chapter organized according to theatrical season and the functioning of each Providence theatre during each season. The book contains lists of attractions which appeared at each theatre during each season, sometimes with dates of performances, names of plays performed, indications of relative financial success, etc. Interspersed throughout the text are brief biographical sketches of notable performers, quotations from the Providence *Journal,* and some suggestions of the author's opinions of those actors whom he had seen. Chapter XXVI concerns the Providence Opera House, of which the author was one of the founding stockholders. Chapter XXVII contains comments on amateur dramatic societies and minor theatres.

Illustrations. None.

Features. Preface; documentation: sources of many quotations are partially identified; appended pre-
Civil War playbills; index.

Actors. General.

332. Williams, Henry L. *The "Queen of the Drama!" Mary*
Anderson: Her Life On and Off the Stage, together
with Select Recitations from All the Great Plays in
Which She Has Delighted Two Continents. New York:
Williams & Co., ©1885. iv, 128 pp.

Approximately one-third of this volume is devoted to an
admiring "life" of Mary Anderson and the remainder is
composed of passages selected from plays and poems.
The biography surveys her life, but it emphasizes her London engagement of 1883. Several brief extracts from
London criticisms are included.

Illustrations. None.

Features. Table of contents; documentation: sources of
most quotations are identified by title of the
periodical only.

Actors. Mary Anderson.

333. Wilson, Francis. *Francis Wilson's Life of Himself.* Boston
and New York: Houghton Mifflin, 1924. xi, 463 pp.

The author's remembrances and reflections on his life and
friends from the 1850s to the 1920s comprise this book.
Most of the material relates to the author's theatrical
career. He includes anecdotes and appreciations of his
own and his associated activities, but he indicates few
dates. Along with many comments on theatrical conditions during the half-century preceeding publication, the
author presents his advice to people seeking careers in the
theatre. Lengthy reminiscences of Edwin Booth and
Joseph Jefferson III are accompanied by shorter comments on scores of other performers, such as Richard

Mansfield, Mrs. John Drew, Nat C. Goodwin, and Julia Marlowe.

Illustrations. Fifty-five, mostly photographs of Francis Wilson and his acquaintances.

Features. Table of contents; list of illustrations; documentation: sources of quotations are identified by author and/or title and/or date; index.

Actors. Edwin Booth, Joseph Jefferson III, Francis Wilson.

334. —. *John Wilkes Booth: Fact and Fiction of Lincoln's Assassination.* Boston and New York: Houghton Mifflin, 1929; rpt. New York: Benjamin Blom, 1972. xv, 322 pp.

In this account of the events leading to and surrounding John Wilkes Booth's assassination of Lincoln and his own death, the author draws upon previously published materials, including official records, unpublished letters by members of the Booth family, and personal interpretations of events. Some information on Wilkes Booth's character and acting career, as well as brief evaluations of his acting ability, are included.

Illustrations. Forty-one photographs, engravings, tintypes, and water colors of John Wilkes Booth and of people and things associated with him.

Features. Preface; table of contents; list of illustrations; documentation: sources of most lengthy quotations are identified by author and title; index.

Actors. Edwin Booth, John Wilkes Booth, John Sleeper Clarke.

335. —. *Joseph Jefferson: Reminiscences of a Fellow Player.* New York: Charles Scribner's Sons, 1906. 354 pp.

The author, who was a personal friend of his subject from 1889 until Jefferson's death in 1905, "has aimed merely to set down the remembrances, mostly anecdotal, which were his over a number of years in connection with [Jefferson] ." These anecdotes, some based on incidents observed by the author and some related to him by Jefferson and others, are combined with the author's reflections on his fellow-actor and with Jefferson's comments on many subjects, such as acting, painting, and playwriting. The author includes a narrative of the 1896 all-star production of *The Rivals.* Many other actors, for example, Edwin Booth, Mrs. John Drew, and Nat C. Goodwin, are mentioned briefly in this interesting volume. Little description of performances and few specific dates are included.

Illustrations. Thirty-three, mostly photographs of Joseph Jefferson III and of other actors.

Features. Preface; table of contents; list of illustrations; documentation: sources of quotations are identified by author and, occasionally, title and/or date; index.

Actors. Joseph Jefferson III, Francis Wilson.

336. —. *Recollections of a Player.* New York: Printed at the DeVinne Press, 1897. 81 pp.

This book is a loosely chronological, anecdotal autobiography. The author traces his career as a minstrel, a stock actor, and, especially, a comic opera star from the late 1870s through the early 1890s. He includes his views on several of his productions and on some fellow actors, but he provides few specific dates.

Illustrations. Fifty-six, primarily photographs of the author and of other actors.

Features. List of illustrations.

Actors. Francis Wilson.

337. Wilson, Garff B. *A History of American Acting.* Bloomington, Indiana: Indiana University Press, ©1966. x, 310 pp.

> Acknowledging the hazards of analyzing performers of the past, the author notes that he was "surprised and gratified" by the frequency with which "a firm outline and a clear image usually emerges from what may seem to be confused or conflicting testimony." He draws from a variety of nineteenth-century sources in composing short essays which stress notable actors' approaches to acting and the style and effect of their performances. Some biographical data is also included. The title of the book is, unfortunately, misleading, for, as the author accurately notes in the introduction, the emphasis of the text is overwhelmingly on nineteenth-century actors. Within this time-period, the volume is a valuable survey of American acting.

> *Illustrations.* Thirty-five, mostly photographs of actors.

> *Features.* Introduction; table of contents; list of illustrations; thorough documentation; index.

> *Actors.* Maude Adams, Viola Allen, Mary Anderson, Lawrence Barrett, Edwin Booth, Dion Boucicault, Mrs. Leslie Carter, Lotta Crabtree, Charlotte Cushman, E. L. Davenport, Fanny Davenport, Clara Fisher, Minnie Maddern Fiske, Edwin Forrest, John Gilbert, Matilda Heron, E. M. Holland, May Irwin, Fanny Janauschek, Laura Keene, John McCullough, Steele MacKaye, Richard Mansfield, Julia Marlowe, Maggie Mitchell, Helena Modjeska, Clara Morris, James E. Murdoch, Henry Placide, Ada Rehan, Otis Skinner, E. H. Sothern, William Warren, Jr.

338. Wilstach, Paul. *Richard Mansfield: The Man and the Actor.* New York: Charles Scribner's Sons, 1908; rpt. Freeport, New York: Books for Libraries, 1970. xvii, 500 pp.

This biography of Richard Mansfield is based on the author's "intimate acquaintance" with his subject, his conversations with Mrs. Mansfield, and his access to the actor's personal papers. The volume contains biographical data (including specific dates), anecdotes, copious quotations from Mansfield's writings and conversations, and some descriptions of Mansfield's performances. Excerpts from Mansfield's correspondence and from reviews are included. The actor's personal and professional qualities are discussed.

Illustrations. Fifty-three, mostly photographs of Richard Mansfield.

Features. Preface; table of contents; list of illustrations; documentation: sources of quotations are identified by author and/or title and/or date; index.

Actors. Beatrice Cameron, Richard Mansfield.

339. Wingate, Charles E[dgar] L[ewis]. *The Playgoers' Year Book, for 1888. Story of the Stage the Past Year, with Especial Reference to Boston.* Boston: Stage Publishing, [1888]. vi, 87 pp.

The main body of this work is a chronological narrative of the theatrical year in Boston, January-December, 1887. Included in the chronicle are synopses of most of the plays new to Boston, brief stage histories of some revivals, quotations from some playwrights and actors concerning their work, the author's brief evaluations of plays and players, and miscellaneous information. Appended are full cast lists of the "principal" productions and lists of the officers of six Boston theatres.

Illustrations. Sixteen photographs, engravings, and drawings of actors and of scenes from plays.

Features. Introduction; dedicatory preface; cast lists of principal productions; lists of Boston theatre officials; index.

Actors. General.

340. —. *Shakespeare's Heroes on the Stage.* New York and Boston: Thomas Y. Crowell, ©1896. x, 348 pp.

Essays concerning major performers of Shakespearian heroes from the time of Burbage to the 1890s comprise this volume. The roles considered are Othello, Iago, King Lear, Shylock, Coriolanus, Macbeth, Hamlet, and Richard III. Anecdotes and contemporary appraisals and descriptions are included, along with a few specific dates. Comments on English and American actors predominate, but Tommaso Salvini and Ernesto Rossi are also included.

Illustrations. Thirty photographs, engravings, and paintings of actors.

Features. Preface; table of contents; list of illustrations; documentation: sources of quotations are identified by author; index.

Actors. Lawrence Barrett, Edwin Booth, E. L. Davenport, Edwin Forrest, John McCullough.

341. —. *Shakespeare's Heroines on the Stage.* New York: Thomas Y. Crowell, ©1895. ix, 355 pp.

The author presents a "brief and anecdotal" stage history of Shakespearian heroines by devoting a chapter each to the following characters: Juliet, Beatrice, Hermione and Perdita, Viola, Imogen, Rosalind, Cleopatra, Lady Mccbeth, Queen Katherine (*Henry VIII*), Portia (*The Merchant of Venice*), Katherina, Ophelia, and Desdemona. He deals with English and American actresses from the Restoration to the 1890s. He includes anecdotes, factual data, critical opinion, description, and, when possible, his own descriptions and evaluations. Although late-nineteenth-century American actresses receive relatively slight attention, the author's occasional critical and descriptive comments on them are of interest.

Illustrations. Fifty-three photographs, paintings, engravings, and drawings of actresses.

Features. Preface; table of contents, list of illustrations; documentation: sources of quotations are identified by author; index.

Actors. General.

342. Winslow, Catherine Mary Reignolds-. *Yesterdays with Actors.* Boston: Cupples and Hurd, 1887; rpt. Freeport, New York: Books for Libraries, 1972. xv, 201 pp.

The author reminisces about her own acting career (as Kate Reignolds) and about many performers and managers with whom she was associated. Although primarily comprised of anecdotes and recollections drawn from the author's personal experience during the third quarter of the nineteenth century, the book does contain some hearsay. The author includes information pertaining to various actors' personal characters, performances, and offstage behavior, but she does not indicate dates of incidents.

Illustrations. Twenty-six photographs and engravings, mostly of actors.

Features. Introduction; table of contents; list of illustrations.

Actors. John Wilkes Booth, John Brougham, Charlotte Cushman, Ben DeBar, Edwin Forrest, Matilda Heron, Laura Keene, Kate Reignolds, Agnes Robertson, E. A. Sothern, Mrs. J. R. Vincent, William Warren, Jr.

343. Winter, William. *The Actor and Other Speeches, Chiefly on Theatrical Subjects and Occasions.* New York: Dunlap Society, 1891; rpt. New York: Burt Franklin, 1970. 80 pp.

This collection of occasional speeches, originally delivered during the period from 1887 through 1891, includes brief, generalized tributes to Lester Wallack, Edwin Booth, and Henry Edwards.

Illustrations. One photograph of the author.

Features. One photograph of the author.

Actors. General.

344. —. *Ada Rehan: A Study.* New York: Printed for Augustin Daly, 1891. 80 pp.

Ibid. 2nd ed., with a new chapter and additional portraits. New York: Printed for Augustin Daly, 1891. 88 pp.

Ibid. New ed., rev. and enl. New York: Privately printed for Augustin Daly, 1891-1898. 211 pp.

1st ed.: This volume of tribute to Ada Rehan includes the author's general appreciation of her acting, a sketch of her career, a review of Augustin Daly's production of *As You Like It* (with special note of Miss Rehan's Rosalind), and a chapter on her London performances by Justin Huntly McCarthy. The chapter on her work in London contains excerpts from several British reviews and some poetic tributes to Miss Rehan by McCarthy. Both Winter and the London critics include descriptions and evaluations of Miss Rehan's acting. An alphabetical listing of her roles, 1874-90, is also inserted into this volume.

2nd ed.: This edition contains the same material as the first edition, except the author adds three photographs and a chapter on Miss Rehan's performances of Lady Teazle, Pierrot (in *The Prodigal*), and the Princess of France (in *Love's Labours Lost*).

New edition, revised and enlarged: While omitting the McCarthy chapter and revising the remainder of the second edition, the author greatly expands his treatment of Miss Rehan's theatrical career in this edition. In addition to those roles evaluated in the earlier editions, the author criticizes many of his subject's other characterizations, most notably those in Shakespearian plays. Excerpts from many English, French, and German reviews of Miss Rehan's performances are included.

Illustrations. 1st ed.: Twenty photographs of Ada Rehan.
　　　　　　2nd ed.: Twenty-three photographs of Ada Rehan.
　　　　　　New edition, revised and enlarged: Twenty-five photographs of Ada Rehan.

Features. 1st ed.: Table of contents; list of illustrations; documentation: sources of quotations are identified by author and/or title and/or date; alphabetical list of Ada Rehan's roles, 1874-90.
　　　　　2nd ed.: Same as those in the first edition.
　　　　　New edition, revised and enlarged: Preface; table of contents; list of illustrations; documentation: sources of quotations are identified by author and/or title and/or date; chronology of Ada Rehan's life, 1860-98; alphabetical list of Ada Rehan's roles, 1874-98.

Actors. (all editions). Ada Rehan.

345. —. *Brief Chronicles.* 3 parts. New York: Dunlap Society, 1889-90; rpt. 3 parts in 1. New York: Burt Franklin, 1970. Pt. I: xiv, 130 pp.; Pt. II: pp. 131-248; Pt. III: pp. 249-339.

"This book is mostly composed of brief biographical sketches of actors and of other persons who have been connected with the American stage in my own time [since, approximately, the middle of the nineteenth century]. All these persons I have seen and most of them I have known. The sketches here collected and reviewed were written by me in various periodicals. . . . In almost every instance the sketch is one that was written upon the moment, to record the death of the person whom it commemorates." The eighty-six sketches differ considerably in length. They contain varying amounts of biographical data, personal appreciation, and professional evaluation.

Illustrations. Three drawings of actors (one in each part).

Features. Preface (Pt. I); table of contents (Pt. I); documentation: sources of quotations are identified by author and/or title and/or date.

Actors. General.

346. —. *Edwin Booth in Twelve Dramatic Characters.* Portraits by W. J. Hennessy. Engraving by W. J. Linton. Boston: James R. Osgood, 1872. 51 pp.

The author's biographical sketch of Edwin Booth occupies the fifty-one numbered pages in this volume. Twelve full-page, idealized engravings of Booth in various roles follow the sketch, each engraving being accompanied by a selection from the appropriate drama. The biography is primarily a narrative, including many specific dates, but it also contains the author's evaluation of several of Booth's characterizations, three lengthy reviews (one each by Winter, George William Curtis, and William Stuart) which include some description of Booth's performances, and a description of Booth's Theatre.

Illustrations. Twelve engravings of Edwin Booth.

Features. List of illustrations; documentation: sources of some quotations are partially identified.

Actors. Edwin Booth.

347. —. *The Jeffersons.* Boston: James R. Osgood, 1881; rpt. New York: Benjamin Blom, 1969. x, 252 pp.

The author sketches the lives and careers of Thomas Jefferson, Joseph Jefferson, Elizabeth Jefferson, Joseph Jefferson II, Charles Burke, and Joseph Jefferson III. Approximately one-seventh of the text concerns the latter actor's career from 1861 to 1880. The chapter on Joseph Jefferson III briefly traces the actor's life and includes the author's lengthy evaluations of Jefferson's versions of *Rip Van Winkle* and *The Rivals*. Partial lists of roles are contained in each chapter.

Illustrations. Ten engravings, paintings, and silhouettes, mostly of members of the Jefferson family.

Features. Preface; table of contents; list of illustrations; documentation: sources of quotations are identified by author and title; bibliography: a partial listing of sources is contained in the preface; index.

Actors. Joseph Jefferson III.

348. —. *Life and Art of Edwin Booth.* New York: Macmillan, 1893; rpt. New York: Greenwood, 1968. xii, 308 pp.

Ibid. New ed., rev. Boston: Joseph Knight, 1894; New York: Macmillan, 1894. 437 pp.

1893 ed.: Deriving his materials primarily from his long friendship with Edwin Booth and from his previous writings on that actor, the author divides this volume into three main sections: "The Life of Edwin Booth," "The Art of Edwin Booth," and "Memorials." The "Life" includes a chronological account of Booth's life and contains factual data, critical comments, anecdotes, an appreciation of the man, and comments on many of Booth's associates. The "Art" section is comprised of the author's evaluations of the actor's major roles and of Booth's performances in those roles, including some descriptions of Booth's portrayals. "Memorials" contains letters and speeches by or concerning Booth, tributes to him, and comments concerning awards and other matters concerning Booth's life.

1894 ed.: "Errors that crept into the first edition of this Memoir have been corrected in [this edition]. The present text is more accurate. A few tables and playbills have been omitted, and a few letters of Booth added."

Illustrations. 1893 ed.: Sixteen illustrations in various media, mostly of Edwin Booth.
1894 ed.: One painting of Booth.
1894 extra illustrated edition (Macmillan): Sixteen illustrations in various media, mostly of Edwin Booth.

Features. 1893 ed.: Preface; table of contents; list of illustrations; documentation: sources of most quotations are partially identified; the "Memorials" section includes a brief chronology of Edwin Booth's life and a chronological listing, with dates, of all theatres in which Booth performed, 1886/87-91.
1894 ed.: Preface; table of contents; documentation: sources of quotations are partially identified; the "Memorials" sections includes a brief chronology of Edwin Booth's life (note: the information on the 1886/87-91 tours is omitted in this edition).

Actors. Edwin Booth.

349. —. *Life and Art of Joseph Jefferson, together with Some Account of His Ancestry and of the Jefferson Family of Actors.* New York: Macmillan, 1894. xv, 319 pp.

This volume is a "complete revision" of the author's earlier *The Jeffersons* (see 347). "The story has been rectified, augmented, re-arranged, and in part re-written, —so that this work is, practically, new. It certainly is more ample and more authentic than its predecessor. . . ." Approximately one-third of the book concerns the post-1860 period. In extending Joseph Jefferson's biographical sketch past 1860, the author emphasizes the actor's off-stage life. In addition to evaluations of Jefferson's Rip Van Winkle and Bob Acres, comments on his portrayals of Caleb Plummer, Mr. Golightly, and Dr. Pangloss are included. The author also inserts comments on several of

Jefferson's contemporaries, including E. A. Sothern, Mark Smith, Laura Keene, and John T. Raymond.

Illustrations. Sixteen photographs and engravings, mostly of Joseph Jefferson III and other actors.

Features. Preface; table of contents; list of illustrations; documentation: sources of most quotations are identified by author and/or title and/or date; appended materials concerning various events and periods in the theatre, including the 1882 tribute to William Warren, Jr., and Joseph Jefferson III's activities as a lecturer; brief chronology of the life of Joseph Jefferson III; index.

Actors. Joseph Jefferson III.

350. —. *Life and Art of Richard Mansfield, with Selections from His Letters.* 2 vols. New York: Moffat, Yard, 1910; rpt. Freeport, New York: Books for Libraries, 1970; rpt. Westport, Connecticut: Greenwood, 1970. Vol. I: 361 pp.; Vol. II: 353 pp.

The author composed this biography at Mansfield's request, drawing information from his twenty-five-year friendship with the actor, hundreds of personal letters from Mansfield, and his own criticisms of Mansfield's performances. The first volume is a narrative of the actor's life, emphasizing the 1883-1907 period, which is interspersed with copious selections from Mansfield's letters and with the author's evaluations of various events in his subject's life. The second volume contains chapters on twenty-seven of Mansfield's portrayals and includes the author's appraisals and occasional descriptions of Mansfield's characterizations. The author devotes the bulk of each of these chapters to play analyses, character analyses, plot outlines, and other subjects which help one to see his critical viewpoint, but which do not directly pertain to Mansfield's portrayals. An excellent summary description of the actor and an invaluable chronology of Mansfield's life are also included in this volume.

Illustrations. Vol. I: Forty-one, mostly photographs of Richard Mansfield.

    Vol. II: Thirty-five photographs of Richard Mansfield as various characters.

Features. Vol. I: Preface; table of contents; list of illustrations; biographical sketch of Erminia Rudersdorff (Mansfield's mother); his mother's will; an appreciation, with a list of stage roles, of Beatrice Cameron (Mansfield's wife).

    Vol. II: Table of contents; list of illustrations; "Summary" (includes a list of Richard Mansfield's stage roles); chronology of Richard Mansfield's productions); appendices attacking Clyde Fitch's authorship of *Beau Brummell* and Paul Wilstach's biography of Mansfield (see 338); index (for both volumes).

Actors. Beatrice Cameron, Richard Mansfield.

351. —. *The Life of David Belasco.* Completed, with a preface, by William Jefferson Winter. 2 vols. New York: Moffat, Yard, 1918; rpt. Freeport, New York: Books for Libraries, 1970; rpt. New York: Benjamin Blom, 1972. Vol. I: xxiii, 530 pp.; Vol. II: xvi, 563 pp.

When William Winter died on June 30, 1917, most of this biography of his long-time friend was in manuscript or unrevised typescript. In the preface, the author's son and aide, William Jefferson Winter, states, "My task has been, substantially, to supply some dates, to fill some blanks, and to edit, coordinate, and join the material left by my father." The bulk of the work is a chronological record of David Belasco's theatrical career through 1917. This record incorporates Belasco's correspondence, his autobiographical writings, cast lists, and the author's narrative, descriptions, and evaluations of his subject's career, plays, productions, and personality. The first volume takes the narrative to the summer of 1900. The second volume continues the chronicle through 1917, with over one-half of this volume devoted to the pre-1911 period. Specific dates are frequently indicated, and brief comments on numerous actors, such as James A. Herne, E. H. Sothern, and George Arliss, are included.

Illustrations. Vol. I: Seventy-three, mostly photographs of David Belasco and of actors.
Vol. II: Sixty-one, mostly photographs of David Belasco and of actors.

Features. Vol. I: Preface by William Jefferson Winter; table of contents; list of illustrations; documentation: sources of quotations are identified by author and/or title and/or date and, rarely, page number; partial list of roles which David Belasco acted (pp. 141-47); list of plays which Belasco directed prior to midsummer, 1882 (pp. 264-67); index.
Vol. II: Table of contents; list of illustrations; documentation: sources of quotations are identified by author and/or title and/or date and, rarely, page number; list of the dramatic works of Belasco (pp. 327-32; includes years of composition and, if an adaptation, source); chronology of the life of Belasco; index.

Actors. Blanche Bates, David Belasco, Mrs. Leslie Carter, Francis Starr, David Warfield.

352. —. *Other Days, Being Chronicles and Memories of the Stage.* New York: Moffat, Yard, 1908; rpt. Freeport, New York: Books for Libraries, 1970. 389 pp.

This work contains discussions of the following topics: American actors of the first half of the nineteenth century, the eight American actors noted below, Adelaide Neilson, and early twentieth-century stage conditions. The late nineteenth-century American actors who are included were personal friends of the author, and the chapters concerning them are mainly reminiscent. These chapters contain varying amounts of biographical data, anecdotes, personal appreciation, and performance criticism. Excerpts from several of the subjects' letters to the author are included.

Illustrations. Seventeen engravings and photographs, mostly of actors.

Features. Preface; table of contents; list of illustrations; appended notes on Mrs. Marshall, Edwin Forrest, E. A. Sothern, Henry Irving and Lawrence Barrett, and William Dunlap; index.

Actors. Mary Anderson, Lawrence Barrett, Dion Boucicault, John Brougham, Charlotte Cushman, Joseph Jefferson III, John McCullough, E. A. Sothern.

353. —. *Shadows of the Stage.* 3 series. New York: Macmillan, 1892-95. First Seires: 387 pp.; Second Series: 367 pp.; Third Series: 351 pp.

The essays composing these three volumes are reprints—in some cases "condensed, improved, and rearranged"—of articles previously published by the author, mainly in periodicals. Primarily appreciations on plays, players, playwrights, productions, and trends of the last half of the nineteenth century, the essays contain varying amount of evaluation, description, and biographical data. Articles on many European and English actors, for example, Irving, Ellen Terry, Salvini, Ristori, and Coquelin, are included.

Illustrations. (each volume). Six photographs and engravings, mostly of actors.

Features. (each volume). Preface; table of contents; list of illustrations; documentation: sources of most quotations are identified by author and/or title and/or date.

Actors. First Series: Mary Anderson, Lawrence Barrett, Edwin Booth, Charlotte Cushman, Charles Fisher, William J. Florence, Mrs. G. H. Gilbert, Joseph Jefferson III, James Lewis, John McCullough, Richard Mansfield, Ada Rehan, Genevieve Ward.

Second Series: Lawrence Barrett, John Brougham, Charlotte Cushman, Edwin Forrest, John Gilbert, James H. Hackett, George W. Jamieson, Jean Davenport Lander, Richard Mansfield, Helena Modjeska, Clara Morris, John E. Owens, Ada Rehan, William Wheatley.

354. —. *Shakespeare on the Stage.* 3 series. New York: Moffat, Yard, 1911-16; rpt. New York: Benjamin Blom, 1969. First Series: 564 pp.; Second Series: xxix, 664 pp.; Third Series: 538 pp.

These three volumes contain information on twenty-one of Shakespeare's plays, focusing primarily on scores of prominent delineators of the plays' major characters. The author considers actors who performed during the period from the Restoration to the first decade of the twentieth century, strongly emphasizing English and American players. The comments on individual actors include, in varying amounts, anecdotes, indications of general interpretation, descriptions of specific stage business and/or line readings, descriptions of costume and/or makeup, and performance criticism. Most of the actors who performed after the middle of the nineteenth century were personally observed by the author. The author also contributes historical and critical comments pertaining to the plays and the roles.

Illustrations. First Series: Forty-eight illustrations in various media, mostly of English and American actors.
Second Series: Fifty-four illustrations in various media, mostly of English and American actors.
Third Series: Forty-three illustrations in various media, mostly of English and American actors.

Features. Preface (each volume); tables of contents (each volume for that volume); lists of illustrations (each volume for that volume); documentation: sources of quotations are identified by author and/or title; indices (Second and Third Series for those volumes).

Actors. (each volume). General.

355. —. *A Sketch of the Life of John Gilbert, Together with Extracts from His Letters and Souvenirs of His Career.* New York: Dunlap Society, 1890; rpt. New York: Burt Franklin, 1970. 55 pp.

This book is more a memorial volume to John Gibbs Gilbert than a biography. It contains appreciations of the actor by the author (a friend of over twenty years) and by Curtis Guild, some biographical data, and several statements by the actor. Among the latter are curtain speeches, numerous letters to the author, a brief autobiographical account (written in 1878), and an essay on the "old stock company."

Illustrations. One drawing of John Gilbert and a facsimile playbill for the testimonial tendered him upon the anniversary of his fiftieth year on the stage (December 5, 1878).

Features. Prefatory note; documentation: sources of quotations are partially identified.

Actors. John Gilbert.

356. —. *The Stage Life of Mary Anderson.* New York: George J. Coombes, 1886. xv, 151 pp.

The author, writing with "a warmth of sympathy, and earnestness of thought, and a fidelity of portraiture," offers his estimate of Mary Anderson's acting to the spring of 1886. The book is composed primarily of reviews originally published in the New York *Tribune* and revised by the author for inclusion in this volume. The bulk of the work directly concerns Miss Anderson's acting, including criticism, description, and general evaluation of the effects of her performance. Some anecdotes and biographical information are included, along with the author's occasional criticism of the plays in Miss Anderson's repertoire. Since the original articles were written over a number of years and there are several reviews of many of Miss Anderson's characterizations, the author presents his view of the actress' development.

Illustrations. One photograph of Mary Anderson.

Features. Preface; table of contents; appended note on Mary Anderson's managers, on her supporting company of 1885-86, and on the extent of her 1885-86 season.

Actors. Mary Anderson.

357. —. *Tyrone Power.* New York: Moffat, Yard, 1913; rpt. New York: Benjamin Blom, 1972. 192 pp.

This biography of (Frederick) Tyrone Power, the Younger, emphasizes the actor's professional stage career from his debut in 1886 through his performance of Brutus in William Faversham's production of *Julius Caesar* in 1912/13. Many specific dates, anecdotes, and evaluations of Power's performances are included, along with the author's lengthy disquisitions on various theatrical topics —mostly criticisms of the dramas in which Power appeared. The author knew his subject personally and had observed most of the actor's principal performances. Brief comments on such other players as George Chaplin, Mrs. Fiske, and Henry Miller are also included.

Illustrations. Twenty-one, mostly photographs of Tyrone Power.

Features. Preface; table of contents; list of illustrations; partial listing of Tyrone Power's roles; "Chronology of the Professional Life of Tyrone Power" (Nov., 1886-Jan., 1913); obituary of Edith Crane (Power's wife); a 1913 letter from Power in reference to his withdrawal from Faversham's production of *Julius Caesar*.

Actors. Fanny Janauschek, Tyrone Power.

358. —. *Vagrant Memories, Being Further Recollections of Other Days.* New York: George H. Doran, 1915; rpt. Freeport, New York: Books for Libraries, 1970. 525 pp.

"My chief purpose in writing these chapters was to provide personal reminiscence, but, while making what I venture to designate authentic vignettes of important and variously interesting actors, I have given essential details of biography and made critical estimates of achievement. . . ." The author also includes letters from several of his subjects. In addition to those American actors noted below, the author comments briefly on such players as Ada Rehan, Clara Morris, and H. J. Montague, and provides substantial discussions of Augustin Daly, Henry Irving, and Johnston Forbes-Robertson. A chapter entitled "The Theatre and Morality" provides an interesting glimpse of the author's general views on the nature and the social role of theatre.

Illustrations. Forty, mostly photographs of actors.

Features. Preface; table of contents; list of illustrations; documentation: sources of quotations are identified by author and/or title and/or date; index.

Actors. Edwin Booth, Mrs. G. H. Gilbert, Matilda Heron, Laura Keene, James Lewis, Julia Marlowe, Mark Smith, E. H. Sothern, James W. Wallack, Jr., Lester Wallack, William Warren, Jr.

359. —. *The Wallet of Time, Containing Personal, Biographical, and Critical Reminiscence of the American Theatre.* 2 vols. New York: Moffat, Yard, 1913; rpt. Freeport, New York: Books for Libraries, 1969; rpt. New York: Benjamin Blom, 1969. Vol. I: xxv, 668 pp.; Vol. II: xiv, 680 pp.

Essays on actors who were prominent from the middle of

the nineteenth century through the first decade of the twentieth comprise the main portion of this work. Comments on dramas, dramatists, managers, and moral concerns are also included. The chapters on actors contain varying quantities of biographical data, anecdotes, generalized appreciation, specific criticism, and performance description. Among the American actors commented upon briefly are James H. Hackett, William J. Florence, Viola Allen, and William H. Crane.

Illustrations. Vol. I: Forty-five, mostly photographs of actors.

Vol. II: Fifty-two, mostly photographs of actors.

Features. Vol. I: Preface; table of contents; list of illustrations; index.

Vol. II: Table of contents; list of illustrations; index.

Actors. Vol. I: Lawrence Barrett, John Brougham, Charles Coghlan, Charlotte Cushman, Charles Fechter, Edwin Forrest, Mrs. G. H. Gilbert, George Holland, James Lewis, John McCullough, Helena Modjeska, Clara Morris, John E. Owens, John T. Raymond.

Vol. II: Maude Adams, Mary Anderson, Blanche Bates, Mrs. Leslie Carter, Minnie Maddern Fiske, Julia Marlowe, Ada Rehan, E. H. Sothern, David Warfield, Frank Worthing.

360. —. *A Wreath of Laurel, Being Speeches on Dramatic and Kindred Occasions.* New York: Dunlap Society, 1898; rpt. New York: Burt Franklin, 1970. xiii, 149 pp.

This volume contains several occasional speeches which were delivered by the author during the period from 1891 through 1898. Among the contents are generalized tributes to Joseph Jefferson III and Henry Irving.

Illustrations. Four photographs of subjects of the speeches and a watercolor of the author.

Features. Preface; table of contents; appended list of persons mentioned in the speeches, with years of birth and death indicated.

Actors. General.

361. Winter, William Jefferson (comp. and ed.). *In Memory of Frank Worthing, Actor: Born at Edinburgh, Scotland, October 12, 1866, Died at Detroit, Michigan, December 27, 1910.* New York: Printed for Distribution, 1911. 79 pp.

This memorial volume contains a biographical sketch of Frank Worthing by Willian Winter, an account of Worthing's funeral, a list of the actor's roles, and tributes to him by Blanche Bates, Grace George, Julia Marlowe, Acton Davies, Henry Miller, Tyrone Power, Jefferson Winter, and Louis V. DeFoe. The biography includes comments on Worthing's major American engagements, 1894-1910, and an evaluation of his acting. The tributes combine personal and professional appreciations.

Illustrations. Six photographs of Frank Worthing.

Features. Prefatory note; table of contents; list of illustrations; list of Frank Worthing's stage roles (extensive, but incomplete).

Actors. Frank Worthing.

362. *Wit and Humor of the Stage: A Collection from Various Sources Classified Under Appropriate Subject Headings.* Philadelphia: George W. Jacobs, 1909. 236 pp.

This book contains scores of "ludicrous happenings here and there, practical jokes, witty stories, and personal anecdotes" attributed to theatre folk. Many American actors, for example, E. A. Sothern, Nat C. Goodwin, and John McCullough, are represented. Although most of the stories are of little import, some provide glimpses of the personalities of the subjects.

Illustrations. One engraving of Joseph Jefferson III.

Features. Prologue; table of contents.

Actors. Joseph Jefferson III.

362a. Young, William C. *Famous Actors and Actresses on the American Stage.* 2 vols. New York: R. R. Bowker, ©1975. Vol. I: xxi, 602 pp.; Vol. II: xi, 603-1298 pp.

The author attempts "(1) to present contemporary evaluations of the abilities of a certain actor or actress; and (2) to relate a performer's philosophy of acting and approach to certain roles." Arbitrarily limiting the subjects of the work to two hundred and twenty-five, the author includes material on native-born, visiting, and foreign-born resident players, attempting to include the most important and the prototypical performers. He includes actors from Lewis Hallam, Jr. to Carol Channing, but emphasizes the eighteenth and nineteenth centuries. In addition to extensive critical, descriptive and theoretical quotations, the work includes some biographical data. Most of the information in this useful collection of artistic portraits is derived from books, New York newspapers, and magazines.

Illustrations. Two hundred and thirty-two photographs, prints, etc., including one or two of each of the actor-subjects.

Features. Preface (Vol. I); introduction (Vol. I); tables of contents (each volume for that volume); lists of illustrations (each volume for that volume); thorough documentation; selected bibliography (Vol. II); index by decades (Vol. II); cumulative index (Vol. II).

Actors. General.

363. Yurka, Blanche. *Bohemian Girl: Blanche Yurka's Theatrical Life.* Afterword by Brooks Atkinson. Athens, Ohio: Ohio University Press, ©1970. xii, 306 pp.

The author reminisces about her life and career from her youth (she was born in 1887) through 1969. Less than one-fifth of the book concerns the pre-1911 period, but this section includes some information on the beginnings of her career—under the management of David Belasco. The remainder of the volume contains anecdotes, narration, and opinions relating to her later career, with comments on such subjects as John Barrymore (she played Gertrude to his Hamlet), E. H. Sothern, the Theatre Guild, Hollywood, and one-woman shows.

Illustrations. Forty-two, mostly photographs of the author, her friends, and her associates.

Features. Preface; table of contents; list of illustrations; documentation: sources of some quotations are identified by author and title; afterword by Brooks Atkinson; index.

Actors. David Belasco, Blanche Yurka.

CONCLUSION

Summary

This study contains annotated entries for three hundred and sixty-three works published in the United States in the English language from 1861 through 1976 which include substantial material on American actors of the 1861-1910 period. The volumes annotated contain a wide variety of materials concerning such actors, including biographical data, performance criticisms and descriptions, personal appreciations, illustrations, anecdotes, and theoretical statements. Among the authors are found some of the actors themselves, many of their personal acquaintances, critics and audience members contemporary to them, and later scholars. When the books annotated in this study are combined with periodical articles of the 1861-1910 period, there results a wealth of material sufficient to enable current-day scholars to study American Actors, 1861-1910, with a high degree of thoroughness.

As in most areas of historical study, critical estimates and, in some cases, "factual" data disagree from one source to another. But, by means of validating historical evidence, by comparing the evaluations and descriptions of the many commentators, and by exercising interpretative judgement, scholars are able to arrive at valid conclusions concerning the lives and performance qualities of late nineteenth- and early twentieth-century American actors. In such works as Charles Shattuck's *The Hamlet of Edwin Booth* (see 281), Joseph Leach's *Bright Particular Star* (see 186), and Marion Moore Coleman's *Fair Rosalind* (see 75), scholars are demonstrating increased interest in collecting and analyzing information and publishing studies of American Actors, 1861-1910. The present project, hopefully one of a series of reference works, is an attempt to facilitate the endeavors of current and future scholars by providing a guide to books which contain information relevant to the study of such actors.

§

Recommendations for Further Research

The following reference projects, carried out with specific reference to American Actors, 1861-1910, would be of aid to scholars in the area: 1) annotated bibliographies of British books; 2) annotated bibliographies of American and British magazine and journal articles; 3) annotated bibliographies and/or indices of American and British newspaper articles; 4) guides to illustration, manuscript, correspondence, and personal papers collections held by libraries, museums, and other repositories; 5) guides to published and unpublished prompt books; and 6) a comprehensive and reliable biographical dictionary of actors.

With the aim of providing guides to materials concerning American actors from the beginning of theatrical activities in the United States until the present time, it is desirable that the reference projects suggested above, as well as the annotated bibliography included in this study, be expanded to cover the pre-1861 and post-1910 periods.

Such reference tools, it is hoped, will encourage and facilitate the following types of scholarly work: 1) definitive biographies of American actors; 2) critical and historical studies of major roles and plays on the American stage; 3) critical reconstructions of notable American performances and productions; 4) studies of nineteenth-century theatre practices in America; and 5) reassessments of the theatre's historical place and function in American society.

It is intended that the annotated bibliography contained herein will be periodically supplemented to include additional works found to be relevant to the study.

INDEX TO ACTORS

Adams, Annie, 257

Adams, Maude, 85, 169, 174, 183, 185, 202, 239, 243, 252, 257, 264, 265, 304, 337, 359

Allen, Viola, 53, 149, 304, 337

Anderson, David C., 291

Anderson, Mary, 15, 37, 72, 113, 149, 174, 195, 207, 227, 236, 249, 272, 311, 332, 337, 352, 353, 356, 359

Anglin, Margaret, 69, 155, 218, 228, 304

Arbuckle, Maclyn, 303

Arden, Edwin, 303

Arliss, George, 13, 14, 34, 135, 208

Arthur, Julia, 53, 304

Bandmann, Daniel E., 19, 224

Barnabee, Henry Clay, 21, 302

Barras, Charles M., 328

Barrett, Lawrence, 24, 38, 39, 42a, 75, 127, 140, 168, 191, 195, 207, 223, 240, 272, 273, 290, 291, 305, 322, 337, 340, 352, 353, 359

Barron, Charles, 275

Barrymore, Ethel, 5, 26, 28, 29, 121, 183, 185, 202, 203, 236a, 252

Barrymore, Georgie Drew, 5, 72

Barrymore, John, 5, 27, 28, 29, 121, 252, 253

Barrymore, Lionel, 5, 28, 29, 121

Barrymore, Maurice, 5, 29, 53, 75, 121, 195, 232, 306

Bates, Blanche, 304, 307, 351, 359

Bates, Helen Leslie, *see* Helen Leslie

Bates, Marie, 149

Beaudet, Louise, 72

Belasco, David, 32, 103, 130, 203a, 307, 351, 363

Bell, Digby, 302

Bellew, Kyrle, 310

Bennett, Mabel Adrienne Morrison, *see* Mabel Adrienne Morrison

Bennett, Richard, 33

Bergere, Valerie, 304

Bingham, Amelia, 149, 304

Blair, John, 303

Blake, William Rufus, 180

Booth, Agnes, 72, 195

Booth, Edwin, 1, 3, 16, 38, 39, 42, 47, 53, 57, 63, 67, 75, 77, 82, 83, 97, 107, 120, 124, 125, 127, 130, 132, 136, 140, 142a, 145, 165, 166, 168, 176, 182, 189a, 191, 195, 197, 207, 208, 209, 214, 216, 232, 236, 239, 246, 249, 252, 254, 266, 268, 269, 272, 273, 278, 281, 281a, 282, 290, 291, 295, 297, 298, 305, 311, 317, 322, 333, 334, 337, 340, 346, 348, 353, 358

Booth, John Wilkes, 30, 68, 107, 120, 182, 191, 197, 223, 254, 273, 282, 309, 334, 342

Booth, Junius Brutus, Jr., 182, 254, 278

Booth, Ogarita Rosalie, 120
Booth, Rachel, 255
Booth, Rita, *see* Ogarita Rosalie
  Booth
Boucicault, Dion, 18, 40, 74, 78,
  125, 126, 157, 195, 207, 208,
  223, 232, 242, 252, 280, 320,
  337, 352
Bowers, Mrs. D. P., 72
Brady, William A., 44, 45
Brougham, John, 49, 136, 180, 207,
  242, 328, 342, 352, 353, 359
Burke, Billie, 55
Burroughs, Marie, 304
Burrows, James, 275

Cameron, Beatrice, 149, 338, 350
Carle, Richard, 302
Carter, Mrs. Leslie, 32, 185, 304,
  307, 337, 351, 359
Cayvan, Georgia, 72, 195
Chanfrau, Francis, 136
Chaplin, George, 257
Clarke, Annie M., 275
Clarke, John Sleeper, 182, 207, 242,
  280, 334
Coghlan, Charles, 18, 311, 315, 359
Coghlan, Rose, 72, 195, 227, 304
Cohan, George M., 71, 103, 220
Cohan, Jerry J., 71
Cohan, Josephine, 71
Collier, William, 121
Conquest, Ida, 304
Corcoran, Katherine, *see* Katherine
  Corcoran Herne
Cosgrave, Luke, 79
Couldock, Charles W., 223
Crabtree, Lotta, 31, 37, 72, 89,
  130, 195, 270, 278, 337
Crane, William H., 53, 81, 149, 195,
  303
Crosman, Henrietta, 304, 305
Cruze, James, 79

Cushman, Charlotte, 46, 63, 130,
  186, 203, 207, 252, 256, 267,
  272, 281a, 296, 311, 324, 337,
  342, 352, 353, 359
Cushman, Pauline, 37

Dailey, Peter F., 302
Daly, Arnold, 139, 239
Daly, Dan, 302
Daniels, Frank, 302
Davenport, E. L., 16, 105, 111, 207,
  224, 232, 281a, 311, 337, 340
Davenport, Fanny, 37, 53, 72, 195,
  232, 337
Davenport, Harry, 159
Davidge, William P., 84
Davies, Phoebe, 304
Dean, Julia, *see* Julia Deane Hayne
DeAngelis, Jefferson, 86, 302
DeBar, Ben, 181, 342
DeMille, Cecil B., 88
DeWolfe, Elsie, 90, 149, 304
Dixey, Henry E., 302
Dodge, Jack, 95
Dodson, J. E., 303
Donnelly, Dorothy, 185
Dow, Ada, 274, 293
Dressler, Marie, 98, 99
Drew, John, II, 5, 26, 83, 92, 94,
  100, 121, 169, 183, 184, 195,
  202, 232, 251, 259, 288, 303
Drew, Mrs. John (Louisa Lane), 5,
  26, 101, 121, 195, 232
Durbin, Maud, 288

Edeson, Robert, 149
Edouin, Willie, 255
Elliott, Gertrude, 118
Elliott, Maxine, 118, 141, 149,
  185, 304
Ellsler, Effie, 72
Ellsler, John A., 107, 224
Eytinge, Rose, 111

Fairbanks, Douglas, 150
Faversham, William, 303
Fawcett, Owen, 227
Fechter, Charles, 63, 74, 115, 205, 207, 242, 246, 266, 269, 272, 280, 311, 359
Field, Kate, 327
Fields, Lou, 173, 222
Fisher, Charles, 180; 195, 251, 353
Fisher, Clara, 337
Fiske, Minnie Maddern, 32, 34, 53, 117, 144, 149, 174, 195, 203, 239, 252, 304, 305, 311, 337, 359
Flockton, Charles P., 294
Florence, Malvina Pray, 195, 207
Florence, William J., 136, 195, 207, 328, 353
Forrest, Edwin, 4, 23, 152, 207, 217, 231, 240, 246, 252, 260, 268, 269, 272, 278, 281a, 282, 317, 328, 337, 340, 342, 353, 359
Fox, George L., 136, 165
Foy, Eddie, 110, 122
Frederick, Pauline, 108

General, 2, 7, 8, 9, 10, 11, 12, 22, 35, 36, 48, 50, 51, 52, 56, 56a, 58, 60, 61, 64, 65, 73, 91, 104, 109, 116, 119, 123, 128, 129, 131, 137, 142, 143, 147, 148, 154, 156, 160, 161, 162, 162a, 164, 167, 171, 178, 187, 199, 200, 201, 204, 206, 211, 215, 219, 229, 230, 238, 244, 247, 248, 250, 258, 261, 263, 277, 285, 286, 287, 301, 308, 313, 314, 316, 325, 329, 330, 331, 339, 341, 343, 345, 354, 360, 362a,
George, F. W., 79
George, Grace, 69, 304
George, Mrs. Grace (Rena Marcells), 79
Gilbert, Mrs. G. H. (Anne Hartley), 83, 134, 251, 353, 358, 359
Gilbert, John, 195, 311, 337, 353, 355

Gillette, William, 53, 76, 124, 130, 135, 169, 183, 184, 202, 208, 303, 305
Golden, John, 138
Golden, Richard, 302
Goodwin, Nat C., 53, 118, 141, 149, 195, 303

Hackett, James H., 57, 353
Hackett, James K., 149, 232, 303
Hall, Pauline, 72
Hampden, Walter, 228
Harlan, Otis, 302
Harned, Virginia, 149, 183, 184, 304
Harrigan, Edward, 149, 179, 195
Hart, Tony, 179
Hart, William S., 153
Haworth, Joseph, 293, 303
Hayne, Julie Dean, 37, 190, 212, 257
Held, Anna, 304
Hemple, Samuel, 328
Henderson, Rita, *see* Ogarita Rosalie Booth
Herne, James A., 53, 106, 132, 239, 303
Herne, Katherine Corcoran, 106
Heron, Bijou, 228
Heron, Matilda, 37, 207, 337, 342, 358
Holland, E. M. 195, 232, 303, 337
Holland, George, 158, 180, 194, 359
Holland, Joseph, 232
Hopper, DeWolf, 159, 173, 292, 302
Hull, Josephine, *see* Josephine Sherwood
Hull, Shelley, 59

Irving, Isabel, 304
Irwin, May, 53, 304, 337

James, Louis, 310, 322
Jamieson, George W., 353
Janauschek, Fanny, 127, 195, 290, 311, 357
Janis, Elsie, 175
Jansen, Marie, 72
Jefferson, Charles Burke, 176
Jefferson, Joseph, III, 38, 41, 53, 81, 82, 96, 112, 130, 141, 149, 159, 176, 177, 189a, 195, 198, 207, 227, 232, 239, 242, 249, 252, 280, 290, 303, 311, 317, 333, 335, 347, 349, 352, 353, 362
Jefferson, Thomas, 176
Jewett, Henry, 303
Jones, Walter, 302
Judah, Mrs. (Mariette Starfield), 278

Keene, Laura, 37, 82, 337, 342, 358
Keene, Thomas, 53
Kelcey, Herbert, 303
Kidder, Kathryn, 304
Knowlton, Dora, 259

Lackaye, Wilton, 303
Lander, Jean Davenport, 353
Lane, Louisa, *see* Mrs. John Drew
Langrishe, John S., 279
Lawrence, Lillian, 304
Leclerq, Charles, 259
Leman, Walter M., 188
LeMoyne, Sarah Cowell, 304
LeMoyne, W. J., 195
Leslie, Helen, 31
Lewis, Catherine, 259
Lewis, James, 83, 100, 251, 353, 358, 359
Lindsay, John Shanks, 79, 190
Logan, Olive, 102, 192, 193

McCullough, John, 66, 69, 170, 207, 252, 272, 278, 281a, 294, 322, 337, 340, 352, 353, 359

MacDowell, Melbourne, 303
McIntosh, Burr, 149
MacKaye, Steele, 111, 196, 337
McHenry, Nellie, 72
Maeder, Clara Fisher, 252
Mann, Louis, 173, 303
Mannering, Mary, 149, 169, 185, 304
Manola, Marion, 72
Mansfield, Beatrice Cameron, *see* Beatrice Cameron
Mansfield, Richard, 53, 69, 70, 83, 130, 141, 149, 151, 163, 183, 184, 195, 227, 239, 252, 303, 311, 317, 337, 338, 350, 353
Mantell, Robert B., 54, 303, 311
Marcells, Rena, *see* Mrs. Grace George
Marlowe, Julie, 25, 37, 53, 60, 149, 169, 174, 183, 185, 195, 252, 274, 293, 304, 311, 318, 337, 358, 359
Martinot, Sadie, 72
Mason, John, 275, 303
Mather, Margaret, 290
Meade, Ed, 213
Menken, Adah Isaacs, 20, 37, 133, 189, 270, 278
Miles, Robert E. J., 224
Miller, Henry, 155, 218, 228, 303
Mitchell, Maggie, 195, 337
Modjeska, Helena, 5, 6, 15, 37, 53, 72, 75, 124, 126, 127, 130, 145, 174, 195, 207, 216, 272, 288, 290, 304, 311, 353, 359
Molony, Kitty, 140
Montgomery, Dave, 300
Morris, Clara, 37, 53, 72, 195, 207, 210, 223, 224, 225, 305, 311, 337, 353, 359
Morris, Felix, 226
Morrison, Lewis, 33
Morrison, Mable Adrienne, 33

Murdoch, James E., 233, 234, 235, 337
Murray, Charles H., 79

Navarro, Mme, de, *see* Mary Anderson
Nazimova, Alla, 103, 228, 252
Nolan, James, 275

Olcott, Chauncey, 149
O'Neill, Annie, 149
O'Neill, James, 40a, 57a, 132a, 189a, 195, 278, 282, 284a, 303
Owens, John E., 136, 181, 224, 241, 353, 359

Palmer, Minnie, 72
Pitou, Augustus, 249
Placide, Henry, 180, 337
Post, Guy Bates, 312
Post, Lillie, 72
Potter, Cora Urquhart, 53, 72, 310
Potter, Mrs. James Brown, *see* Cora Urquhart Potter
Power, Tyrone, II, 232, 357
Powers, James T., 255, 302
Pray, Malvina, *see* Malvina Pray Florence

Raymond, John T., 195, 207, 359
Reed, Roland, 303
Rehan, Ada, 12, 37, 53, 72, 83, 92, 93, 94, 100, 114, 151, 174, 195, 210, 240, 251, 259, 262, 280, 283, 284, 288, 290, 304, 311, 337, 344, 353, 359
Reignolds, Kate, 82, 342
Riccardo, Corona, 304
Richman, Charles J., 303
Ring, James H., 275
Robertson, Agnes, 207, 232, 242, 342
Robson, Eleanor, 185
Robson, May, 149, 304
Robson, Stuart, 53, 81, 141, 195, 303

Rock, Ida, 140
Russell, Annie, 53, 149, 169, 183, 185, 304
Russell, Lillian, 37, 53, 72, 98, 99, 173, 221, 222, 237
Russell, Sol Smith, 141, 195, 303
Ryan, Kate, 275

Salvini, Alexander, 195, 223
Sanders, Mary, 304
Seabrooke, Thomas Q., 302
Seymour, William, 46, 275
Shannon, Effie, 304
Shaw, Mary, 304
Sherwood, Josephine, 59
Sinclair, Catherine, 37
Skinner, Maud Durbin, *see* Maud Durbin
Skinner, Otis, 40, 42a, 53, 75, 149, 208, 252, 288, 290, 303, 312, 337
Smith, Mark, 358
Sothern, E. A. 18, 63, 87, 163, 205, 207, 232, 242, 245, 266, 276, 280, 294, 328, 342, 352
Sothern, E. H., 25, 53, 103, 124, 126, 149, 151, 183, 184, 195, 232, 245, 274, 293, 294, 303, 311, 337, 358, 359
Starr, Frances, 32, 351
Stevens, Emily, 34
Stoddart, James H., Jr., 53, 195, 299
Stone, Ed, 300
Stone, Fred, 300
Sykes, Jerome, 302

Taber, Robert, 25, 274
Taylor, Emma, 83
Taylor, Laurette, 80, 203, 305a
Templeton, Fay, 53
Thompson, Denman, 43, 189a, 195

Thorne, Charles R., Jr., 141, 195
Tiffany, Annie Ward, 149
Truax, Sarah, 312
Tyree, Elizabeth, 304
Tyler, Odette, 304

Urquhart, Isabella, 72

Vaders, Emma, 140
Vincent, Mrs. J. R., (Mary Ann), 195, 275, 294, 342
Vokes, Rosina, 72

Wainwright, Marie, 72
Walker, George, 62, 271
Wallack, James W., Jr., 111, 358
Wallack, Lester, 136, 195, 207, 232, 266, 310, 311, 319
Walsh, Blanche, 304
Ward, Genevieve, 146, 242, 321, 353
Warde, Frederick, 322, 323

Warfield, David, 149, 173, 307, 351, 359
Warren, William Jr., 17, 21, 63, 177, 195, 272, 275, 305, 337, 342, 358
Watkins, Harry, 289
Weathersby, Eliza, 141
Weber, Joe, 173, 222
Wheatley, William, 136, 328, 353
Whiffen, Thomas, 326
Whiffen, Mrs. Thomas (Blanche Galton), 326
Williams, Bert, 62, 172, 271
Williams, Fritz, 303
Wilson, Francis, 149, 183, 184, 292, 302, 333, 335, 336
Wilson, George W., 275
Wood, Mrs. John, 242
Wood, Rose, 33
Worthing, Frank, 359, 361

Yurka, Blanche, 363

INDEX TO TITLES

About Stage Folks, 160

Acting and Actors, Elocution and Elocutionists, 240

The Actor and Other Speeches, 343

Actors and Actresses of Great Britain and the United States, 207

Actors and Authors, 285

The Actors' Birthday Book, 48

The Actor's Heritage, 102

Actors on Acting, 73

An Actor's Tour, 19

Ada Rehan, 344

After All, 90

The Amazing Career of Sir Giles Overreach, 16

America's Players, 130

American Portraits, 1875-1900, 41

The American Stage, 7

American Stage Celebrities, 8

The American Stage of To-Day, 103

The American Stage of To-Day: Biographies and Photographs of One Hundred Leading Actors and Actresses, 10

The American Stage. Schiller Theatre Souvenir, 9

The American Theatre: A Sum of Its Parts, 11

The American Theatre as Seen by Its Critics, 1752-1934, 229

Among the Great Masters of the Drama, 272

Analytic Elocution, 233

Annals of the New York Stage, 238

Apropos of Women and Theatres, 192

Arnold Daly, 139

The Art of Acting, 40

The Art of Acting: A Discussion, 78

As God Made Them, 42

At the New Theatre and Others, 104

The Autobiography of Cecil B. DeMille, 88

The Autobiography of Joseph Jefferson, 177

Autobiographical Sketch of Mrs. John Drew, 101

Backstage with Actors, 239

Backstage with Henry Miller, 228

The Bancrofts, 18

The Barrymores, 5

Before the Footlights and Behind the Scenes, 193

Behind the Scenes with Edwin Booth, 140

The Bennett Playbills, 33

Bert Williams, 271

The Best Plays of 1894-1899, 61

The Best Plays of 1899-1909, 199

The Best Plays of 1909-1919, 200

Between Actor and Critic, 38

The Biographical Encyclopedia & Who's Who of the American Stage, 263

Birds of a Feather Flock Together,

87

Blood-and-Thunder, 305a

Bohemian Girl, 363

Both Sides of the Curtain, 321

Breakfast in Bed, 276

Brief Chronicles, 345

Bright Particular Star, 186

The Career of Dion Boucicault, 320

Catalogue of Dramatic Portraits in the Theatre Collection of the Harvard College Library, 147

Celebrated Comedians of Light Opera and Musical Comedy in America, 302

Charles Albert Fechter, 115

Charles Frohman, 202

Charlotte Cushman, 324

Charlotte Cushman: Her Letters and Memories of Her Life, 296

Chicago Stage, 286

Clowning Through Life, 122

Clyde Fitch and His Letters, 230

Companions on the Trail, 131

Confessions of an Actor, 27

Crowding Memories, 3

Curiosities of the American Stage, 165

The Curse of the Misbegotten, 40a

Daniel Frohman Presents, 124

Darling of Misfortune, 191

David Belasco, 203a

Dear Josephine, 59

Diamond Jim, 221

Diary of a Daly Debutante, 259

A Dictionary of the Drama, 2

Dion Boucicault, 157

Doubling Back, 213

Douglas Fairbanks, 150

Drama Cyclopedia, 287

The Drama of Yesterday & To-Day, 280

The Dramatic List, 242

Dramatic Opinions and Essays, 283

The Dramatic Year (1887-88), 127

Driftwood of the Stage, 161

Duet in Diamonds, 237

Edward Loomis Davenport, 105

Edwin Booth (Copeland), 77

Edwin Booth (Hutton), 166

Edwin Booth in Twelve Dramatic Characters, 346

Edwin Booth: Recollections by His Daughter, 39

Edwin Forest, 23

Edwin Forrest: First Star of the American Stage, 217

Edwin Forrest: The Actor and the Man, 152

The Elder and the Younger Booth, 67

Eminent Actors in Their Homes, 149

The Eminent American Comedienne Marie Dressler in The Life Story of an Ugly Duckling, 98

Enchanting Rebel, 189

Encore, 125

Epoch, 196

The Escape and Suicide of John Wilkes Booth, 30

Ethel Barrymore, 236a

Eugene O'Neill, 57a

The Fabulous Forrest, 231

Fair Rosalind, 75

Familiar Chats with Queens of the Stage, 72

Family Circle, 288

Famous Actor-Families in America, 232

Famous Actors & Actresses and Their Homes, 183

*Famous Actors and Actresses on

the American Stage, 362a

Famous Actors and Their Homes, 184

Famous Actors of the Day in America, 303

Famous Actresses and Their Homes, 185

Famous Actresses of the Day in America, 304

Famous American Actors of To-day, 195

A Few Memories, 236

Fifty Years Back Stage, 258

Fifty Years in Theatrical Management, 187

Fifty Years of Make-Believe, 322

The Fighting Man, 44

First Nights and First Editions, 292

The Fools of Shakespeare, 323

Footlight Favorites, 313

Footlight Flashes, 84

Footlights and Spotlights, 290

Footlights on the Border, 129

Footprints and Echoes, 81

Forty-Odd Years in the Literary Shop, 119

Forty Years Observation of Music and the Drama, 142

Forty Years on the Stage, 22

Francis Wilson's Life of Himself, 333

French Theatre in New York, 206

From Candles to Footlights, 279

From Phelps to Gielgud, 15

Fun I've Had, 316

Genevieve Ward, 146

Genius and Other Essays, 297

George Henry Boker, 42a

George M. Cohan, 220

The Golden Age of New Orleans Theater, 181

Good Night, Sweet Prince, 121

Good Troupers All, 198

Great Artists of the American Stage, 314

The Great Chicago Theatre Disaster, 110

Great Stars of the American Stage, 35

The Green Room Book, 143

A Group of Comedians, 180

A Group of Theatrical Caricatures, 136

Hamlet from the Actor's Standpoint, 246

The Hamlet of Edwin Booth, 281

Harvest of My Years, 250

Helena Modjeska, 6

Heroines of the Modern Stage, 174

A History of American Acting, 337

History of the American Stage, 50

The History of the Boston Theatre, 1854-1901, 308

The History of the Fourteenth Street Theatre, 298

A History of the New York Stage, 51

A History of the Philadelphia Theatre, 1878-1890, 204

History of the Providence Stage, 1762-1891, 331

History of the San Francisco Theatre, 278

A History of the Theatre in Salt Lake City from 1850 to 1870, 154

Holland Memorial, 158

The Illusion of the First Time in Acting, 135

The Illustrated American Stage, 169

In Memory of Frank Worthing, 361

In Memory of John McCullough, 170

Index to the Portraits in Odell's

"Annals of the New York Stage,"
171
*Intimate Recollections of Joseph
Jefferson,* 176

"Jack" Dodge, 95
James A. Herne, 106
The Jeffersons, 347
John Barrymore, 253
John Drew, 92
*John McCullough as Man, Actor and
Spirit,* 66
John Wilkes Booth, 334
Joseph Jefferson at Home, 96
*Joseph Jefferson: Reminiscences of
a Fellow Player,* 335
Julia Marlowe, 25
Julia Marlowe: Her Life and Art, 274
Julia Marlowe's Story, 293

Kate Field, 327
Keeping Off the Shelf, 326

Ladies of the Footlights, 37
The Lady of the Gardens, 91
The Last Tragedian, 291
The Laugh Makers, 56a
Laurette, 80
Lawrence Barrett, 24
Leading Ladies, 203
*Leaves from the Autobiography of
Tommaso Salvini,* 277
*Letters of Mr. and Mrs. Charles Kean
Relating to Their American Tours,*
60
Letters to Harriet, 218
Life and Art of Edwin Booth, 348
Life and Art of Joseph Jefferson,
349
Life and Art of Richard Mansfield,
350
*Life and Memories of William War-
ren,* 17

*The Life and Remarkable Career
of Adah Isaacs Menken,* 20
*The Life and Work of David Belas-
co,* 307
*The Life, Crime, and Capture of
John Wilkes Booth,* 309
The Life of a Star, 223
The Life of Augustin Daly, 83
A Life of Charlotte Cushman, 256
The Life of David Belasco, 351
Life of Denman Thompson, 43
Life of Edwin Forrest, 4
*The Life of Edwin Forrest, with
Reminiscences and Personal Re-
collections,* 260
The Life of Henry Irving, 47
The Life of Laura Keene, 82
Life on the Stage,
*Life, Stories, and Poems of John
Brougham,* 49
*The Life Story of an Ugly Duck-
ling,* 98
Life Was Worth Living, 262
Lillian Russell, 222
*The Little Church Around the
Corner,* 194
Lord Dundreary, 245
Lotta's Last Season, 31

The Mad Booths of Maryland, 182
*The Marie Burroughs Art Port-
folio of Stage Celebrities,* 56
Mary Anderson, 113
The Masks of King Lear, 268
The Masks of Othello, 269
Masters of the Show, 249
The Matinee Idols, 58
Maude Adams, 85
Maude Adams: A Biography, 243
*Maude Adams: An Intimate Por-
trait,* 264
The Melancholy Tale of "Me", 294
Memorial Celebration of the Six-

tieth Anniversary of the Birth of Edwin Booth, 214

Memories, 26

Memories and Impressions of Helen Modjeska, 216

Memories of a Hostess, 162

Memories of a Manager, 126

Memories of an Old Actor, 188

Memories of Daly's Theatres, 93

Memories of Fifty Years, 319

Memories of One Theatre, 94

The Memories of Rose Eytinge, 111

Memories of the Professional and Social Life of John E. Owens, 241

Merely Players, 317

The Merry Partners, 179

The Mimic World, 193

Modjeska, 145

Monarchs of Minstrelsy, 261

The Mormons and the Theatre, 190

Mrs. Fiske, 144

Mrs. Fiske and the American Theatre, 34

Mrs. Fiske, Her Views on Actors, Acting, and the Problems of Production, 117

My Aunt Maxine, 118

My Crystal Ball, 201

My Life and Memories, 69

My Life East and West, 153

My Own Story, 99

My Ten Years in the Studios, 13

My Years on the Stage, 100

Nat Goodwin's Book, 141

The Negro in the American Theatre, 172

New National Theatre, Washington, D.C., 164

The New York Mirror Annual and Directory of the Theatrical Profession for 1888, 116

Nobody, 62

Noted Men and Women, 227

Old Boston Museum Days, 275

Once a Clown, Always a Clown, 159

One Man in His Time, 289

O'Neill, 132a

O'Neill: Son and Playwright, 284a

Other Days, 352

Our Actors and Actresses, 242

Our Recent Actors, 205

Outside Broadway, 219

Papers on Acting, 208

Pauline Frederick, 108

A Pictorial History of the American Theatre, 36

A Pictorial History of the American Theatre, 100 Years, 1860-1960, 36

A Pictorial History of the American Theatre, 1860-1970, 36

A Pictorial History of the American Theatre, 1900-1950, 36

A Pictorial History of the American Theatre, 1900-1951, 36

A Pictorial History of the American Theatre, 1900-1956, 36

A Pictorial History of the Great Comedians, 56a

Pioneer Theatre in the Desert, 212

Players and Plays of the Last Quarter Century, 305

Players and Playwrights I Have Known, 74

The Players Blue Book, 301

Players of a Century, 247

Players of the Present, 64

The Playgoers' Year Book, for 1888, 339

Plays and Players, 167

Plays of the Present, 65

A Plea for the Spoken Language,

234

A Portfolio of Players, 251

Portrait of a Family, 112

Portraits of the American Stage, 1771-1971, 252

Prince of Players, 273

Principles of Playmaking, 209

The Print of My Remembrance, 306

The "Queen of the Drama", 332

Queen of the Plaza, 133

Recollections of a Player (Stoddart), 299

Recollections of a Player (Wilson), 336

Reminiscences, 226

Reminiscences of a Dramatic Critic, 63

Reminiscences of DeWolf Hopper, 159

Reminiscences of Henry Clay Barnabee, 21

Richard Mansfield, 338

Rip Van Winkle Goes to the Play, 210

"Rip Van Winkle": The Autobiography of Joseph Jefferson, 177

Roadside Meetings, 132

Robert Mantell's Romance, 54

Rolling Stone, 300

The Romance of an Old Playhouse, 257

The San Francisco Stage, 128

San Francisco Theatre Research, 278

The Secrets of a Showman, 70

Seven Daughters of the Theatre, 318

Shadows of the Stage, 353

Shakespeare from the Greenroom, 57

Shakespeare on the American Stage, 281a

Shakespeare on the Stage, 354

Shakespeare's Heroes on the Stage, 340

Shakespeare's Heroines on the Stage, 341

Shakespearian Players and Performances, 295

Shaw's Dramatic Criticism (1895-98), 284

Sherlock Holmes and Much More, 76

Showman, 45

Silhouettes of My Contemporaries, 1

Silver Theatre, 325

Six Years at the Castle Square Theatre, 123

Sixty Years of the Theatre, 311

Sketch of the Life of George Holland, 158

A Sketch of the Life of John Gilbert, 355

Sketches of Tudor Hall and the Booth Family, 197

So Far, So Good!, 175

Some Players, 53

The Stage, 235

The Stage and Its Stars, 244

Stage and Screen, 46

The Stage as a Career, 162a

Stage Confidences, 225

The Stage in America: 1897-1900, 151

The Stage Life of Mary Anderson, 356

The Stage Memories of John A. Ellsler, 107

The Stage Reminiscences of Mrs. Gilbert, 134

Stage-Struck John Golden, 138

Steeplejack, 163

The Story of a Theatre, 137

The Story of a Young Edwin Booth,

254

The Sunny Side of the Street, 330

*Talks in a Library with Laurence
  Hutton*, 168
Theatre Tonight, 79
The Theatre of Augustin Daly, 114
The Theatre Through Its Stage Door,
  32
Theatrical and Circus Life, 178
*The Theatrical Manager in England
  and America*, 97
Theatrical Sketches, 310
The Theatrical 'World' for 1893, 12
The Theatrical 'World' of 1894, 12
The Theatrical 'World' of 1895, 12
The Theatrical 'World' of 1896, 12
Then Came Each Actor, 142a
These Things are Mine, 215
This One Mad Act, 120
Titans of the American Stage, 282
*The Triumphs and Trials of Lotta
  Crabtree*, 89
Troupers of the Gold Coast, 270
Trouping, 189a
Trouping in the Oregon Country,
  109
Twelve Great Actors, 266
Twelve Great Actresses, 267
The Twentieth Century Theatre,
  248
*Twenty Years on Broadway and the
  Years It Took to Get There*, 71
Twinkle Little Star, 255
The Turnover Club, 148
Tyrone Power, 357

The Unlocked Book, 68
Up the Years from Bloomsbury,
  14

A Vagabond Trouper, 86
Vagrant Memories, 358

Wags of the Stage, 328
The Wallet of Time, 359
We Barrymores, 29
We Three, 28
Weber and Fields, 173
Whatever Goes Up−, 315
Who's Who in Music and Drama,
  156
Who's Who in the Theatre, 329
Who's Who on the Stage, 52
Who's Who on the Stage, 1908, 52
William Vaughn Moody, 155
Wit and Humor of the Stage, 362
With a Feather on My Nose, 55
A Woman of Parts, 312
A Wreath of Laurel, 360

Yesterdays with Actors, 342
The Young Maude Adams, 265

INDEX TO AUTHORS

Abbott, Lyman, 1
Adams, Samuel Hopkins, 80
Adams, William Davenport, 2
Agate, James, 70
Aldrich, Mrs. Thomas Bailey (Lilian Woodman), 3
Alger, William Rounseville, 4
Alpert, Hollis, 5
Altemus, Jameson Torr, 6
Anderson, Mary, 236
Archer, William, 12
Arliss, George, 13, 14, 135
Arthur, Sir George C. A., 15
Atkinson, Brooks, 80, 253
Austin, F. A., 52
Ayres, Alfred, 240

Baldwin, Raymond P., 89
Ball, Robert Hamilton, 16
Ball, William Thomas Winsborough, 17
Bancroft, Lady Marie, 18
Bancroft, Sir Squire, 18
Bandmann, Daniel E., 19
Barclay, George Lippard, 20
Barnabee, Henry Clay, 21
Barnes, John H., 22
Barrett, Lawrence, 23
Barrie, James M., 202
Barron, Elwyn Alfred, 24
Barry, John Daniel, 25
Barrymore, Ethel, 26
Barrymore, John, 27, 28
Barrymore, Lionel, 29

Bates, Finis Langdon, 30
Bates, Helen Marie Leslie, 31
Belasco, David, 32, 271
Bennett, Joan, 33
Binns, Archie, 34
Blum, Daniel, 35, 36
Bodeen, DeWitt, 37
Booth, Edwin, 38, 39
Boucicault, Dion, 40, 78
Bowen, Croswell, 40a
Bradford, Gamaliel, 41, 42
Bradley, Edward Sculley, 42a
Brady, James Jay, 43
Brady, William A., 44, 45
Brazier, Marion Howard, 46
Brereton, Austin, 47
Briscoe, Johnson, 48
Brougham, John, 49
Brown, John Mason, 229
Brown, Thomas Allston, 50, 51
Browne, Walter, 52
Brunner, H. C., 251
Buck, Lillie West Brown, 53
Bulliet, Clarence Joseph, 54
Burke, Billie, 55
Burke, John, 237
Burroughs, Marie, 56

Cahn, William, 56a
Carlisle, Carol Jones, 57
Carpenter, Frederic I., 57a
Carroll, David, 58
Carson, William Glasgow Bruce, 59, 60

Chapman, John, 61
Charters, Ann, 62
Chinoy, Helen Krich, 73
Cibber, Colley, 260
Clapp, Henry Austin, 63
Clapp, John Bouve, 64, 65
Clark, Barrett H., 279
Clark, Susie Champney, 66
Clarke, Asia Booth, 67, 68
Clarke, Joseph Ignatius Constantine,
    69
Clement, Clara Erskine, 324
Cobb, Irvin S., 138
Cochran, Charles Blake, 70
Cohan, George Michael, 71, 228
Cohen, Alfred J., 72
Cole, Toby, 73
Coleman, John, 74
Coleman, Marion Moore, 75
Cook, Doris Estelle, 76
Copeland, Charles Townsend, 77
Coquelin, Constant, 78
Cosgrave, Luke, 79
Courtney, Marguerite Taylor, 80
Crane, William H., 81
Creahan, John, 82

Dale, Alan, 72
Daly, Joseph Francis, 83
Davidge, William Plater, 84
Davies, Acton, 85
DeAngelis, Jefferson, 86
DeFoe, Louis V., 32
DeFontaine, Felix Gregory, 87
DeMille, Cecil Blount, 88
Dempsey, David, 89
DeWolfe, Elsie Anderson, 90
Dier, Mary Caroline Lawrence, 91
Dithmar, Edward Augustus, 92, 93,
    94, 251
Dodge, John Mason, 95
Dole, Nathan Haskell, 96
Donohue, Joseph W., Jr., 97

Downer, Alan S., 171, 177
Downey, Fairfax, 293
Dressler, Marie, 98, 99
Drew, John, II, 100, 101
Drew, Mrs. John (Louisa Lane),
    101

Eaton, Walter Prichard, 102, 103,
    104
Edgett, Edwin Francis, 64, 65, 105
Edwards, Herbert J., 106
Ellsler, John Adam, 107
Elwood, Muriel, 108
Ernst, Alice Henson, 109
Everett, Marshall, 110
Eytinge, Rose, 111

Fabian, Monroe H., 252
Fairbanks, Letitia, 150
Farjeon, Eleanor, 68, 112, 177
Farrar, J. Maurice, 113
Felheim, Marvin, 114
Field, Kate, 115
Fiske, Harrison Grey, 116, 240
Fiske, Minnie Maddern Davey, 117,
    140
Forbes-Robertson, Diana, 118
Forbes-Robertson, Sir Johnston,
    262
Ford, James Lauren, 119
Forrester, Izola Louise, 120
Fowler, Gene, 121
Foy, Eddie, 122
French, Charles Elwell, 123
Frohman, Daniel, 124, 125, 126,
    202
Fuller, Edward, 127
Furnas, Joseph Chamberlin, 315

Gagey, Edmond McAdoo, 128
Gallegly, Joseph S., 129
Gard, Robert E., 130
Garland, Hamlin, 131, 132

Gebbie, George, 244
Gelb, Arthur, 132a
Gelb, Barbara, 132a
Gerson, Noel Bertram, 133
Gerson, Virginia, 230
Gielgud, Sir John, 15
Gilbert, Mrs. Anne Hartley, 134
Gillette, William, 135
Gisby, Barnard, 19
Gladding, W. J., 136
Glover, Lyman B., 137
Golden, John, 138
Goldsmith, Berthold H., 139
Goodale, George P., 160
Goodale, Katherine (Kitty Molony),
   140
Goodwin, Nathaniel Carl, 141
Grau, Robert, 142
Grebanier, Bernard, 142a
Griffith, Frank Carlos, 144
Gronowicz, Antoni, 145
Grossman, Edwina Booth, 39
Gustafson, Zadel Barnes, 146

Hall, Lillian Arvilla, 147
Hall, William T. "Biff", 148
Hamm, Margherita Arlina, 149
Hanaford, Harry Prescott, 156
Hancock, Ralph, 150
Hapgood, Norman, 151
Harlow, Alvin F., 86, 122
Harrington, Mildred, 99
Harrison, Gabriel, 152
Hart, William Surrey, 153
Hayes, Helen, 36
Hayne, Donald, 88
Henderson, Myrtle E., 154
Hennessey, W. J., 346
Henry, David Dodds, 155
Herne, Julie A., 106
Hibbert, Henry George, 12
Hines, Dixie, 156
Hogan, Robert Goode, 157

Holbrook, Stewart, 109
Holcomb, William H., 95
Hopper, DeWolf, 159
Horton, Judge William Ellis, 160,
   161
Howe, Mark Antony DeWolfe, 162
Hubert, Philip G., Jr., 162a
Huneker, James Gibbons, 163, 283
Hunt, Bampton, 143
Hunter, Alexander, 164
Hutton, Laurence, 165, 166, 167,
   168, 207, 251, 319

Irving, Henry, 78
Isaacs, Edith Juliet R., 172
Isman, Felix, 173
Izard, Forrest, 174

Janis, Elsie, 175
Jefferson, Eugenie Paul, 176
Jefferson, Joseph, III, 177
Jennings, John Joseph, 178

Kahn, Ely Jacques, Jr., 179
Keese, William Linn, 180
Kendall, John Smith, 181
Kibbee, Lois, 33
Kilby, Quincy, 308
Kimmel, Stanley Preston, 182
Kobbe, Gustav, 183, 184, 185
Koch, E. DeRoy, 52
Kooken, Olive, 34

Leach, Joseph, 186
Leavitt, Michael Bennett, 187
Lees, C. Lowell, 212
LeGallienne, Eva, 254, 298
Leman, Walter Moore, 188
Leslie, Amy, 53
Lesser, Alan, 189
Lewis, Paul, 133
Lewis, Philip C., 189a
Lindsay, John Shanks, 190

Linton, W. J., 346
Lloyd, Harold, 56a
Lockridge, Richard, 191
Logan, Olive, 192, 193

MacAdam, George, 194
McClintic, Guthrie, 312
McKay, Frederic Edward, 195
MacKaye, Percy, 196, 218
Mahoney, Ella V., 197
Malveryn, Gladys, 198
Mantle, Burns, 91, 199, 200
Marbury, Elisabeth, 201
Marcosson, Isaac Frederick, 202
Margaret, 310
Marinacci, Barbara, 203
Marker, Lise-Lone, 203a
Marshall, Thomas Frederic, 204
Marston, John Westland, 205
Martin, Charlotte M., 134
Mason, Hamilton, 206
Matthews, James Brander, 40, 78,
    135, 207, 208, 209, 210, 211, 251
Matthews, John F., 284
Maughan, Ila Fisher, 212
Meade, Edwards Hoag, 213
Middleton, George, 215
Modjeska, Helena, 216
Moody, Richard, 217
Moody, William Vaughn, 218
Moore, Isabel, 168
Moore, Lester L., 219
Morehouse, Ward, 220
Morell, Alfred Parker, 221, 222
Morris, Clara, 223, 224, 225
Morris, Felix, 226
Morrissey, James W., 227
Morse, Frank Philip, 228
Moses, Montrose Jonas, 229, 230,
    231, 232
Murdoch, James Edward, 233, 234,
    235

Navarro, Mary Anderson de, 236
Newman, Shirlee Petkin, 236a

O'Connor, Richard, 237
Odell, George Clinton Densmore,
    238
O'Neill, Shane, 40a
Ormsbee, Helen, 239
Osmun, Thomas Embley, 240
Owens, Mrs. John E. (Mary
    Stephens), 241

Parker, John, 329
Pascoe, Charles Eyre, 242
Patterson, Ada, 243
Paul, Howard, 244
Pemberton, Thomas Edgar, 245
Phelps, Henry Pitt, 246, 247
Phelps, William Lyon, 248
Pinero, Arthur W., 12
Pitou, Augustus, 249
Polkinhorn, Joseph H., 164
Pollock, Channing, 250
Power-Waters, Alma Shelley, 253,
    254
Powers, James T., 255
Price, William Thompson, 256
Putnam, G. H., 168
Pyper, George Dollinger, 257

Quinn, Germain, 258

Ranous, Dora Knowlton Thomp-
    son, 259
Rees, James, 260
Rice, Edward LeRoy, 261
Rigdon, Walter, 263
Robbins, Phyllis, 264, 265
Robertson, Walford Graham-, 262
Robins, Edward, Jr., 266, 267
Rogers, Will, 99
Rosenberg, Marvin, 268, 269
Rourke, Constance, 270

Rowland, Mabel, 271
Rowlands, Walter, 272
Ruggles, Eleanor, 273
Russell, Charles Edward, 274
Ryan, Kate, 275

Sadik, Marvin, 252
Sala, George Augustus, 276
Salvini, Tommaso, 277
Schoberlin, Melvin, 279
Scott, Clement William, 280
Semmes, David, 130
Shattuck, Charles Harlen, 281, 281a
Shaw, Dale, 282
Shaw, George Bernard, 12, 283, 284
Sheaffer, Louis, 284a
Sherman, Robert Lowery, 285, 286, 287
Sherwood, Garrison P., 61, 199, 200
Shipman, Louis Evan, 136
Shipp, Cameron, 29, 55
Shore, Viola Brothers, 138
Skinner, Cornelia Otis, 288
Skinner, Maud Durbin, 289
Skinner, Otis, 40, 289, 290, 291
Smith, Harry Bache, 292
Sothern, Edward Hugh, 293, 294
Sprague, Arthur Colby, 295
Stebbins, Emma, 296
Stedman, Edmund Clarence, 297
Steinberg, Mollie B., 298
Stoddart, James Henry, Jr., 299
Stone, Fred Andrew, 300
Stone, Melville E., 81
Storms, A. D., 301
Stout, Wesley Winans, 159
Strang, Lewis Clinton, 302, 303, 304, 305

Tarkington, Booth, 100
Taylor, Douglas, 65, 101
Taylor, Dwight, 305a
Thomas, Augustus, 306

Thornton, Willis, 107
Timberlake, Craig, 307
Tompkins, Eugene, 308
Towne, Charles Hanson, 255
Townsend, George Alfred, 309
Townsend, Margaret, 310
Towse, John Ranken, 311
Tree, Sir Herbert Beerbohm, 329
Truax, Sarah, 312
Trumble, Alfred, 313, 314
Tyler, George Crouse, 315

Varney, George Leon, 21
Veiller, Bayard, 316

Wagenknecht, Edward, 317, 318
Waldron, James A., 240
Wallack, (John Johnstone) Lester, 319
Walsh, Townsend, 320
Ward, Genevieve, 321
Wards, Frederick B., 322, 323
Watermeier, Daniel Jude, 38
Waters, Clara Erskine Clement, 324
Watson, Margaret G., 325
Wells, Henry W., 208
Wendell, Evert Jansen, 64
Werner, Edgar S., 240
Weston, Effie Ellsler, 107
Whiffen, Mrs. Thomas (Blanche Galton), 326
Whiteing, Richard, 321
Whiting, Lilian, 327
Whitton, Joseph, 328
Wilder, Marshall Picknev, 330
Willard, George Owen, 331
Williams, Henry B., 11
Williams, Henry L., 332
Willis, John, 36
Wilson, Francis 333, 334, 335, 336
Wilson, Garff B., 337
Wilstach, Paul, 338

Wingate, Charles Edgar Lewis, 195, 339, 340, 341

Winslow, Catherine Mary Reignolds-, 342

Winter, William, 10, 38, 49, 251, 299, 343, 344, 345, 346, 347, 348, 349, 350, 351, 352, 353, 354, 355, 356, 357, 358, 359, 360

Winter, William Jefferson, 351, 361

Woollcott, Alexander, 117

Young, William C., 362a

Yurka, Blanche, 363